Praise for *The Circular Revolution*

T0293183

'Practical, actionable and written to deliver results. Binder and Braun's how-to guide for business leaders looking to embrace sustainable business models and a regenerative mindset is both timely and valuable.'

**Paul Polman, business leader,
campaigner, co-author of *Net Positive***

'The circular business models described in this book have been a source of inspiration for us on our circularity journey. As one of the major topics of the future, circularity certainly needs to be on every business leader's agenda.'

**Judith Wiese, Managing Board Member of Siemens AG;
Chief People and Sustainability Officer**

'An essential book for innovative business models for the circular economy. This is a compelling guide to innovation with impact!'

**Alexander Osterwalder, co-creator of the Business
Model Canvas; founder of Strategyzer**

'Having dedicated much of my life to environmental conservation and sustainability, I am continually inspired by insightful perspectives that challenge us to think differently about our relationship with the planet. *The Circular Business Revolution* offers a practical framework for sustainable business models, shedding light on the urgent need for action and the transformative power of collective efforts.'

**André Hoffmann, Vice-Chairman of Roche;
environmentalist and philanthropist**

'Leaders today must have the tools to navigate the future of sustainability. *The Circular Business Revolution* offers a blueprint that aligns profitability with environmental stewardship and transforms challenges into opportunities. This is an essential read for any leader committed to meaningful impact.'

Jessica Sibley, TIME Chief Executive Officer

'Circular bio-economy is the oldest concept on planet Earth; since nature is based on the principles of a circular economy, nothing is lost and everything has its purpose. We humans, as part of nature, should abide by the same principles. This is logical in theory, but not so clear yet in practice and this valuable contribution is well addressing exactly this gap.'

**Janez Potočnik, Co-Chair of the UN International Resource Panel;
former European Commissioner for Research and Environment**

'Just the right book for first-time and experienced innovators who seek to implement circular economy business models. Enjoy discovering new opportunities and useful worksheets that will help you to take action!'

Marc Gruber, Professor of Entrepreneurship and Technology Commercialization at EPFL; co-author of *Where to Play - 3 Steps for Discovering your Most Valuable Market Opportunities*

'This book provides a well-structured and comprehensive guidance to any executive willing to look beyond the unsustainability of our current economy, and to engage with the transformation towards circular business practices. At a time when regeneration is becoming an existential mandate, it can be very helpful for many struggling to find practical responses to the always difficult question: "What should we change?"'

Carlos Alvarez Pereira, Secretary General of the Club of Rome

The Circular
Business Revolution

Pearson

At Pearson, we believe in learning – all kinds of learning for all kinds of people. Whether it's at home, in the classroom or in the workplace, learning is the key to improving our life chances.

That's why we're working with leading authors to bring you the latest thinking and best practices, so you can get better at the things that are important to you. You can learn on the page or on the move, and with content that's always crafted to help you understand quickly and apply what you've learned.

If you want to upgrade your personal skills or accelerate your career, become a more effective leader or more powerful communicator, discover new opportunities or simply find more inspiration, we can help you make progress in your work and life.

Every day our work helps learning flourish, and wherever learning flourishes, so do people.

To learn more, please visit us at **www.pearson.com**

The Financial Times

With a worldwide network of highly respected journalists, *The Financial Times* provides global business news, insightful opinion and expert analysis of business, finance and politics. With over 500 journalists reporting from 50 countries worldwide, our in-depth coverage of international news is objectively reported and analysed from an independent, global perspective.

To find out more, visit **www.ft.com**

[JULIA BINDER
MANUEL BRAUN]

The Circular Business Revolution

A practical framework for sustainable business models

Pearson

Harlow, England • London • New York • Boston • San Francisco • Toronto • Sydney • Dubai • Singapore • Hong Kong
Tokyo • Seoul • Taipei • New Delhi • Cape Town • São Paulo • Mexico City • Madrid • Amsterdam • Munich • Paris • Milan

PEARSON EDUCATION LIMITED
KAO Two
KAO Park
Harlow CM17 9NA
United Kingdom
Tel: +44 (0)1279 623623
Web: www.pearson.com

First edition published 2024 (print and electronic)
© Julia Binder and Manuel Braun (print and electronic)

ISBN: 978-1-292-45896-0 (print)
       978-1-292-45895-3 (ePub)

British Library Cataloguing-in-Publication Data
A catalogue record for the print edition is available from the British Library

Library of Congress Cataloging-in-Publication Data
Names: Binder, Julia (Professor of sustainable innovation) author. | Braun,
    Manuel (Director at Systemiq), author.
Title: The circular business revolution : a practical framework for
    sustainable business models / Julia Binder, Manuel Braun.
Description: First edition. | Harlow, England ; New York : Pearson, 2024. |
    Includes bibliographical references and index.
Identifiers: LCCN 2024010270 | ISBN 9781292458960 (paperback) | ISBN
    9781292458953 (epub)
Subjects: LCSH: Circular economy. | Sustainable development.
Classification: LCC HC79.E5 B555 2024 | DDC 338.9/27--dc23/eng/20240326
LC record available at https://lccn.loc.gov/2024010270

10 9 8 7 6 5 4 3 2 1
28 27 26 25 24

Cover design by Nick Redeyoff
Cover image courtesy of Lizzy Burt

Print edition typeset in 9.75/12 Helvetica Neue LT Pro by Straive

NOTE THAT ANY PAGE CROSS REFERENCES REFER TO THE PRINT EDITION

Contents

While we work hard to present unbiased, fully accessible content, we want to hear from you about any concerns or needs with this Pearson product so that we can investigate and address them:

- Please contact us with concerns about any potential bias at https://www.pearson.com/report-bias.html

- For accessibility-related issues, such as using assistive technology with Pearson products, alternative text requests, or accessibility documentation, email the Pearson Disability Support team at **disability.support@pearson.com**

About the authors

Julia Binder, professor of Sustainable Innovation and Business Transformation at IMD Lausanne, is a renowned thought leader recognised on the 2022 Thinkers50 Radar list for her work at the intersection of sustainability and innovation. With over a decade devoted to sustainability research and teaching, she actively supports business leaders in driving meaningful change to address global challenges. Before joining IMD, Julia initiated a sustainability initiative at EPFL and co-led a large-scale European project on sustainable innovation at TUM. Outside the professional realm, Julia dives into the joyful chaos of motherhood, takes on the challenge of speedy cooking, gardens passionately and occasionally indulges in sports – finding satisfaction in the beauty of everyday life.

Manuel Braun is an expert in the domain of sustainability and resource productivity, working at the intersection of research and practice. He is director at Systemiq, a global think tank focused on sustainable systems change, where he leads the circular business programme. Manuel holds a PhD from the Technical University of Munich and is actively engaged in teaching and executive training programmes across Europe. Previously, he spent eight years at McKinsey & Company, leading sustainable product development and design projects across industries. Manuel is a nature enthusiast in the professional realm and beyond. He is a passionate alpinist and loves to spend time with his family exploring the great outdoors – whether on foot, mountain bike or ski.

Authors' acknowledgements

We would like to express our deepest gratitude to the many people who helped to make this book happen. We wish to thank our families, who continuously motivated us to follow our passion for writing this book, who encouraged us throughout this journey and who allowed us to lose track of time. A big thank you to Lisa, Vincent and Noah, as well as Pietro, Leonardo and Alessandro for your unconditional support and for being an incredible source of energy, balance and fun.

We are deeply grateful to Alexander Osterwalder, Martin Stuchtey, Andrew Winston, Joe Murphy, Oliver Brunschwiler and Talke Schaffrannek for engaging in insightful conversations and generously contributing their perspectives to this book. Special thanks to Bill Sharpe for developing the Three Horizons framework and sharing feedback and experiences. We would like to thank Matthias Ballweg, Susanne Kadner and the whole Circular Republic team for the collaboration and the invaluable discussions. A special thanks goes to the system change leaders at Systemiq for being continuous sparring partners: Sophie Herrmann, Morten Rossé, Felix Philipp, Marco Daldoss Pirri, Carl Kühl, Tilmann Vahle, Achim Teuber, Marlene Kick, Clara von Luckner, Marie Wehinger, Theo Gott and many more.

We also owe gratitude to the many practitioners and experts across domains for the inspiring conversations that informed our work: Anja Eisenreich, Fabian Takacs, Marvin Henry, Julian Kirchherr, Philipp Forster, Jan Konietzko, Paul Woelkenberg, Marianne Kuhlmann, Benedikt Braig, Katharina Peterwerth, Caroline Stern, Tom Szaky, Yvonne Swoboda, Aurel Stenzel, Christoph Bornschein, Patrick Hypscher, Jan-Christoph von der Lancken, Justus Kammüller, Johannes Weirather, Bertram Kloss, Florian Schmieg, Christian Deger, Ulf Oesterlin, Hana Milanov, Marc Gruber and Wolfgang Jenewein. There are many more we should thank. We are grateful for so many conversations over the last years that helped us to learn and shape our ideas!

We extend our heartfelt appreciation to the entire IMD team, with special gratitude to Knut Haanaes, Delia Fischer and Paul Milner for their unwavering support and commitment. We are equally thankful to the numerous participants in our programmes who willingly served as 'guinea pigs', providing real-life examples and contributing to the continuous improvement of our worksheets and frameworks.

Importantly, we would like to thank the icons in the domain of circular economy, whose visionary thought leadership and dedicated efforts have shaped and built this field over the years. The work in this book stands on the shoulders of giants, and we are profoundly thankful for their enduring contributions.

We are grateful for the support of our publisher, specifically Eloise Cook and Yashmeena Bisht, for the professional guidance throughout this process. Our appreciation extends to the team of Housatonic for designing the artwork and being great partners.

We offer our appreciation and gratitude to you, the reader. We truly hope that these pages help you on the journey towards your circular and regenerative business future. Thank you for the engagement and personal leadership against the triple crisis!

Publisher's acknowledgements

Text credits

26 Martin Stuchtey: Quotes by Neale Donald Walsch; 26 Martin Stuchtey: Quotes by Kaz Nejatian; 40 Andrew Winston: Kantor, D. (2012) Reading the Room: Group dynamics for coaches and leaders, Jossey-Bass.; 40 Andrew Winston: Janni, N. (2022) Leader as Healer: A new paradigm for 21st century leadership, LID Publishing.; 40 Andrew Winston: Kantor, D. (2012) Reading the Room: Group dynamics for coaches and leaders, Jossey-Bass.; 40 Andrew Winston: Adapted from David Kantor (2011) Reading the Room: Group Dynamics for Coaches and Leaders; 40 Andrew Winston: Adapted from Kantor, D. (2012) Reading the Room: Group Dynamics for Coaches and Leaders. Jossey-Bass; 46 The Royal Society: Genovese, M. A. (2015) The Future of Leadership: Leveraging influence in an age of hyper-change (Leadership: Research and Practice), Routledge.; 48 Elsevier: Transforming David Kantor's Four Player model of Team Roles. https://www.renewalassociates.co.uk/2023/06/transforming-david-kantors-four-player-model-of-team-roles/; 47 Joe Murphy: Katzenbach, J. R. and Smith, D.K. (2009) The Discipline of Teams, Harvard Business Review Classics.; 47 Joe Murphy: Quotes by Henry Ford; 47 Joe Murphy: Sinek, S. (2009) Start with Why: How great leaders inspire everyone to take action, NY Portfolio.; 47 Joe Murphy: Adapted from Lencioni, P. (2002) The Five Dysfunctions of a Team: A leadership fable. John Wiley & Sons; 47 Joe Murphy: Quotes by Robert Frost; 49 Ørsted A/S: Quotes by Stephen Covey; 52 Lush ltd: Adapted from Scharmer's model of the Four Fields appears in Isaacs W. (1999) Dialogue and the Art of Thinking Together. Bantam Doubleday Dell Publishing Group; 52 Alpro: David Bohm, On Dialogue, Taylor & Francis; 53 Vaude: Quotes by Nancy Rothbard; 55 Freitag: Quotes by Alain de Botton; 56 Oliver Brunschwiler: Horst W. J. Rittel and Melvin M. Webber, Jun., 1973 Dilemmas in a General Theory of Planning, Springer.; 56 Oliver Brunschwiler: Quotes by Keith Grint; 56 Oliver Brunschwiler: Ronald Heifetz and Donald L. Laurie From the Magazine (December 2001) The Work of Leadership, Harvard Business Publishing; 62 Julia L. K. Nußholz: Quotes by Andy Cook; 63 Alexander Osterwalder: Adapted from William Isaacs, Dialogue and the Art of Thinking Together, Journal of Organizational Change Management, Penguin Random House; 63 Alexander Osterwalder: Quotes by Eleanor Roosevelt; 63 Alexander Osterwalder: Mike Clayton, The Influence Agenda: A Systematic Approach to Aligning Stakeholders for Driving Change: A Systematic Approach to Aligning Stakeholders in Times of Change, Palgrave Macmillan; 63 Alexander Osterwalder: Quotes by Pablo Picasso; 120 Springer Nature Limited: Quotes by Peter Drucker; 147 Dwight D. Eisenhower: Pete Samson MAY 20, 2022, Brompton Bike CEO Shares His Vision For Cleaner, Happier Cities, Mr Feelgood; 152 Robert Bosch GmbH: Sarah Rozenthuler

2016, Systemic dialogue: a gateway to purpose-led leadership, Sift Limited; 152 SAP SE: Southwest Airlines: Our Purpose and Vision; 157 Ellen MacArthur Foundation: Quotes by Steve Jurkovich; 175 Charlton Grant LTD: Ebert, C., Hurth, V. and Prabhu, P., (2018) The What, the Why and the How of Purpose: A guide for leaders, Chartered Management Institute and Blueprint for Better Business White Paper, https://www.managers.org.uk/~/media/Files/Reports/Guide-for-Leaders-White-Paper.pdf.; 175 Talke Schaffrannek: Polman, P. and Winston, A. (2021) Net Positive: How courageous companies thrive by giving more than they take, Harvard Business Review Press.; 175 Talke Schaffrannek: Quotes by Margaret Mead; 175 Talke Schaffrannek: Isaacs(1999), Dialogue: The Art of Thinking together, Doubleday; 179 Patagonia, Inc: Quotes by David Thoreau; 179 Patagonia, Inc: Quotes by Oliver Wendall Holmes; 180 Ørsted A/S: Quotes by Mahatma Gandhi; 183 Hermann Hesse: President Barack Obama, Remarks by the President at Rally on Health Insurance Reform, THE WHITE HOUSE September 12, 2009.; 183 The Roddick Foundation: President Barack Obama, Remarks by the President at Rally on Health Insurance Reform, THE WHITE HOUSE September 12, 2009.

Image credits

COV IMD: IMD Logo; COV Lizzy Burt: Lizzy Burt; 2,5,6,8,9,10,10,11,14,16, 19,22,23,24,27,35,38,42,50,51,60,66,64,65,69,83,95,107,119,133,136,137, 142,144,145-146,149,150,156,159,160,161,165,169,172 houstanic.eu.

SQUARING THE CIRCLE?

Getting started

1

Squaring the circle?

Imagine squaring a circle in the world of geometry, a challenge that has confounded mathematicians for centuries. Their quest was to construct a square with an area precisely equal to that of a given circle using only a compass and straight edge. This seemingly impossible task serves as a powerful analogy for the colossal task of reshaping our current linear economy into a circular one. Just as mathematicians grapple with the intractable nature of squaring a circle, we, too, face considerable complexities when it comes to circularising the way we do business. The shift from a linear economy to a circular one can seem as impossible as this age-old mathematical puzzle, which explains why the promise of the circular economy has not materialised yet. In this book, we will embark on a journey through the intricate and often perplexing landscape of the circular economy. We will explore the circular economy's inherent challenges, its remarkable potential and the innovative solutions and business model opportunities that can bridge the gap between our linear past and the circular future we aspire to create. As we delve into the principles and business model patterns that govern the circular economy, we will discover that the impossible can become possible, and the improbable can turn into the inevitable. Welcome to the fascinating world of circular business models, where we aim to transform complexity into opportunity and, just perhaps, square the circle of sustainable prosperity.

Ask yourself

- Have you observed signals for change or critical pressure points facing your organisation if you continue with business as usual?
- Do you have a clear vision of where your organisation wants to position itself in a sustainable future?
- How can you identify opportunities to reinvent yourself in the context of the shift towards a sustainable, circular and regenerative economy?
- How well-prepared is your organisation to strategically innovate for circularity, navigating the dynamic pathway with creativity?
- Is your organisation structurally and culturally ready for a successful transformation towards circularity?

If you don't have an answer yet, you're not alone. In our work and research with leading companies and the people who run them, we encountered the same uncertainty over and over again: the vision and theoretical promise of the circular economy is convincing and appealing, but it does not appear feasible nor actionable for a business to implement.

We agree – and disagree! We agree that the conversation around a circular economy has often been too abstract or philosophical. For many business decision makers it seems somewhat distant from their day-to-day corporate reality, where they are facing the pressure to deliver tangible economic results quickly. At the same time, we disagree that it can't be done. This book is the result of our two individual journeys that culminated in a shared passion and vision to show that a circular business world is desirable – and feasible. We derive our insights from encounters with thought leaders, experts, pioneers and multiple case examples that prove that a different economy is possible.

Using a decade's worth of research, insights and best practices we address the fundamental question: *How do we envision, design and implement circular business models?* Drawing upon analyses of hundreds of real-world cases we illustrate how a circular business transformation can unite environmental and economic impact. Beyond that, we shed light on the critical bottlenecks that must be overcome to succeed on this revolutionary journey.

Moving from 'licence to operate' to 'licence to innovate'

Let us now introduce you to the guiding structure that will shape your journey into the world of circularity. This practical framework challenges conventional thinking through a new approach to sustainable business transformation centred around circular business model innovation (Figure 1.1). This innovative journey takes you beyond the standard linear model of business success. At the core of our framework are three distinct horizons that span over time, from the present reality to the emerging future. It embraces a different way of looking at the world and our economy, a circular paradigm, which could change how you see sustainability, innovation and the future of your business. We hope this

Figure 1.1. Circular business revolution framework

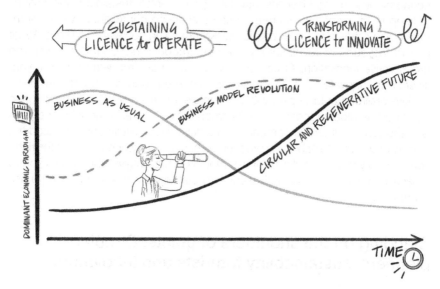

(inspired by the Three Horizons framework by Bill Sharpe and International Futures Forum[1])

framework sparks new ideas, helping you on the practical journey of building winning circular business models.

The first horizon, 'Business as usual', represents the current status quo where companies operate within the bounds of traditional, linear business models and value creation. This is the realm of your current success. However, we invite you to look at your case from outside-in and delve deep into the signals for change that challenge this status quo. Most business leaders agree that their current business will likely experience significant disruptions over the next 10–15 years. The primary focus will be on understanding the constraints of the current system and recognising the urgent call for change.

In contrast, the horizon 'Circular and regenerative future' invites you to shape a vision of what the future of business might look like for your organisation. Here, we embrace the emergence of a new circular and regenerative business paradigm – a vision for the future success of your business that is future-proof and resilient against external shocks. Consider it a north star for a net positive future that does not exceed the limits of our planetary boundaries but, instead, fosters positive externalities. It represents a transformative change towards a future where your company cultivates new relationships and builds new ecosystems with the goal of achieving regenerative outcomes.

The horizon of 'Business model revolution' serves as the critical bridge between the linear business models of the past and the circular, regenerative economy we envision in the not-so-distant future. Business model innovation empowers companies to proactively address the inefficiencies of their current value chain. Yet, many innovations today merely sustain the existing linear economy, where organisations introduce (incremental) sustainable innovations to keep their 'licence to operate', such as ensuring compliance with environmental regulations and adapting to quickly changing societal conditions. What is truly needed are revolutionary business models that enable circular and regenerative innovation. At its core, circular business models represent your 'licence to innovate'. They optimise for resource productivity and harmonise positive environmental impact with profitable economic value – a concept often perceived as utopian today. We will introduce five business model archetypes and showcase numerous companies that have successfully demonstrated the viability of such sustainable and prosperous business practices. Scaling the right, commercially viable circular business models is the catalyst that allows you to proactively shape a transformative pathway that aligns with your future business imperative.

Standing on the shoulders of giants: Circular pioneers, sustainability futurists and innovators

On our journey to develop a practical framework for sustainable and circular business models, we've drawn inspiration from the dynamic intersection of three influential streams of thought and practice: the pioneers of circular thinking, sustainability futurists as well as innovation and business model visionaries

Figure 1.2. Sources of inspiration

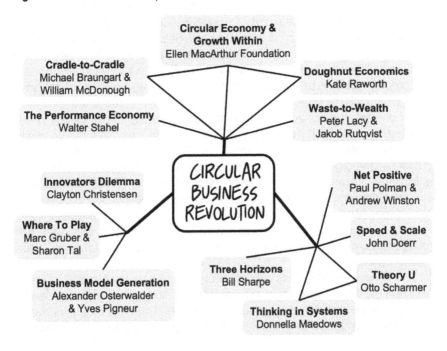

(Figure 1.2). This fusion creates a rich foundation of concepts and experiences aimed at catalysing change in how we conduct business and interact with the world. These varied inspirations serve as guiding lights, illuminating the path towards a future that is not just more prosperous, but also inherently sustainable and regenerative.

Your circular business revolution at a glance

We are excited to embark on this explorative journey into the world of circularity and regenerative thinking with you. Envision this as an expedition – an exploration that spans the past, present and future of your business landscape. As part of this journey we invite you to craft a roadmap for a pathway designed not just to adapt to change but to truly thrive in. We will delve into the practical details of how to translate transformative opportunities into practical applications.

Turning the circularity promise into business reality in four steps

This book will guide you through four steps to support you in designing your circular business model opportunities. We will present a rich set of real-world examples to inspire your imagination, along with practical tips and tricks for turning your aspirations into transformative action.

Step 1. Sense broadly – Understand the signals for change

Dive into the signals for change that challenge your traditional business case and linear business models. The primary focus will be to gain a clear understanding of the constraints within your current system and 'business-as-usual' approach. We will help you in sensing your emerging context and anticipating the most pressing signals.

Step 2. Think ahead – Envision a circular and regenerative future

Break with the past and present to envision what the business landscape of the future might look like for you. Shift your mindset to embrace a new, circular business paradigm. We will guide you in formulating an ambitious vision for your circular and regenerative business future. The north star guiding the 'theory for change' for your business.

Step 3. Revolutionise! – Explore and prioritise circular business models

Delve into five revolutionary business models archetypes. This will enable you to creatively explore the opportunities, which can harmonise positive environmental impact with profitable economic value. Seize your 'licence to innovate' and articulate your opportunity set. We will help you to think from the 'future back' and craft your transformative pathway.

Step 4. Get ready – Leverage organisational enablers for driving progress

Explore the essential organisational enablers to turn your vision into reality, your ideas into action. We will assist you in enhancing your circular business acumen, enabling you to navigate emerging barriers more effectively. Strengthen your readiness to catalyse the circular business transformation across the dimensions of strategy, execution and people.

Navigating the circular business model archetypes and patterns

At the heart of our comprehensive framework are five circular business model archetypes, each equipped with a specific icon for quick identification (Figure 1.3). Underlying these archetypes, you'll discover 15 carefully crafted

Figure 1.3. Circular business model archetypes

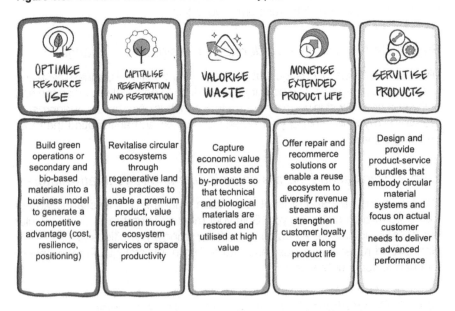

OPTIMISE RESOURCE USE	CAPITALISE REGENERATION AND RESTORATION	VALORISE WASTE	MONETISE EXTENDED PRODUCT LIFE	SERVITISE PRODUCTS
Build green operations or secondary and bio-based materials into a business model to generate a competitive advantage (cost, resilience, positioning)	Revitalise circular ecosystems through regenerative land use practices to enable a premium product, value creation through ecosystem services or space productivity	Capture economic value from waste and by-products so that technical and biological materials are restored and utilised at high value	Offer repair and recommerce solutions or enable a reuse ecosystem to diversify revenue streams and strengthen customer loyalty over a long product life	Design and provide product-service bundles that embody circular material systems and focus on actual customer needs to deliver advanced performance

business model patterns serving as inspiration to help you identify the most impactful opportunities for your business. These patterns transcend industries, providing a universal language for strategic innovation, and have the power to align environmental impact with concrete business value. Within each business model pattern you will find a thorough exploration of its industry relevance accompanied by a wealth of case examples that offer valuable insights. While we highly encourage thorough exploration of all five archetypes, as doing so can trigger non-obvious ideas and opportunities, you can also directly delve into a specific archetype that you believe holds particular relevance for your business.

A practical and hands-on approach

This book is designed to be both practical and interactive, seamlessly integrating theoretical insights and real-world case examples with reflection exercises and worksheets. Our goal is to empower you to actively craft your own circular transformation pathway, step by step, ensuring a hands-on and personalised journey towards implementing circular business models. Aligned with the four steps outlined previously, we have developed four guiding worksheets that will help you crystallise your insights, refine your strategy and solidify your path towards a successful circular transformation. These tools serve as companions ensuring that the journey from inspiration to implementation is tailored to your specific needs.

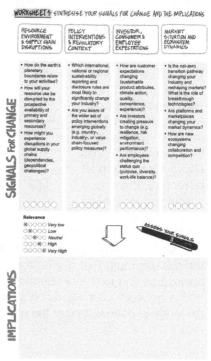

Worksheet 1 – Understand the signals for change and the impact on your organisation

This worksheet addresses the limitations of the traditional 'business-as-usual' strategy, which may excel under normal circumstances but pose challenges in the face of changing conditions. It provides a structured methodology to identify the most relevant signals for change – whether they stem from resource disruptions, regulatory pressure or shifting market dynamics. Through this proactive examination of your case and future operational landscape, several implications emerge indicating that your current approach may no longer be fit for purpose.

Worksheet 2 – Envision a circular and regenerative future and define your ambition

This worksheet guides you in defining your ambition level for both your environmental impact and business aspirations. With a strategic time frame of 10–15 years this exercise encourages visionary thinking, fostering fundamental

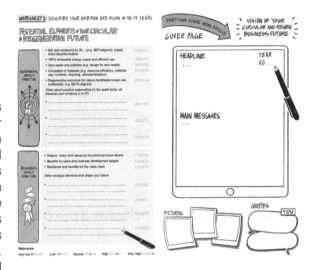

changes without being too distant. At the core of this worksheet is the 'Newspaper headline' exercise, an impactful tool for crafting your future horizon. You are encouraged to vividly envision a world where your desired change has manifested.

Worksheet 3 – Explore and prioritise circular business model opportunities and map your pathway

This worksheet starts with a synthesis of your emerging opportunity ideas. After initially evaluating the economic and environmental impact potential, the focus shifts to identifying which opportunities

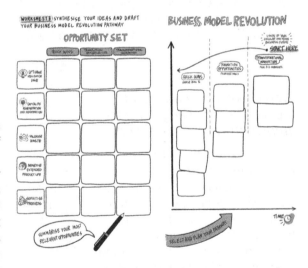

are most relevant to achieve your vision. Employing a 'future back' approach, this step involves exploring transformative innovation opportunities in the distant future that align closely with your envisioned path. Next, work backwards and turn your attention to transition opportunities which act as a bridge between your aspirational future and current business reality. Finally, the journey grounds itself in the present, introducing quick-win opportunities.

Worksheet 4 – Leverage organisational enablers for action by assessing your circular readiness

This worksheet focuses on assessing your readiness for realising your circular business transformation. It offers a readiness scan that can help you to learn about the success factors, particularly tailored to your prioritised business models. Key considerations encompass the people layer, emphasising foundational skillsets and leadership to drive change across the organisation; the strategic layer, providing direction and strategic alignment; as well as the execution layer, building the operational backbone for your journey.

Good to know!

Embrace the journey!

You can certainly use this book to just get some inspiration or compare cases and best practice examples. However, if you're eager to transition from idea to action, we invite you to join us on the comprehensive journey from start to finish. Anticipate some twists and turns as you navigate between different steps. 'Explore, experiment, learn, adapt' – as you will learn later in Chapter 4 from Alexander Osterwalder. Enjoy the process!

Tailored to YOU!

Whether you're just starting to explore circularity or you are already actively advancing a circular business agenda, this book caters to your unique journey. While structured as a holistic experience, recognising that every company has different needs and starting points, the decision of when to join us depends on your prior knowledge and experience. But in any case, be prepared to ask yourself tough questions and challenge your ambition level, such as the one Andrew Winston (co-author of *Net Positive*) poses in Chapter 3: 'Is the world better off because your business is in it?'

Positive mindset!

The triple planetary crisis – climate change, biodiversity loss and pollution – demands a proactive solutions mindset. Because every company is part of the problems we are facing, they are also playing an important role in being part of the solution. We invite you to embrace an opportunity mindset, as articulated by sustainability pioneer Martin Stuchtey in Chapter 2: 'It's too late to be a pessimist'. This perspective shift not only recognises the challenges, but also empowers you to contribute positively to resolving the critical issues ahead of us.

Engage your team!

The book is organised in a way to guide you through this journey one step, one reflection and one worksheet at a time. You may not have all the exact answers, that's not a problem you can work with assumptions, but the true value lies in collaboratively using the worksheets as this will help you to ensure a sense of ownership among your team, speak the same language, spark collective creativity and venture in the same direction. In the words of Talke Schaffrannek, Circularity leader at BASF (Chapter 5): 'You have to enable the collective expertise and energy to develop circular solutions.' To ensure all voices are heard it's oftentimes a good idea to start with individual reflections on the worksheets before engaging in collaborative discussions.

Who benefits from joining us on this revolutionary journey?

Senior leaders and executives

If you are an executive or senior business leader you will gain insights into circular strategies that hold the potential to mitigate risks, tap into new value pools, improve resource productivity and contribute to overall value chain resilience!

Sustainability specialists

As a sustainability specialist or practitioner, deepen your knowledge and practical understanding of circular economy principles and business model design. Explore case studies and best practices for how to successfully drive circularity within your organisation.

Innovation managers

As an innovation manager, you can leverage this book to explore new avenues for product and service development that create market differentiation and a competitive edge through circular business models.

Supply chain professionals

If you are a supply chain expert or practitioner you may gain valuable insights into optimising resource use and building new ecosystems. Circular supply chain practices help to advance supply chain resilience and align with corporate sustainability goals.

Start-up founders

As a (prospective) entrepreneur, benefit from this book by discovering opportunities to build new ventures. Either with circular models at the core and from the ground up, or by working on enabling technologies or the required infrastructure! This is an opportunity space with tailwind through growing consumer preferences and interested investors.

Policy makers

If you are a government official or working at the policy–business interface, equip yourselves to create supportive enabling conditions that incentivise businesses to adopt circular practices, addressing the challenge of balancing economic growth with sustainable development.

Educators and researchers

If you are an academic, use this book to stay informed about the latest developments in circular economy concepts and enrich your curricula to ensure students are well prepared for a future where sustainable practices are integral to successful business operations.

Investors and financial analysts

As an investor or analyst, understand the impact of circular strategies on investment decisions and portfolio management to navigate a market where circular practices are increasingly seen as indicators of long-term success and stability.

Let's get started to see opportunities where others see only risks, turning the uncertainty of future changes into a strategic asset for your company. Are you prepared to embark on this journey? If so, make yourself comfortable to challenge your perspectives, ignite your creative spirits and join us on this exploratory journey into the fascinating world of circularity!

Signals for change: What is your emerging future?

2

Reinventing your business models servoo as the key to turning emerging challenges into opportunities that will drive you closer to your ambitious objectives. This chapter will integrate an 'inside-out' understanding of your value creation system with an 'outside-in' awareness of your ever-evolving operational context and environment. While the 'inside-out' perspective provides you with an all-encompassing view of your value creation system, it's crucial to underscore the importance of cultivating a robust 'outside-in' perspective. This will not only ensure your 'licence to operate' – the necessary measures to meet evolving environmental requirements – but also secure your 'licence to innovate'. Understanding your signals for change helps you to identify areas where you can gain a competitive edge through cost savings or where you can tap into new market opportunities. Try to anticipate the future operational environment for your specific case, which is likely poised to be disruptive.

2.1 Inside-out perspective on value creation

Many of the challenges we face today stem from the inherent limitations of prevailing linear value-creation systems. This concept, often referred to as 'linear lock-in' or 'take-make-waste' represents our current dominant economic model (see Figure 2.1). In essence, we can find inefficiencies at every stage of linear value chains. These inefficiencies commence at the design stage, where a staggering 80 per cent of a product's environmental impact is determined.[1] Next, consider how we extract and source natural resources, such as mining raw materials or logging for wood. These resources then undergo extensive processing, passing through multiple stages across different businesses, with very limited traceability, before eventually becoming a finished product. Frequently, inefficiencies emerge from underutilised capacities, like machines operating below their full potential or trucks running at less than full capacity. The resulting product is then sold and used by a single customer for its entire lifespan. For many companies it remains unknown who the actual end-consumer really is. The products often fail to realise their full potential, whether due to functional limitations, planned obsolescence or emotional factors. Ultimately when these products no longer serve a purpose, valuable materials and components frequently degrade into waste, often finding their way into incineration processes. From a company perspective, this is typically described by a linear value chain; highly dependent on the respective company, but along similar patterns and often mirroring some common challenges within sectors. Here are three illustrative examples:

- **Textiles and fashion:** In traditional (fast) fashion, clothes are mass-produced, sold and unfortunately often used infrequently before being discarded into the general waste stream. This practice contributes significantly to waste and pollution problems. Shockingly, statistics reveal that 60 to 90 per cent of clothing ends up either in landfills or being incinerated.[5] To put it in perspective, this is roughly equivalent to a truckload of clothes being buried or burned every second.[6]

- **Food and agriculture:** In conventional agriculture and food, the processes involve the growth and harvesting of crops followed by sales. Food is produced, shipped and sold typically along a complex

Figure 2.1. Traditional linear value-creation systems

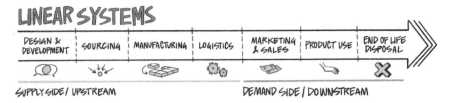

(inspired by Nordic Innovation,[2] Sitra[3] and Lacy and Rutqvist[4])

and opaque value chain. The Food and Agriculture Organization estimates that around 14 per cent of the world's food is lost between harvesting and retail markets, with an additional 17 per cent wasted at the retail level or by consumers.[7] This means roughly one-third of food goes to waste.

- **Plastics and packaging:** The rapid growth of global plastics production, especially for packaging, coupled with the predominant linear economic model that includes single-use packaging, has given rise to a significant amount of plastic waste. A problem that is expected to almost double globally by 2040.[8] Alarmingly, under business-as-usual assumptions, only about 13 per cent of this plastic waste undergoes recycling, approximately 31 per cent is landfilled or incinerated, while a staggering 56 per cent is mishandled, often leaking into land or oceans, or being openly burned.

Many of the systemic challenges we face today are deeply ingrained in our linear economic systems.[9] Linear systems prioritise the productivity of workers and labour over the efficient use of resources. Negative externalities stemming from economic activities, such as the social and environmental costs associated with waste and pollution, are often passed on to society and nature. Within these systems, value creation hinges on the production and sales of as many products as possible, fostering both overproduction and overconsumption. Producers often bear limited responsibility for what happens with their products and associated waste at the end of their life cycle. Additionally, our global and fragmented supply chains often lack transparency, creating opaque value chains. This lack of visibility makes it challenging to trace the origins and current states of materials, hindering efforts to implement sustainable solutions effectively. Furthermore, insufficient collection and reverse logistics infrastructure pose formidable barriers, making it nearly impossible to design and execute recovery strategies efficiently. Inadequate sorting and pre-processing exacerbate the problem, often making the cost-efficient recirculation of materials back into the economy challenging. These challenges underscore the need for comprehensive and systemic shifts towards more sustainable and circular economic models.

Mapping your value chain will help you to identify current inefficiencies from 'cradle to grave', encompassing all stages from resource extraction to the end of a product's life. Unlocking circular opportunities requires an understanding of your value chain and its inefficiencies. Doing this 'upstream' can reveal challenges that are related to resource extraction, while insights 'downstream' can reveal inefficiencies beyond your immediate sphere of influence. Understanding the inefficiencies in your value chain will help to shape your environmental impact ambition and also put a spotlight on various economic opportunities. These opportunities may include the conversion of waste into value, optimisation of product, machinery and logistics utilisation for improved unit economics, or harnessing untapped opportunities to create more value from products with extended life cycles. Of course, the specifics of your value chain will strongly depend on your position in the overall value creation process (such as a mining and materials provider, machinery company, producer of goods, or operations and service provider).

Inside-out perspective – Get started right now!

To begin this journey, we encourage you to map your current value chain and systematically collect observations of the potential inefficiencies you encounter. The following worksheet will help you to run this exercise (Figure 2.2). Try to take a perspective on the complete life cycles of your most relevant products, even if you may have some information and knowledge gaps. First, imagine your value chain steps and consider the inefficiencies that immediately come to your mind. There are five emerging clusters of types of inefficiencies, some of which are listed in the worksheet, but not exhaustively. Then, second, evaluate the significance of these inefficiencies in the context of your operations and overall sustainability objectives. Third, think about the implications: How do these challenges influence your current and future business?

As a source of inspiration for editing the worksheet, let's look at the different types of inefficiencies and revisit the **example from textiles and fashion**.

- Overuse of costly, unsustainable and scarce resources
  - *Very high use of fossil-based resources:* Products mostly rely on virgin feedstock, mainly plastics (63 per cent) and cotton (26 per cent).[10]
  - *Very high reliance on primary resources:* Recycled material use is very minimal (2 per cent). This mostly comes from other industry waste (e.g. PET bottles), not from textile-to-textile recycling.[11]
- Negative externalities on natural capital or social capital
  - *Pressure on land, water and ocean use change:* Unsustainable material production (e.g. cotton) has significant insecticide and pesticides use.
  - *Pollution:* Washing synthetic textiles contributes to 35 per cent of microplastics leakage into the environment due to plastic microfibres.[12]
  - *High climate/CO_2 emission intensity:* Value chain has impact on global emissions (2–10 per cent of CO_2 emissions, depending on source), with material production (20 per cent), product use (20 per cent) and wet processing (15 per cent) having highest shares.[13]
- Significant waste generation at low material value
  - *Radical cost optimisation focus:* Low-quality clothing items are often discarded after seven to eight wears.[14]
  - *High amounts of processing waste:* Textile dyeing is the second largest polluter of water globally.[15]
  - *Limited transparency on compliance in the value chain:* Production often in developing and low-wage countries with limited transparency on social and environmental standards and regulation.
- Low productivity or underutilised capacities in product use
  - *Low utilisation:* Overall clothing utilisation decreased significantly over the last two decades.

Figure 2.2. Taking stock of linear system challenges

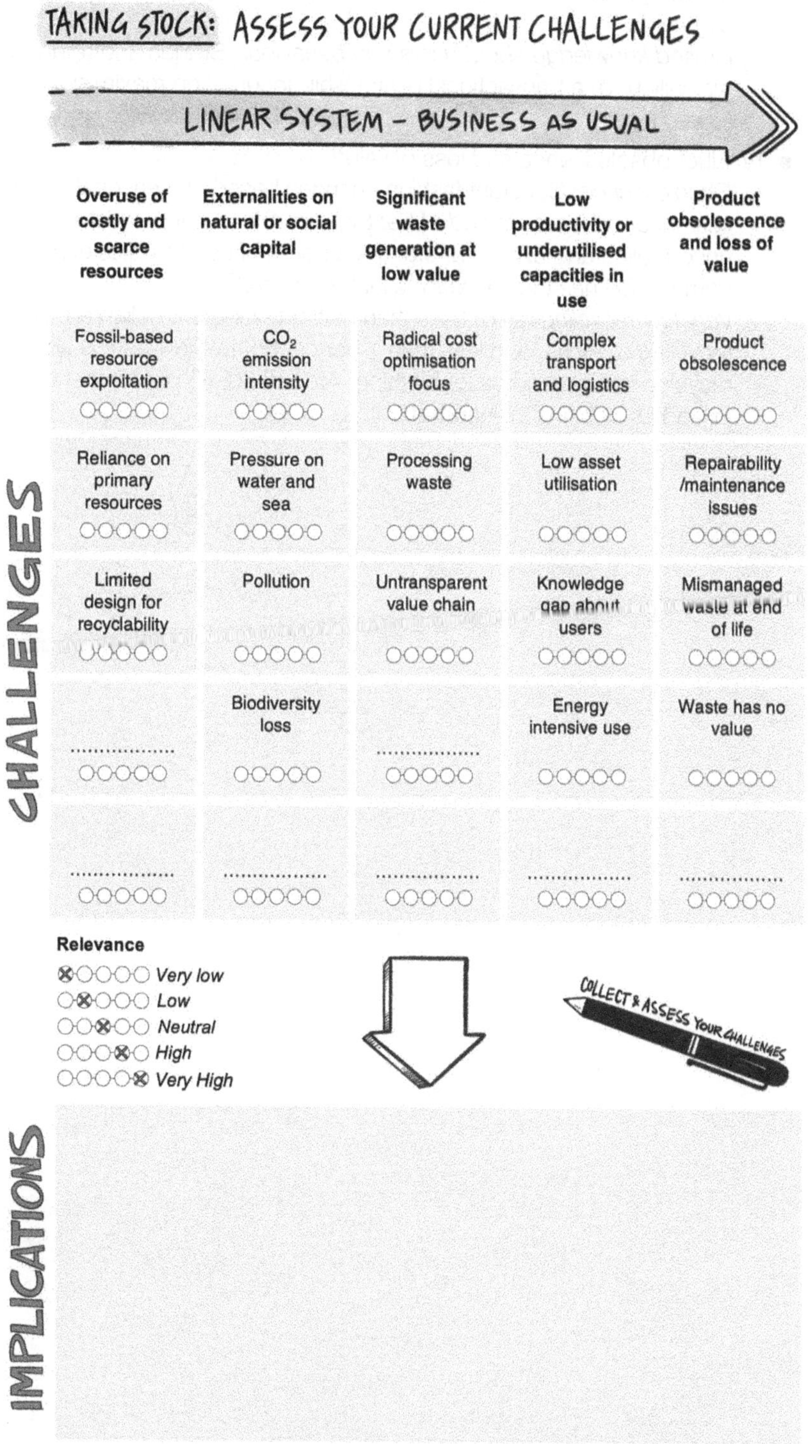

TAKING STOCK: ASSESS YOUR CURRENT CHALLENGES

LINEAR SYSTEM – BUSINESS AS USUAL

CHALLENGES

Overuse of costly and scarce resources	Externalities on natural or social capital	Significant waste generation at low value	Low productivity or underutilised capacities in use	Product obsolescence and loss of value
Fossil-based resource exploitation ○○○○○	CO_2 emission intensity ○○○○○	Radical cost optimisation focus ○○○○○	Complex transport and logistics ○○○○○	Product obsolescence ○○○○○
Reliance on primary resources ○○○○○	Pressure on water and sea ○○○○○	Processing waste ○○○○○	Low asset utilisation ○○○○○	Repairability /maintenance issues ○○○○○
Limited design for recyclability ○○○○○	Pollution ○○○○○	Untransparent value chain ○○○○○	Knowledge gap about users ○○○○○	Mismanaged waste at end of life ○○○○○
.... ○○○○○	Biodiversity loss ○○○○○	.... ○○○○○	Energy intensive use ○○○○○	Waste has no value ○○○○○
.... ○○○○○	.... ○○○○○	.... ○○○○○	.... ○○○○○	.... ○○○○○

Relevance
⊗○○○○ Very low
○⊗○○○ Low
○○⊗○○ Neutral
○○○⊗○ High
○○○○⊗ Very High

COLLECT & ASSESS YOUR CHALLENGES

IMPLICATIONS

- *Inefficient transport and logistics:* Return rates in fashion e-commerce typically range from 20 to 40 per cent, varying by regions and segments.[16]
- *Limited knowledge about users and behaviour:* Brands and retailers typically have a transactional relationship focused on maximising (one-off) sales.
- Product obsolescence and loss of value
  - *Obsolescence:* Constant fashion changes based on seasonal trends.
  - *Mismanaged waste at end of life:* Significant amount of waste is uncontrolled and exported, e.g. the amount of used textiles exported from the EU has tripled over the last 20 years.[17]
  - *Very low recycling rates:* Less than half of textiles are collected for recycling or reuse, and less than 1 per cent of textile waste is actually recycled into new fibres for clothing. Around 60–90 per cent ends up in landfills or being incinerated.[18]

2.2 Outside-in perspective on your future operating context

Do disruptions come expected or unexpected? Natural cosmetics company Weleda faced a surprise almost overnight. Two of its products, a rosemary hair tonic and hair oil, became unexpectedly popular on TikTok, where the Gen-Z praised their effectiveness and shared their results. This led to a surge in sales, but also a challenge in sourcing enough rosemary to meet the demand. Weleda had been collecting rosemary from the wild in Spain, where it grows abundantly and organically. However, due to climate change and drought, the area was suffering from a decline in plant diversity and quality. After conducting several trials, Weleda found a suitable partner in France, a farmer who agreed to grow rosemary for them. This was a risky venture as rosemary takes time to mature and yield a harvest. To support the farmer Weleda helped him with their agronomy team and a compost project which improved the soil health, reduced the carbon footprint and enhanced the biodiversity of the farm. Weleda's story is an example of how a company found an innovative solution to address a severe supply chain shortage without compromising on environmental and social standards. A happy end in their case.

Just like many company leaders, you may have realised that your organisation's future operating context is set for disruption. In facing fundamental challenges ahead, the capability to innovate will emerge as *the* critical factor for long-term success. The convergence of technological advancements, evolving consumer needs and new business models has frequently showcased how organisational contexts can rapidly shift. Think of digital photography and smartphones reshaping the photography industry, or digital music platforms like iTunes and Spotify that have transformed the music industry. The emergence of ride-sharing services and the electrification of the car, propelled by regulatory shifts, is currently disrupting the mobility sector. In the past two decades, digitalisation was the driving force for disruption; now, the next two decades will be steered by sustainability. For instance, the chemical industry is grappling with the need to reduce their dependence on fossil-based carbon feedstock. The agricultural industry quickly demands more resilient operating practices and business models due to resource scarcity (e.g. water shortages) and intense weather conditions related to climate change (e.g. heatwaves). The energy industry is in its transition as renewable energy adoption accelerates, underpinned by supportive policies. In light of these multifaceted developments, one constant emerges: disruptions are reshaping corporate operational environments at a significant scale and at an accelerating pace. Creating both danger and possibilities, risks and opportunities, depending on your perspective.

It is therefore crucial to embrace this transformative context by developing a solid outside-in understanding of the relevant signals for change for your company. This means drafting a holistic picture of the changing business environment and distilling the most relevant signals for your specific case. It is helpful to interpret the future operating context in terms of its implications, ranging from keeping your 'licence to operate' (i.e. essential must-dos to meet the new requirements of the changing environment) to seizing your 'licence to innovate'

Figure 2.3. Signals for change

RESOURCE ENVIRONMENT & SUPPLY CHAIN DISRUPTIONS	POLICY INTERVENTIONS & REGULATORY CONTEXT	INVESTOR, CONSUMER & EMPLOYEE EXPECTATIONS	MARKET SITUATION AND ECOSYSTEM DYNAMICS
• Resource scarcity and increasing price volatility • Pressure on global and fragmented supply chains • End-to-end supply chain transparency and traceability • Supply chain decarbonisation • Regenerative land use practices	• Increasing reporting/ disclosure requirements • Specific sustainability regulation (e.g. deforestation-free supply chains) • Complexity across and within markets and regions • Interaction with policy makers	• ESG becoming an investing imperative • Consumers demand green and fair products • Employee activism related to corporate sustainability • Sustainability becomes key in attracting and retaining talents	• Changing competitive environment • Breakthrough technologies • Platform economy and new market places • Exclusive ecosystem partnerships • Collaborating with competitors (coopetition)
↓ BOUNDARIES	↓ UNCERTAINTY	↓ CHANGE	↓ DISRUPTION

LINEAR SYSTEM – BUSINESS AS USUAL →

(i.e. areas to achieve competitive advantage via cost savings or market opportunities). Your emerging future can be structured along four categories (Figure 2.3).

Resource environment and supply chain disruptions

Resource scarcity and a run for net-zero resources are shifting the power dynamics in many industries, tilting the balance towards the supply side. The pursuit of resource availability puts pressure on already volatile supply chains. We encourage you to adopt a resource-focused viewpoint and look at your company's position, considering its sectoral and regional context. The goal of this exercise is to develop a clear hypothesis about your resource environment in 5–10 years. We will begin with a comprehensive overview and progressively refine your outlook step by step.

How do the Earth's planetary boundaries relate to your activities?
The planetary boundaries are critical thresholds that define the safe operating space for humanity within Earth's ecological system. The framework, developed by scientist Johan Rockström and his colleagues, provides a more granular perspective of our planet's triple crisis: climate, biodiversity and pollution. More

specifically, the boundaries encompass nine biophysical processes: climate change, water use or erosion of biodiversity among others (Figure 2.4).[19] Crossing these thresholds risks destabilising the Earth's system. In simple terms, planetary boundaries function as safety limits preserving the Earth's health and equilibrium. While the nine boundaries have been individually defined, they are intricately interconnected. As of September 2023, scientists quantified for the first time all planetary boundaries. Six out of nine boundaries have transgressed the threshold for increasing risk to people and irreversible change.

The planetary boundaries is a global framework with high materiality to your business. You can take two different perspectives here. First, consider how each of the planetary boundaries impacts your business. To make it more relatable,

Figure 2.4. Planetary boundaries framework

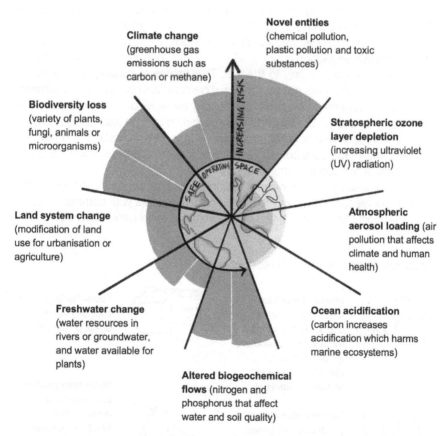

(based on Azote for Stockholm Resilience Centre, based on analysis in Richardson *et al.*[20]; biodiversity loss differentiates between functional and genetic; freshwater change separates blue and green water; biogeochemical flows cover phosphorus and nitrogen) take a specific planetary boundary and think about how it aligns with your area of operations. How do these natural processes influence your organisation? Second, building on your current value chain, which of your corporate activities have the most significant impact on the planetary boundaries? Nature risk is business risk, including physical risks due to damage of ecosystems or transition risks such as changes in demand or difficulties to meet regulatory requirements.[21]

How will your resource use be disrupted by the prospective availability of primary and secondary resources?

The scarcity of resources and raw materials can cause significant disruptions in supply chains. Behind the perspective of planetary boundaries, global resource use plays a critical role. For example, approximately 50 per cent of global emissions arise from resource extraction and processing, and more than 90 per cent of biodiversity loss and water stress, according to the International Resource Panel (IRP).[22] Following the approach of the IRP, resources include land, air, water and materials. Economic actors, in particular, use material resources to produce goods and services for our socio-economic systems. Material resources can be differentiated into four categories (Figure 2.5).

From a global perspective, absolute material resource use is still increasing. Global material extraction more than tripled between the 1970s and 2020 to 92 billion tonnes, according to the IRP. This relates to roughly 12 tonnes per capita in terms of annual average material demand and consumption, whereby high-income countries consume significantly more resources per capita than low-income countries. Global trade is particularly reliant on fossil fuels and metal ores. Some material resources, such as copper, lithium, cobalt and platinum group metals (PGMs), are considered as critical raw materials due to their supply vulnerabilities or economic importance.

From a company perspective, it's fundamental to understand and quantify your current resource use. Do you have information about your company's overall resource consumption? If not, you may develop an initial perspective using a few

Figure 2.5. Types of material resources

 Biomass (such as timber for industrial use or energy, crops for food, crop residues, grazed biomass, biomass for energy, biobased materials)

 Fossil fuels (such as coal, gas, crude oil, oil shale, petroleum)

 Non-metallic minerals (such as sand, gravel, limestone, plaster, clay)

 Metal ores (such as iron, aluminium, copper, other non-ferrous metals, precious metals)

(building on definitions by the International Resource Panel[23])

simple steps. First, to understand and categorise your absolute material resource use, use the total weight of purchased goods, or extrapolate an average weight of materials that are used to produce and package the organisation's primary products and services (e.g. the weight in tonnes for a specific year). Then apply the above resource typology or a structure that suits your specific context. Are you heavily dependent on a specific material resource? Try to differentiate your material inflows between primary and secondary resources. Primary material consumption refers to the use of virgin material resources for your production. Secondary materials refer to recovered and recycled materials that have already been used. Next, estimate the amount and type of waste generated. Particularly for solid waste, are you able to estimate the absolute volumes and, more importantly, do you have insights into the proportion that is diverted from disposal or incineration, directed instead towards material recovery operations (such as reuse or recycling)? Lastly, assess your resource outflows. In this final step, concentrate on the products and materials leaving the factory gates (i.e. what material resources leave the organisation, including the waste lens). If you are intentionally designing your products for reuse or recycling, do you have any data on the success of these efforts, such as confirmation that they are being effectively recycled?

How might you experience disruptions in your global supply chains?

The vulnerability of your global supply chains can be significant, particularly when your resource requirements heavily depend on specific materials, especially primary mined resources or scarce resources, and specific geographical supply regions. These risks are exacerbated when your supply chains are exposed to potential geopolitical conflicts or natural disasters, such as earthquakes, droughts, floods and, wildfires. Certain value chains exhibit inherent dependencies in their resource environment, and this is particularly evident in the case of many metals. For instance, the supply of critical raw materials like magnesium, cobalt and lithium often hinges on single regions or countries. China, for example, plays a pivotal role as the primary supplier, providing over 80 per cent of the global magnesium supply and over 90 per cent of many heavy rare earth elements. Cobalt predominantly comes from the Democratic Republic of Congo, while more than 75 per cent of lithium is sourced from Chile or Australia. The supply of PGMs heavily relies on South Africa and Russia. It's worth noting that recycling and refining from secondary sources are becoming increasingly vital in mitigating these dependencies. As the demand for resources continues to rise, particularly in the context of electrification and the energy transition, these specific regional supply dependencies could pose a significant risk. A disruption in the supply chain becomes a pressing concern for company operations.

It has become an important priority for many companies to advance their resource use strategy in order to create more resilient supply chains and implement their ambitious sustainability targets (e.g. net zero by 20xx, scope 1-2-3-decarbonisation). This leads to a competition for net-zero resources, such as recyclates, or renewables and their derivatives, or sustainable biomass. For example, for some high-quality plastic recyclate streams, such as recycled PET, there is already a situation of supply shortage versus high demand. Strategic thinking around the resource environment and potential supply chain disruptions is thus also needed for secondary materials.

Generally, also consider that having a high supply concentration on a limited number of suppliers, production facilities or transportation channels can make your supply chain vulnerable to disruptions if one or more of them encounter issues.

Food for thought

How will your resource and supply chain environment look like in 10 years from now?

In light of the planetary boundaries, the availability of primary and secondary resources and potential disruptions in global supply chains, can you project how your resource and supply chain environment will evolve over the next decade? Consider your organisation's specific resource consumption patterns and supply chain dependencies, and explore how these factors may shape the future of your organisation.

Meet a sustainability pioneer

Martin Stuchtey: 'It's too late to be a pessimist'

'The world is currently experiencing supply-side inflation, supply-chain disruptions, geo-political resource competition and a run for net-zero resources. All these factors suggest that any future model of prosperity generation will benefit from our ability to decouple from non-renewable resources. The circular economy lies at the core of this systemic change providing economic, social and ecological benefits – and independence.'

Martin Stuchtey is professor for Industrial Systems in Transition at the University of Innsbruck and founder of The Landbanking Group and Systemiq. In our conversation, he illustrated that, over the last 15 years, the circular economy movement has evolved significantly. It becomes clear that replacing the linear and extractive patterns of production and consumption though a circular and regenerative paradigm is the cheapest and fairest way to address the crises related to climate, biodiversity and cost of living.

However, according to Martin, this transformation is not happening at the required pace and requires more emphasis on unleashing natural capital. Given the speed of our Earth system changing, restoring and preserving natural ecosystems has never been more important. 'Nature is critical infrastructure that we need to thrive as companies, economies, and societies. We need to invest into natural capital at scale and shift land-use to circular and regenerative practices at scale, towards nature positive outcomes.' The Landbanking Group is building an end-to-end platform for natural capital, leveraging technology to create regenerative, circular and climate-resilient supply chains. It is an example of a new breed of companies that are deeply embracing circular and regenerative thinking with optimism – taking responsibility and rethinking business.

Policy interventions and regulatory context

Regulators around the world are introducing policy interventions with increasing pace and ambition levels. These interventions can be broadly categorised into two key aspects. First, they pertain to the regulatory landscape for sustainable business practices, particularly concerning reporting and disclosure (Figure 2.6). Second, they encompass a diverse spectrum of emerging policy measures that span from economic tools like fiscal tax adjustments, subsidies and public procurement policies, to the establishment of standards such as eco-design, and the implementation of bans or mandates, such as those targeting single-use products. These policy interventions manifest in various forms across different regions of the world with Europe taking a prominent leadership role, notably propelled by the policy frameworks established by the European Commission.

Figure 2.6. Emerging reporting and disclosure developments (selected examples)

ILLUSTRATIVE

VOLUNTARY

GUIDING STANDARDS

TCFD   Taskforce on Climate-Related Financial Disclosures (TCFD)

TN FD   Taskforce on Nature-Related Financial Disclosures (TNFD)

GRI   Global Reporting Initiative (GRI)

TARGET SETTING

Science Based Targets initiative (SBTi) and Science Based Targets Network (SBTN)

REPORTING PLATFORMS

CDP

Carbon Disclosure Project

MANDATORY

REGULATORY STANDARDS & TAXONOMIES

 International Sustainability Standards Board (ISSB) Sustainability Accounting Standards Board (SASB)

 ISO International Organization for Standardization

EFRAG European Financial Reporting Advisory Group (EFRAG)
- EU Taxonomy Regulation
- Corporate Sustainability Reporting Directive (CSRD)
- Sustainable Finance Disclosure Regulation (SFDR)
- Ecodesign for Sustainable Products Regulation (ESPR)
- Corporate Sustainability Due Diligence Directive (CSDDD)
- Green Claims Directive
- Packaging and Packaging Waste Directive
- Carbon Border Adjustment Mechanism (CBAM)

NATIONAL REGULATIONS (EXAMPLES ONLY)

Australia – Prudential Practice Guidance on Climate Change and Financial Risks

US – Climate Disclosures for Public Companies; National Framework for Advancing the U.S. Recycling System regulation; California Climate Corporate Accountability Act

China – ESG-related amendments to the disclosure rules for listed companies; Guidance for enterprise ESG disclosure; Circular Economy Promotion Law

UK – Sustainability Disclosure Standards

Which reporting and disclosure rules are most likely to significantly change your industry?

With respect to the corporate reporting landscape, voluntary measurement and disclosure initiatives have paved the way for emerging mandatory regulation standards. For example, the main bodies proposing rules for environmental, social and governance (ESG) reporting (e.g. EFRAG, ISSB, SEC) are building on the guidance of the Task Force on Climate-Related Financial Disclosures (TCFD). Within the frame of voluntary initiatives, the Science Based Targets initiative (SBTi) has done pioneering work to develop a leading framework for setting corporate decarbonisation pathways, which is being adopted increasingly globally and, in many ways, developing into an implicit standard for ambitious companies. Building on the momentum of SBTi, now science-based targets for air, land, biodiversity, freshwater and the ocean are being developed by the Science Based Targets Network (SBTN).

Regulators and standard setters worldwide are introducing mandatory disclosure requirements in various shapes and colours. This is driven by the ambition to reach (inter)national commitments as well as the pressing need for immediate action to manage the exposure to climate-related risks and protect economic and financial stability. Particularly in Europe, the policy framework of the European Green Deal has paved the way for a set of policy interventions, including the Corporate Sustainability Reporting Directive (CSRD) affecting nearly 50,000 companies to report to this standard. Within that framework, there is also a specific standard (E5) dedicated to resource use and the circular economy.

Are you aware of the wider set of policy interventions emerging globally, beyond reporting and disclosure?

Several policies, which differ widely across regions, aim at supporting the transition to more sustainable economic systems and specific industries. China, for example, is introducing a series of laws to accelerate more responsible resource use, such as the Circular Economy Promotion Law, the Circular Economy Development Strategy or the CE action plan. The US has introduced the National Recycling Strategy and the Resource Recovery and Circular Economy Act. Europe has linked resource-related policies to the European Green Deal and Circular Economy Action Plan.

Within and across all these policy initiatives, regulators employ a diverse toolkit of measures. Taking Europe as an example, these regulations may encompass bans or mandates, like the ban on single-use plastics, as well as standards such as the Ecodesign for Sustainable Products Regulation. Additionally, green procurement policies are implemented to stimulate new business models or technologies. Producer ownership levers, including the Extended Producer Responsibility schemes for packaging or Waste from Electrical and Electronic Equipment (WEEE), are also in play. Moreover, economic instruments, such as dedicated investments, grants and subsidies contribute to the regulatory landscape. Effective fiscal instruments can also manifest as tax adjustments, such as virgin material taxes or VAT adjustments. Understanding the relevant policy interventions necessitates a specific focus on the respective national applications, and even adaptations at specific regional, state or city levels.

The implications of different policy types, whether related to disclosure and reporting, standards, regulatory instruments or economic instruments, may have regional or local specifications. For globally operating organisations with a range of products across industries, navigating this intricate environment can be highly complex.

Food for thought

With a perspective on 10 years ahead, what are your hypotheses given current developments in your regulatory context?
How do you anticipate these evolving regulations to impact your business operations, supply chains and overall sustainability strategies over the next decade? Are you adequately prepared to adapt to future regulatory shifts and to leverage emerging opportunities?

Investor, consumer and employee expectations

Many companies are confronted with increasing expectations to act on their environmental and social performance – both from their internal and external stakeholders. Maintaining your 'licence to operate' requires a strategic response to these expectations.

How are customer expectations changing?

Consumer and customer expectations undergo a radical shift whereby sustainability is no longer an optional add-on, but manifesting itself as a key purchasing criterion. This observation is backed by a multitude of market research. For example, studies suggest that climate change, pollution and waste are top of consumers' concerns,[24] or point to an increased willingness to pay for sustainable products[25] and found that online searches for sustainable goods have increased by 71 per cent globally between 2016 and 2021. The WWF and the *Economist* refer to this increase in global awareness and demand for sustainability as a 'global eco-wakening'.[26] It is important to note that despite an increase in eco-conscious purchasing behaviour, it would be a fallacy to assume that customers are opting for a more environmentally friendly alternative by default. In fact, consumers are now considering environmental performance criteria *alongside* traditional purchasing criteria, such as performance and price, and will decide for the product that offers the highest personally perceived net value.

In the B2C space, for example, looking into everyday consumer packaged goods, a recent study by McKinsey and NielsenIQ focused on analysing actual purchasing behaviour. This research found that products making ESG-related claims showed an average of 28 per cent cumulative growth over a five-year period (2018–2022), versus 20 per cent for products that did not make such ESG-related claims.[27] Overall, the younger generations seem to be a stronger driving force behind sustainable buying behaviour, yet, at the same time their purchasing power is currently lower than that of older generations. A recent survey among US consumers found that sustainability is more important than brand names, especially for Gen-Z.[28] For example, the global recommerce market, such as market platforms that sell preloved fashion, is experiencing strong tailwinds, particularly driven by the millennials and Gen-Z.[29]

In the B2B space, customer expectations of their suppliers are undergoing a significant shift. An increasing number of organisations is committing to ambitious net-zero climate goals.[30] They realize that achieving these goals is only possible by decarbonizing their global supply chains, including their Scope 3 emissions. Supply chain emission reduction strategies require B2B customers to integrate sustainability into their procurement principles and supplier engagement.[31]

Food for thought

Is sustainability becoming an increasingly relevant criteria for your current and especially future customers?
Imagine your customer portfolio in 10 years. What are the specific factors that are becoming more important (such as sustainable product attributes, climate impact and carbon footprint performance, waste reduction, quality, premium products, supply chain transparency, flexibility, convenience and experiences)?

How are investors creating pressure to change?

Many companies face greater investor scrutiny, especially with a lens on their sustainability performance and the corresponding financial implications, and also with respect to the exposure to risks and opportunities. The concept of ESG has rapidly gained relevance among investors. A study conducted by EY in 2020 revealed that only 32 per cent of investment teams had conducted a structural and formal review of a company's performance on environmental and social aspects in 2018. Remarkably, within a span of two years, this number increased to 73 per cent indicating an increased emphasis on structured ESG due diligence.[32] The same study also found that, during this period, a growing number of companies failed to adequately disclose the ESG risks that could potentially impact their business models. Similarly, PwC's global investor survey in 2022 highlighted investors' demand for companies to report on the relevance of sustainability to their business models (69 per cent), yet 87 per cent of respondents expressed that corporate reporting often includes unsubstantiated sustainability claims.[33] While investors are also confronted with more stringent sustainability regulations, there is a market-driven rationale at play. As Serafeim noted in 2020, the market valuation premium for companies with strong sustainability performance has been on the rise since 2010 supported by a positive public sentiment momentum.[34]

Yet, the emphasis on sustainability is not restricted to public equity investors alone. Private equity and venture capital investors are increasingly seeking investments in companies that will win in the era of climate change and resource productivity. In fact, investments in climate tech start-ups increased by a remarkable 24-fold over a decade, reaching over USD 50 billion of annual investment in 2021, according to Dealroom data.[35]

In sum, investors expect their (potential) investments to mitigate risk while capitalising on opportunities. This entails evaluating a company's sustainability performance with an emphasis on financial results. By adopting a future-oriented investment lens, investors aim to get a granular understanding of emerging financial risks and opportunities.

Food for thought

Is your pressure to change being driven by the expectations of investors?
This could encompass factors such as enhancing resilience, mitigating risks, ensuring compliance, improving environmental performance, positioning your company to seize market opportunities or making a positive social impact. Examining your current capitalisation table and how it may transform in the future is essential. This evaluation will help you to anticipate changing investor expectations.

How are employees challenging the status quo?

Both current employees and incoming talent are increasingly drawn to workplaces that contribute to a sustainable future and align with their values. A growing body of research underscores the significance of purpose in the workplace. For instance, a study by McKinsey revealed that nearly 90 per cent of employees across all levels are seeking purpose in their lives, with 70 per cent indicating that their work significantly contributes to defining their sense of purpose. At the same time there appears to be a 'purpose gap'. While a majority of executives and upper management believe that they can embody their purpose in their day-to-day work, around 85 per cent of managers and frontline employees expressed disagreement and uncertainty about their ability to do so.[36]

Talents now expect their work to provide a sense of purpose. This concept of purpose is multidimensional, spanning dimensions such as social equality, environmental stewardship, or professional autonomy and continuous learning. Employers are consequently faced with the intricate task of not only recognising but actively nurturing these diverse facets, supporting their employees in fulfilling their personal needs. PwC research demonstrated that across different regions and cultural contexts (including China, Germany, India, UK, US), 65 per cent of individuals aspire to work for companies with a strong social conscience.[37] Notably, other surveys found that 9 out of 10 people would be willing to sacrifice 23 per cent of their future earnings for a job with meaning.[38] Sustainability has emerged as an important factor for talents when choosing a company to work for. Research by Anthesis examined various age groups' sentiments regarding company choice based on sustainability credentials. The results revealed an age-related correlation: Gen-Z respondents ranked sustainability considerations the highest at 67 per cent, yet even among individuals categorised as 'over 55', 40 per cent claimed to search for sustainability credentials in their employers.[39] These figures underscore that sustainability credentials are no longer merely a 'nice-to-have' but have become an imperative in today's workforce.

Food for thought

How are your employees challenging the status quo and demanding change in your business?
Looking a decade ahead, it becomes increasingly clear that sustainability will play a pivotal role in both attracting and retaining talent. In your view, which factors hold the greatest significance for your organisation (such as a sense of purpose, diversity and inclusion, work–life balance, supply chain responsibility, human rights, sustainable innovation, or social and community impact)? Regarding these key factors, how would you characterise the expected level of ambition among your company's employees in the next 10 years?

Market situation and ecosystem dynamics

Is the net-zero transition pathway changing your industry and reshaping value pools? What is the role of breakthrough technologies?
The net-zero transition requires an economic, industry and market transformation at a scale that involves all sectors and countries. Solving the climate crisis has a clear action plan: decarbonising the grid, electrifying transportation, revolutionising agriculture and food, as well as reducing industrial emissions and removing carbon.[40] Market disruptions typically take the form of an S-curve: (1) concepts and solutions are developed, then (2) enter a niche market stage marked by performance and cost improvements, then (3) transition to the mass market stage as soon as specific tipping points are reached that facilitate rapid scaling, before they (4) enter late market stage where these new solutions reach saturation and become the new industry norm.[41] According to an analysis by Systemiq, there are several examples for such tipping points already in progress or on the horizon:[42]

- **Automotive sector:** Battery electric vehicles surpassing the cost, range and convenience of petrol and diesel cars
- **Power sector:** The combined use of solar, wind and storage becoming more cost efficient than establishing new coal or gas power plants

- **Food sector:** Plant-based proteins becoming cheaper than meat while maintaining equivalent taste and nutritional values
- **Agriculture sector:** Preserving land and fostering nature-based solutions (including Carbon credits, or ecosystem service payments) proving financially more attractive than converting land for non-sustainable practices like monocultures or extensive forestry.

Typically, it requires a convergence of various forces working in synergy to create a supporting momentum (i.e. positive, reinforcing feedback loop) to help a system move towards a tipping point. Several technologies are core to that low carbon transition. Tipping points are often cost driven and/or convenience driven. However, the adoption of an S-curve is not guaranteed.

For example, governmental regulation can facilitate early market entry through subsidies and support in scaling through regulatory measures. Investments are a key contributor, from public, financial and corporate actors. Businesses, whether established corporations or innovative start-ups, can collaborate with early adopters, build new collaborations and reinvent business models to amplify the scaling of sustainable solutions.

The acceleration of adoption and the shift towards net zero often bring about structural changes in industries, thereby giving rise to new markets and value pools. The automotive sector serves as a good example. Positioned between niche and mass market stage, the wider mobility transition results in a fundamental transformation of product portfolios. This includes a technological shift towards electrified vehicles, the rise of shared mobility offerings and increased connectivity that is supporting the journey from advanced driver assistance systems to autonomous vehicles. These changes create new avenues for value creation, opening the doors for innovative business models to emerge. In the dynamic landscape of the evolving mobility ecosystem, both newcomers like tech companies and start-ups as well as traditional automakers are diversifying and adopting innovative strategies to ensure success. A recent study estimates that the ongoing net-zero transition is unlocking significant opportunities across various industries, potentially contributing to over USD 12 trillion in annual sales by 2030. Notably, the transport and mobility sector is expected to account for a significant share, ranging from USD 2.3 to 2.7 trillion per year.[43]

Are platforms and marketplaces changing your market dynamics?

Your evolving market landscape may also face disruption from the platform economy and its innovative business models that orchestrate more streamlined value exchanges among various stakeholders, including producers and consumers. Platforms establish open and participatory infrastructures for interactions with a focus on scaling and leveraging network effects. Essentially platforms create the enabling conditions through technology and data, as well as governance and rules.[44] Platforms and marketplaces may play a crucial role in steering industries towards sustainability, showcasing their influence in facilitating collaborative consumption for productive product use. This is exemplified by the transformation of mobility through solutions like ViaVan or Uber, the extension of product life cycles via recommerce platforms like eBay or Vinted, or the extraction of value from discarded goods through material trading platforms such as Metalshub or Cirplus. Platforms have the power to reshape competitive dynamics within a market, for example by connecting consumers directly with producers (e.g. farm-to-fork business models such as Gebana, food sharing such as Too Good To Go), enabling global reach (e.g. handmade or upcycled products by Etsy) or optimising supply chain interactions. Ultimately platforms have the power to structurally transform industries, shifting from traditional, static market structures to dynamic and adaptable competitive landscapes – thereby expanding the playing field from 'industry to arena'.[45]

How are new ecosystems changing collaboration and competition?
Many industries and markets are transforming towards ecosystems characterised by new forms of interaction among economic actors. Successfully engaging in ecosystems can enhance companies' productivity and can address complex challenges that are difficult to tackle alone. This, in turn, significantly impacts the wider market ecosystem where participating or abstaining from such ecosystems can result in competitive advantages or disadvantages. Sustainability is not a single-company game. Networks can be key for sharing knowledge or offering access to best practices and learnings (e.g. Ellen MacArthur Foundation network). Influential networks can also be regional/local or industry focused. Alliances can be an effective way to enable collaborative action and support policy advocacy to address challenges. For example, the Energy Transitions Commission catalysing the net-zero energy transition or the Alliance to End Plastic Waste aiming to tackle plastic waste. Additionally, new data ecosystems (such as Catena-X) may shape innovation and standards.

Food for thought

What are your hypotheses regarding the market dynamics, breakthrough technologies and new ecosystems within your industry?
As you consider the ongoing transition towards a net-zero economy and the emergence of new value pools, technologies, platforms and ecosystems, it's crucial to pinpoint the potential implications for your organisation. This assessment will help you better understand how your business may be impacted and enable you to formulate a proactive response.

Outside-in perspective – Get started right now!

The prevailing 'business-as-usual' strategy often proves effective for day-to-day business, but when confronted with the signals for change this pattern comes under pressure and may no longer be fit for purpose. The signals for change suggest that the traditional 'business-as-usual' trajectory may decline, leading to a potential erosion of your success over time. The following worksheet (Figure 2.7)

Figure 2.7. Worksheet to assess signals for change and implications

WORKSHEET 1: SYNTHESISE YOUR SIGNALS FOR CHANGE AND THE IMPLICATIONS

RESOURCE ENVIRONMENT & SUPPLY CHAIN DISRUPTIONS	POLICY INTERVENTIONS & REGULATORY CONTEXT	INVESTOR, CONSUMER & EMPLOYEE EXPECTATIONS	MARKET SITUATION AND ECOSYSTEM DYNAMICS

SIGNALS FOR CHANGE

- How do the earth's planetary boundaries relate to your activities?
- How will your resource use be disrupted by the prospective availability of primary and secondary resources?
- How might you experience disruptions in your global supply chains (dependencies, geopolitical challenges)?

- Which international, national or regional sustainability reporting and disclosure rules are most likely to significantly change your industry?
- Are you aware of the wider set of policy interventions emerging globally (e.g. country-, industry-, or value chain-focused policy measures)?

- How are customer expectations changing (sustainable product attributes, climate action, quality, convenience, experience)?
- Are investors creating pressure to change (e.g. resilience, risk mitigation, environment performance)?
- Are employees challenging the status quo (purpose, diversity, work-life balance)?

- Is the net-zero transition pathway changing your industry and reshaping markets? What is the role of breakthrough technologies?
- Are platforms and marketplaces changing your market dynamics?
- How are new ecosystems changing collaboration and competition?

Relevance

⊗○○○○ *Very low*
○⊗○○○ *Low*
○○⊗○○ *Neutral*
○○○⊗○ *High*
○○○○⊗ *Very High*

 ASSESS YOUR SIGNALS

IMPLICATIONS

serves as a comprehensive tool to consolidate emerging signals for change that have the potential to disrupt your company's future operational landscape. It synthesises insights gathered from the preceding sections, aiming to provide a holistic understanding of the pressure points challenging the status quo and its associated negative externalities. Although it might feel like being locked into the current linear system and practices you must pose yourself a critical question: Will the linear business pattern be superseded by a new, more productive and sustainable pattern in the long term?

Chapter 2 – In a nutshell

- **Current economic value creation and supply chains typically follow a linear flow, presenting systemic challenges deeply embedded in these linear systems.** Challenges include the overuse of resources, significant waste generation, product obsolescence and loss of value, low productivity, or underutilised capacities, as well as negative externalities on natural capital or social capital.

- **Many business leaders realise that the future operating context of their organisation will be disrupted by resource scarcity and shifting power dynamics towards the supply side.** Limited availability of resources puts pressure on already volatile supply chains. The extent of disruption may be particularly high if you are depending on specific critical resources.

- **Consumer, investor and employee expectations are undergoing a radical shift with sustainability emerging as a key determinant.** Shifting stakeholder expectations could become your primary driving force if your next generation of customers, shareholders or employees hold fundamentally different perspectives.

- **Regulators worldwide are introducing policy interventions with increasing pace and ambition levels.** This may be particularly disruptive to your future business environment if your ability to operate is fundamentally challenged by policy interventions (e.g. single-use plastics bans).

- **Your market situation may be impacted by structural changes driven by the net-zero transition, breakthrough technologies or new competitive dynamics.** The extent of disruption might be clearly characterised by a specific paradigm shift in your market (e.g. energy transition, electrification).

- **These signals for change will have specific implications for your organisation.** These implications will determine your 'licence to operate' (i.e. essential must-dos to meet the new requirements of the changing environment), but also shape your 'licence to innovate' (i.e. areas to achieve competitive advantage through cost savings or market opportunities).

CIRCULAR PARADIGM

LINEAR PATTERN

Towards a circular and regenerative future

3

To embark on the transformative journey of a circular business revolution, it's vital to have a clear vision of your destination. This section is designed to guide you in developing a visionary perspective and theory of change. Together, we will address a fundamental question: How can you transition from a linear value-creation model to one rooted in circular and regenerative principles? At its core, a circular value-creation system thrives on intentional regenerative and restorative design. It focuses on retaining the highest possible value of products and materials by optimising resource productivity. As you delve into the foundational concepts of the circular economy, we aim to empower you to craft an ambitious vision for your own organisation. While your existing vision, mission and purpose provide an important grounding, we will challenge you to think beyond the present limitations. We encourage you to explore unconventional ideas that focus on maximising positive externalities rather than minimising negative ones. Let's paint a vibrant picture of a desirable, net-positive future!

Meet a sustainability thought leader

Andrew Winston: 'Is the world better off because your business is in it?'

'Right now, companies have an opportunity. They should play an active role in addressing the most significant collective challenges of our time.' In our conversation with Andrew Winston, co-author of *Net Positive*, alongside Paul Polman, the urgency and opportunity of creating a net-positive world took centre stage. Andrew defined net positive as 'the idea that businesses should give more to the world than they take. Net positive businesses improve well-being for everyone they impact and at all scales. They also partner with others to tackle the big challenges we face, such as climate change, inequality and biodiversity loss.' Andrew emphasised that net positive is not merely a moral obligation but also a strategic imperative. In a world marked by escalating volatility, uncertainty, complexity and ambiguity, embracing a net-positive pathway becomes paramount for long-term success and resilience.

In the pursuit of net positive, Andrew highlighted the central role of innovation, particularly circular innovation. He asserted that 'innovation is the key to unlocking the potential of net positive. It's about finding new ways to create value that are not only sustainable, but also regenerative and restorative. It's about solving problems that matter, not only for your customers, but also for society and the planet. It's about embracing the opportunities of the digital and green revolutions, and harnessing the power of technology, science and nature.' He emphasised that 'circular innovation is one of the most powerful forms of innovation, as it aligns with the principles of nature, which operate in cycles and balances. By keeping the full scope of emissions in view, circularity drives decarbonisation for so-called Scope 3 emissions, which is on every business agenda now. By adopting circular practices, businesses can minimise their negative impacts and maximise their positive ones, both for themselves and for society.'

Providing practical guidance for businesses, Andrew advocated for a comprehensive approach. He stressed the importance to innovate, collaborate and instigate systemic change. 'You need to rethink your products, services and business models, and find new ways to create sustainable value. You also need to partner with others, such as NGOs, governments, customers and competitors, and work together to address the root causes of the problems we face, and to scale up the solutions.' Referring to their book, he reiterated: 'the real net-positive question is, "Is the world better off because your business is in it".'

Envisioning the future

Close your eyes for a moment and step into the year 2040 when your city has undergone a remarkable transformation. As you stroll through its streets the evidence of the circular economy is everywhere. In your city the notion of waste has been redefined. No longer are discarded items perceived as trash, instead they are seen as valuable resources in continuous cycles of rebirth. Smart and well-planned use of space has helped to create more liveable neighbourhoods. The urban landscape is a living testament to the paradigm shift towards circularity and regeneration. You listen to the birds and take a deep breath. You enjoy the fresh air and realise that there is no constant background noise of combustion engines and no smell of car exhaust fumes. The sky is clearer and brighter. Look up, and you will find rooftop gardens adding a touch of green to the skyline. Fresh grass scents mix with the earthy fragrance of carbon-absorbing green havens. The concrete jungle of the past has transformed into an ecosystem where businesses thrive while contributing to environmental restoration.

In this version of your future the concept of planned obsolescence is a distant memory. Products are crafted for optimised resource use and with longevity in mind. Furniture and belongings are no longer disposable but cherished companions in your life. It's a world where 'buy, use, discard' is replaced with 'access, cherish, and takeback'. In 2040 you may subscribe to services rather than stockpiling possessions. Need a ride? A sleek electric car, part of a shared fleet, arrives within moments. Electronic devices, fashion, home appliances or sport equipment – are easy to choose and use, with services that are optimised for flexibility and peace of mind, replacing product ownership. This shift isn't just about reducing stuff, it's a newfound sense of freedom. In this future vision the city seamlessly embraces the ideas of using fewer materials, decoupling prosperity from resource extraction and breaking away from the old, linear way of consuming. The city's dedication to natural cycles and appreciation of biodiversity shines through in daily life. From recycling materials to sharing services each action adds to the delicate balance of nature, aligning with a sustainable vision that cares for and protects the environment. As you navigate this revitalised city, it's evident that the circular economy isn't just a theoretical concept; it's a lifestyle and business paradigm where human actions harmonise much more with the natural world's rhythms.

As we return to the present, it's only natural to reflect on what role your businesses will play. How will your company succeed in creating business value and, at the same time, have a meaningful impact on the environment? In this vision for 2040 humanity not only survives but thrives through the powers of imagination, innovation, creativity and sustainability. Nature is part of the solution to mitigate climate change and design an economy that operates within planetary boundaries. Business leaders play a pivotal role in shaping this emerging future. The decisions you take today carry profound implications for a world that aspires to be regenerative, circular and deeply collaborative. Just as the 2040 vision depicted here, your imaginative thinking, innovative strategies and creative problem-solving abilities can cultivate a business environment where hope and optimism drive progress.

3.1 The circular economy

Imagine the linear economy as a river and the circular economy as a lake.[1] In the linear economy natural resources flow into base materials, components and products for sale, passing through multiple value-adding stages often with little consideration for the ultimate destination of products and waste. The circular economy, on the other hand, resembles a lake. It aims to keep resources in continuous production cycles, promoting efficiency and longevity while circulating resources at their highest possible value. Walter Stahel, one of the founding fathers of this idea, uses this analogy to illustrate the systemic thinking required for a shift towards a more circular and performance-focused industrial economy.

A circular economy emphasises sustainable production on the supply side and responsible consumption on the demand side (Figure 3.1). It turns linear value chains into circular value chains by 'closing the loop' and optimising for resource productivity while regenerating nature. Moving to a circular economy offers a means to enhance resource productivity, decoupling economic activities from resource consumption and its associated environmental impacts, thereby creating new opportunities.

The circular economy draws its inspiration from nature where the concept of waste is virtually non-existent. Although the fundamental ideas are not new the concept is gaining momentum across the globe. Regulation is creating a new policy environment with supporting enabling conditions. The European Commission has outlined a comprehensive circular economy action plan integral to the

Figure 3.1. The circular economy framework

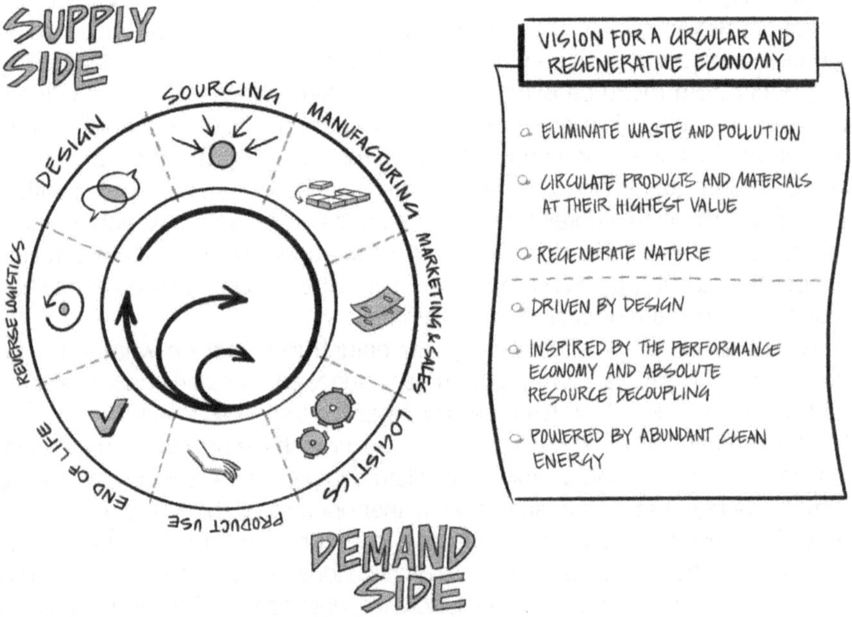

(building on Ellen MacArthur Foundation,[2] McDonough and Braungart,[3] Stahel,[4] Stuchtey et al.,[5] Sitra[6] and Lacy et al.[7])

realisation of the European Green Deal and its decarbonisation agenda. This plan represents a systemic shift towards enhancing societal well-being, meeting human needs and simultaneously reducing its dependence on primary resources and energy. The shift presents an extraordinary economic opportunity with the potential to generate up to EUR 1.8 trillion in annual economic benefits and to create 700,000 new jobs in Europe alone by 2030 (according to the Ellen MacArthur Foundation[8] and the European Commission[9]). Importantly, the accelerating digitalisation over the last two decades is shaping an important backbone for the circular economy and creating new opportunities that were not possible before. Computational power, data analytics and connectivity are enabling circular economy practices to be more cost effective. Although the much-needed circular infrastructure is not yet in place in most regions (e.g. reverse logistics or recycling at scale), there are more and more companies embracing the circular economy as a strategic paradigm. Not only have thousands of corporates committed to the circular economy across sectors, including industry leaders like Philips, Unilever, BMW, SAP, BNP Paribas and many others, but also small and mediums-sized enterprises and start-ups are increasingly disrupting this space. With this backdrop, it's time to delve deeper into the heart of this paradigm and explore the fundamental ideas that underpin it.

Core ideas and principles

Eliminate. Circulate. Regenerate. These three principles, as highlighted by the Ellen MacArthur Foundation,[10] are the cornerstones of the circular economy:

1. **Eliminate:** In the circular economy the aim is to eliminate waste and pollution entirely. This involves embracing the principle of 'closing the loop' and respecting natural cycles, which operate without generating waste. Effective systems should focus on designing out negative externalities (e.g. soil/water/air/plastic pollution).
2. **Circulate:** The goal is to keep products and materials in continuous circulation at their highest value. This means ensuring that embedded technical or biological resources remain in use and maintain high productivity throughout their life cycle.
3. **Regenerate:** Drawing inspiration from natural processes, the circular economy operates in harmony with regenerative natural systems. It leaves room for nature and contributes to the generation of natural capital.

To achieve highly productive and regenerative systems it's crucial for these principles to synergise. This involves operationalising various 'R-strategies' (see below, e.g. repair, reuse/redistribute, refurbish/remanufacture, recycle) and embracing new design paradigms. Design choices that follow the cradle-to-cradle principles, as proposed by McDonough and Braungart,[11] or designs inspired by nature, in the realm of biomimicry as articulated by Benyus,[12] can lead the way. The ultimate goal is to create systems that are inherently circular and regenerative *by design*. Intentional design serves as the central catalyst for this transformation influencing not only the design of products and services but also the redesign of the systems within which we operate. The Ellen MacArthur Foundation plays a pivotal role as a thought leader and field builder in advancing the circular economy movement.

Design for cradle-to-cradle: Transitioning from eco-efficiency to eco-effectiveness

Cradle-to-Cradle (C2C), envisioned by William McDonough and Michael Braungart, embodies a philosophy of designing products with the potential for infinite circulation ensuring that materials and nutrients remain within closed-loop systems. It underpins the design principles of the circular economy extending down to the molecular level, including material and nutrient choices, such as chemicals, which enable both technical and biological cycles. C2C challenges the traditional focus on eco-efficiency, which aims to minimise negative impacts incrementally. Instead it champions the idea of eco-effectiveness, a holistic and regenerative approach that seeks net-positive improvements. This mindset drives integrated circular systems rooted in C2C design principles. In these systems, resources are chosen and used like nutrients, circulating safely in biological or technical cycles, essentially forming a 'material bank'. C2C has also evolved into a certification standard for products, with organisations like EPEA (Environmental Protection Encouragement Agency, founded by Michael Braungart), facilitating the assessment and continuous optimisation of C2C principles.

Performance economy and absolute decoupling

The concept of the circular industrial economy, initially shaped by Walter Stahel in 1976, underscores the importance of moving from a product-centric approach to a performance economy.[13] This perspective adopts a systems lens on the circular economy and emphasises the importance of focusing on product performance, outcomes, services, actual needs and utility (through renting or sharing) instead of product sales and ownership. For example, providing mobility solutions, instead of merely selling cars. Manufacturers retain ownership of the products and focus on enabling access through rental, sharing or tailoring product–service combinations to meet specific outcomes. This approach transfers the responsibility for a product's entire life cycle, including disposal, back to producers. It incentivises the development of more circular material systems and creates opportunities to optimise solutions based on user needs rather than focusing solely on products. This approach signifies the fundamental systemic change underlying the circular economy. It revolves around fulfilling functional and societal needs while optimising resource productivity and achieving absolute decoupling. The term 'decoupling' means delinking the natural resource use (and environmental impacts) from economic activity (and human well-being) to transition to a more sustainable industrial economy.[14]

Abundant clean energy

The circular economy system should be powered by renewable and clean energy sources.[15] This includes the use of renewable energy and energy-efficient practices not only in the production of goods and services, but also in wider system operations. Clean and affordable energy, derived from solar, wind, hydropower or geothermal energy solutions, should be coupled with decentralised strategies and advanced energy storage solutions. This transition to abundant clean energy is pivotal for enhancing the overall environmental performance of the circular economy akin to the historical role fossil fuels played in the past two centuries.

The current state of the global economy reflects a circularity rate of only 7.2 per cent. The Circularity Gap Report (2018–2023) annually assesses global progress in achieving circularity. This figure indicates that out of the around 100 billion tonnes of materials extracted from the Earth each year, currently just 7.2 per cent are reintegrated into the economy through circular practices. This marks a notable decline from the 8.6 per cent achieved in 2020, with the widening of the gap attributed to the simultaneous increase in global material extraction.[16]

Introducing the circular R-strategies

Very practically, how are environmental benefits created in the circular economy? The so-called R-strategies offer a simple framework. These strategies provide guidance for restoring resources in the technical material cycles as well as regenerating resources within the biological cycles. They describe key levers that embrace circularity and establish a priority rank order. As a rule of thumb, note that levers that are higher on the list (R0) achieve a higher level of circularity with fewer resources and less environmental pressure compared with those lower on the list (R9). The following overview describes the levers, building on Potting *et al.*,[17] considering adaptations of Henry *et al.* and other R-conceptualisations.[18]

- **R0 – Refuse:** This strategy involves making a product redundant by either abandoning its function or substituting the same function with a different product.

- **R1 – Rethink/regenerate:** The focus here is on fundamentally optimising a product for more intensive use and improved functional performance. It also involves rethinking how the product fulfils its function while contributing to the regeneration of nature, such as delivering ecosystem services.

- **R2 – Reduce:** Central to this strategy is increasing efficiency in product design, manufacturing or use. It includes consuming fewer natural resources (e.g. avoiding virgin materials), eliminating waste and minimising the use of hazardous materials.

- **R3 – Re-use:** This strategy extends a product's life by ensuring that discarded products in good condition continue fulfilling their original function, typically by another consumer, ideally replacing the need for a new product.

- **R4 – Repair:** Repairing and maintaining defective products to bring them back in use is the essence of this strategy. It ensures that products can be used again and continue to provide their intended function.

- **R5 – Refurbish:** This strategy involves modernising or restoring old products to extend their lifespan and keep them relevant and up to date in current contexts.

- **R6 – Remanufacture:** Parts of discarded products are used in new products with the same function, promoting the reuse of components and extending their life.

- **R7 – Repurpose:** Discarded products or their parts find new life in different functions, which can be achieved through practices such as upcycling.

- **R8 – Recycle:** This strategy involves processing materials to obtain recycled materials of the same quality (goal of maintaining high quality) or lower quality (downcycling). The goal is to maximise the useful application of materials at the end of the product and component life cycle.

- **R9 – Recover:** Recovering embodied energy through processes like incineration of materials or composting/anaerobic digestion.

These R-strategies underpinning the circular economy enable value creation systems to operate in closed loops, with the goal to keep these loops as small as possible. For example, utilising the stock of products more productively creates a smaller loop than the process of recycling. Smaller loops also tend to be more profitable and efficient. This principle aligns with the priority order of the R-strategies, emphasising the retention of resource value. Walter Stahel encapsulates this approach by advising, 'Don't repair what is not broken, don't remanufacture what can be repaired, don't recycle what can be remanufactured'.[19] He further underscores that smaller loops, such as re-use, repair and remanufacture, are best executed at local or regional levels. These cascading principles are not limited to technical products like machinery, furniture, buildings or fashion, they also apply to biological cycles, particularly in the realm of food. Here, rethinking regenerative agricultural practices, reducing food waste, reusing by-products and returning nutrients to the soil play pivotal roles. We will revisit these R-strategies later to illustrate how they generate environmental benefits across various business models.

Circular business models

In your transition from a linear to a circular economy product design and strategic business model innovation take centre stage.[20] Business models are key to practically implementing the R-strategies and unlocking their full impact potential. To simultaneously achieve environmental benefits and create economic value through circularity the primary focus should squarely be on business models. Drawing from a comprehensive analysis of over 110 circular economy definitions,

Meet a circularity expert

Joe Murphy, Ellen MacArthur Foundation: 'The HOW is often the main challenge'

'Tackling the global challenges of climate change, biodiversity loss and pollution requires a fundamental and systemic change, and the circular economy stands out as such a systemic solution. Instead of pursuing linear growth we should focus on embracing a circular economy guided by the examples and principles that nature demonstrates every day: zero waste, circular, regenerative. By design.' We had the opportunity to interview Joe Murphy, executive lead at the Ellen MacArthur Foundation (EMF). As a circular pioneer, the EMF has played a central role in shaping the field and thought leadership agenda of the circular economy over the last decade. Joe and his colleagues have built the leading global network of companies, start-up innovators, investors, public authorities, academia, cities and change makers committed to the circularity agenda. Joe emphasised that the circular economy combines environmental and systemic benefits alongside economic advantages for companies and society. According to him, 'the transition is significantly accelerating, but requires deeper collaboration and higher ambition.' He outlined common barriers to progress noting that policy makers can improve the enabling conditions, such as structurally shifting taxation from labour to resources, which would create incentives to safe natural resources and optimise the business case.

'Given the speed and scale of the required transition, also companies should double down on their ambition levels to scale circular economy business models. This may require them to rebuild or reconfigure entire value chains – and to shape completely new partnerships.' While leading companies express genuine interest in building such new forms of collaboration, many face 'inertia for reinvention, because everybody is busy and there is lots of friction'. Shaping new circular ecosystems hence requires real leadership and can benefit from neutral facilitators like EMF and other innovation networks that help to connect the dots. In reflecting on recommendations, Joe stressed that 'the HOW is often the main challenge, you need to build the process muscle for exploring circular business models and ecosystem innovation.' Second, he emphasised the importance of embracing design as a key driving force for circular solutions. Finally, he highlighted the need to accelerate the transition from ambition to action, drawing parallels to venture building, as a crucial step to unlock the regenerative potential of the circular economy.

Kirchherr and colleagues describe the circular economy as 'an economic system that is based on business models which replace the end-of-life concept [. . .]'. This implies either advancing or transforming your existing business model(s) or developing new business models to capture emerging opportunities.[21]

However, the true challenge lies in translating the circularity principles and levers into tangible, real-world circular business models. Successful circular business models must articulate a clear *value proposition*, delineate the mechanisms for *value creation and delivery* and *capture value (revenue minus costs)*, as advocated by Osterwalder and Pigneur.[22] Transitioning from a linear to circular value-creation system requires business models that radically optimise resource productivity on both the supply and demand sides. The next chapter will focus entirely on concrete business models with the transformative power to decarbonise, dematerialise and regenerate. We will introduce a methodology designed to assist you to explore the most relevant business models. This will allow you to define your opportunity set and zoom in on a well-defined transformation plan that outlines where to start and where your journey will lead. This may enable you to build entirely new ecosystems.

Your future ambition level must guide your circular business transformation. Business models serve as tools to seize opportunities and to catalyse the transition from the linear system into a circular future of sustainable value creation. Therefore, it's essential to start by clearly defining your ambition and the destination towards which you are heading.

3.2 Your future horizon

Imagine a future where your organisation thrives in a circular and regenerative ecosystem leaving a positive impact on the environment and society. A future vision, where your business success goes hand in hand with environmental benefits. This vision of the future is not a lofty aspiration, it's a carefully crafted destination that embodies your commitment to sustainability and responsible business practices. Now, let's reverse engineer this vision. Instead of starting from your present state we begin with this compelling vision of a circular and regenerative future. From here we carefully explore the steps, strategies and transformations that will lead us there.

A circular and regenerative design vision describes a new emerging pattern, your future aspirations combining business impact and purpose with an environmental ambition (Figure 3.2); a completely new paradigm where circular and regenerative thinking is the norm. This transformative shift in mindsets compels us to intentionally design products and services with the goal of achieving regenerative outcomes. A vision that does not overshoot the limits of our planetary boundaries, but instead fosters positive externalities. A theory of change that signifies a shift towards a future where companies must cultivate new relationships and build new ecosystems that sustain us. While this shift may feel distant it's an inevitable transformation that must eventually come to the forefront.

What could be an ambitious environmental vision for your organisation?

Defining an environmental impact ambition is multidimensional and highly specific to any organisation. It often involves particular areas of emphasis, and the crucial step is to outline the aspired outcomes tailored to your specific circumstances.

First, given the global climate emergency every transformative horizon needs to embed a decarbonisation objective, such as a **net-zero ambition**. This objective should encompass the entire scope of your emissions, including those originating from the supply chain, particularly purchased goods and their embedded footprint. Linked to that, the target to rely fully on renewable energies and its efficient use is a priority for many companies and may already be a specific objective for you. However, it's equally important to adopt a comprehensive perspective that considers the product's entire life cycle, including its usage phase.

> **Ørsted** is one of the first energy companies to set a validated net-zero target aligned with the Science Based Targets initiative (SBTi). This ambitious goal extends across the entire value chain, encompassing emissions from Scope 1 to 3. To achieve their reduction targets, Ørsted has launched a supply chain decarbonisation programme aimed at improving climate transparency and action. They also focus on improving circular resource utilisation to secure access to critical raw materials and reduce environmental risks associated with virgin resource extraction and processing. Ørsted envisions 'a world that runs entirely on green energy'.

Figure 3.2. Worksheet for developing the vision of your circular and regenerative business future

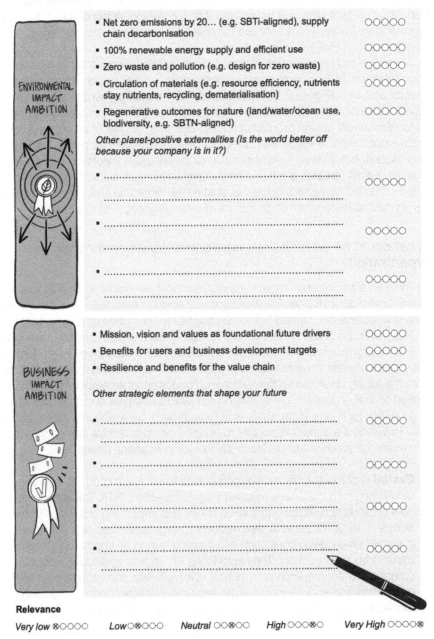

WORKSHEET 2: DESCRIBE YOUR AMBITION AND VISION IN 10-15 YEARS

POTENTIAL ELEMENTS of YOUR CIRCULAR & REGENERATIVE FUTURE

ENVIRONMENTAL IMPACT AMBITION

- Net zero emissions by 20... (e.g. SBTi-aligned), supply chain decarbonisation ○○○○○
- 100% renewable energy supply and efficient use ○○○○○
- Zero waste and pollution (e.g. design for zero waste) ○○○○○
- Circulation of materials (e.g. resource efficiency, nutrients stay nutrients, recycling, dematerialisation) ○○○○○
- Regenerative outcomes for nature (land/water/ocean use, biodiversity, e.g. SBTN-aligned) ○○○○○

Other planet-positive externalities (Is the world better off because your company is in it?)

- .... ○○○○○
  ....

- .... ○○○○○
  ....

- .... ○○○○○
  ....

BUSINESS IMPACT AMBITION

- Mission, vision and values as foundational future drivers ○○○○○
- Benefits for users and business development targets ○○○○○
- Resilience and benefits for the value chain ○○○○○

Other strategic elements that shape your future

- .... ○○○○○
  ....

- .... ○○○○○
  ....

- .... ○○○○○
  ....

- .... ○○○○○
  ....

Relevance

Very low ⊗○○○○   *Low* ○⊗○○○   *Neutral* ○○⊗○○   *High* ○○○⊗○   *Very High* ○○○○⊗

DRAFT YOUR FUTURE NEWS ARTICLE

COVER PAGE

VISION OF YOUR
CIRCULAR AND REGEN
BUSINESS FUTURE

HEADLINE
...

YEAR
20......

MAIN MESSAGES
...

PICTURES

QUOTES

YOU

Your future environmental vision may also encompass additional outcomes stemming from **circularity principles**, spanning from the supply side to the demand side. For example, you might articulate a vision of achieving zero waste. Realising this goal would require not only intentional design improvements but also a broader perspective on pollution that goes beyond the direct control of an organisation. Additionally, you may anchor your vision in the optimised state of circular resource flows and resource productivity. This could involve specifying objectives like secondary material commitments, resource efficiency and dematerialisation.

> **Lush**, a global cosmetics brand, is committed to achieving zero waste through innovative practices. They aim to create a 'cosmetic revolution to save the planet' (among the top strategic goals in their 'master plan'). Their shops feature vegan products with minimal or no packaging, including more than half available as 'naked products'. When packaging is necessary, Lush prioritises recycled materials, reporting 100 per cent of recycled plastic packaging since 2008. They also offer a bring-it-back recycling scheme to customers.

Expanding further, your environmental ambition may extend to preserving and restoring ecosystems, aiming for **regenerative outcomes for nature**. It will depend on your specific situation, which relevant ecosystem outcomes you want to contribute to. Biodiversity measures the richness of nature, air quality supports health and well-being, soil provides the nurturing ground for plants, water cycles and quality is key to sustain any ecosystem and of course carbon is the building block of life and energy. For example, your future vision may establish targets for land use, such as halting the conversion of natural ecosystems, reducing land footprint or promoting landscape engagement through regenerative, restorative and transformational practices.[23]

> **Alpro** is a Belgian company that produces plant-based foods and beverages. They are well-known for their wide range of plant based products such as soy, almond or oat drinks, representing an alternative to dairy products. Alpro's mission is to 'help people make positive choices when it comes to food'. They run a comprehensive sustainability programme, including the support of farmers on their regenerative agriculture journey. They aim to achieve 'zero impact operations' and the team is working with the Science-Based Targets for Nature (SBTN) corporate engagement programme to set the first targets.

Ultimately, as a company, your purpose goes beyond profit; it's about making the world a better place. Paul Polman and Andrew Winston summarise an essential question that business leaders face today: **Is the world better off because your company is in it?**[24] Regardless of whether you rely on technical or biological materials to produce your goods and services, your role in the future is not merely about minimising harm but actively contributing positively to the environment and society. This requires adopting a regenerative mindset, going beyond sustainability, aiming to repair and enhance the ecosystems and communities affected by your operations. Your environmental impact aspiration may thus encompass a multitude of additional elements, reflecting a commitment to making a positive and lasting difference in the world.

Vaude, a family-owned outdoor brand, has embedded sustainability into the heart of its strategy. Their robust guiding vision, 'Improving the quality of life with sustainable outdoor products and future-oriented business strategies' sets the tone for their commitment. The breadth of Vaude's sustainability programme spans product design, environmental performance and social responsibility. For example, a rigid material policy guides the full set of materials used. The programme deeply integrates circular economy practices and business models, aiming to extend product life and close material loops.

How does your business ambition shape your circular and regenerative vision?

Long-term strategic goals often serve as guardrails to consider in your circular vision, and some foundational elements are already shaping the path forward. In particular, **the cultural bedrock of your organisation, including its vision, mission and values**, holds the seeds of the future in the present. For example, specific strong values might have been your recipe for success in the past and will continue to anchor your journey towards the future. These cultural anchors are the lifeblood of many successful organisations, pivotal in shaping and achieving a circular vision. When your employees love working for you, it's not just about a pay cheque. It's a reflection of a healthy culture that empowers your team to be active stewards of your mission and act as change agents for sustainability and innovation.

Haniel, a family-owned company with a rich history in various industries since its founding in 1756, serves as a good case example. The strategy and culture of Haniel, along with its diverse company portfolio, are encapsulated by the German word 'enkelfähig', which means readiness for future generations. This concept embodies living in a values-oriented way and practising entrepreneurial thinking, where sustainability is integral to long-term economic success. The vision of 'enkelfähig' serves as a guiding light in shaping the development of products and services at Haniel. Emphasising a dedication to long-term thinking, this vision is focused on creating value for future generations, ultimately paving the way for a future worth living.

Your future business ambition can seamlessly integrate the **core benefits that your products and services provide to customers**. You might focus on meeting specific human needs, such as sustainable mobility, housing or healthy food and nutrition. Your technology might be leveraged to solve some of the critical real-world sustainability challenges. The scale of this impact may already be outlined by specific **business development** targets like product portfolio expansion, technological advancements or revenue and profitability. While your latest strategic planning can provide direction, it shouldn't limit your future aspirations. Your products and services will always be a crucial element of your circular vision because they represent the tangible output of your efforts. In a circular economy, your products are designed for longevity, high quality, ease of repair and end-of-life materials recycling or upcycling. Or you may embrace a shift towards a service-oriented culture, focusing on offering services instead of solely selling products.

Siemens, the global technology company, underscores its value proposition for customers across three key pillars: decarbonisation and energy efficiency, resource efficiency and circularity and people-centricity and societal impact. Siemens particularly emphasises its commitment to addressing global sustainability challenges, leveraging technologies to decarbonise sectors that account for almost three-quarters of global emissions, including mobility, infrastructure, industry and healthcare. Their strategic dedication to sustainability and future aspiration is set by a framework titled DEGREE, which stands for Decarbonisation, Ethics, Governance, Resource efficiency, Equity, Employability.

Enhancing the **resilience of value chains** has emerged as a strategic priority. Your organisation may be driven by the aspired outcome of increasing stability against external shocks, such as price volatility and resource scarcity. Closed-loop business models and circular operations can yield significant value in this regard. Your business model might strategically integrate take-back and resource recovery. In a circular future scenario, your operations embrace sustainable sourcing and production methods, cultivating fair and equal relationships that benefit suppliers, customers and other value chain partners.

Johnson Matthey (JM) is an over 200-year-old global speciality chemicals company with a focus on sustainable technologies. JM is one of the largest providers and especially recyclers of platinum group metals (PGMs) – platinum, palladium, rhodium, ruthenium, iridium and osmium. Their strategic goal is to catalyse the net-zero transition by 'embedding sustainability into everything' they do. JM is expanding its circular services into growth segments such as hydrogen fuel cells and electrolyser materials. An integrated circular solution can help to close material loops, strategically secure resource supply and increase resilience for both JM and customers. Refined PGMs can have ap- proximately 98 per cent lower footprint compared to primary PGMs.

Building blocks for turning your circular vision into business reality

Can you imagine what a newspaper or magazine article might look like in 10–15 years, summing up your remarkable achievements?

If you fast forward into the future, your future horizon will not be an aspired ambition anymore; it will have materialised into tangible outcomes. The 'Newspaper headline' exercise serves as a potent tool for crafting your future horizon. It encourages you to vividly envision a world where your desired change has become a reality. By framing your vision as a newspaper headline this exercise provides a concrete and relatable snapshot of your ultimate goal. It enables you to grasp and visualise the outcome clearly. This approach shifts your focus to the actual results, compelling you to think about what specific actions, changes and events were necessary to bring about that achievement.

Food for thought

Which magazine shall write about your impact in 10–15 years from now?
What will be the big headline of this article? What key messages should be highlighted in this piece? Who are the individuals that should be showcased, and what would they say about your journey? What will you say about your business and its transformative role in shaping the future?

The newspaper article exercise is relying on the method of backcasting (also referred to as 'future back'). Backcasting is a strategic planning approach that turns traditional forecasting on its head. It effectively forces you to reverse engineer the path to success and to define a theory of change. It uncovers the critical steps and factors that contribute to the envisioned future. Instead of extrapolating the future from the past and present, including current trends, it starts with a clear vision of the desired future and then works backwards to identify the necessary steps to bring that vision to life. This process sparks creative thinking and inventive problem-solving by challenging you to envision a better future and then figure out how to make it a reality.

It's a powerful tool for setting goals, whether on a personal, organisational or societal level, by concentrating on the destination and the means to reach it, rather than relying on past experience and present trends. One of the fundamental principles of this future-back thinking is that it empowers you to become a proactive agent of change rather than a passive observer of the future. Instead of making incremental adjustments to the current state you break away from unsustainable patterns of the past and present to imagine a world where the change you aspire to see has been realised.

FREITAG is a values-driven company that places people and the planet at the core of its mission. 'Intelligent design for a circular future' serves as their purpose and the driving force behind their operations. In 1993 they pioneered the circular business model of producing bags made from old, repurposed truck tarps. FREITAG aligns its overarching strategic goals, projects and daily work with this purpose. FREITAG has developed an impressive business model aligned with circular economy principles. Their circular vision encompasses various elements: fostering a values-based culture, creating circular products, operations and services, as well as inspiring a circular community.

Meet a circularity pioneer

Oliver Brunschwiler: 'Purpose is boss'

In our conversation with Oliver Brunschwiler, FREITAG's former CEO and now board member, the company's commitment to circularity and sustainability became vividly evident. Brunschwiler emphasised that 'purpose is boss at FREITAG, NIKIN, EBP and other brands I am co-accountable for', and this dedication goes beyond mere words; it's deeply ingrained in their corporate culture. It's not just a top-down approach; it extends to every level of the organisation, fostering alignment and a shared sense of purpose among employees. As Oliver put it, 'FREITAG colleagues are the stewards of our circular vision.' FREITAG is committed to investing in the ongoing development and training of its workforce. By prioritising employee education, the company aims to enhance skills and ensures that its team is well-equipped to meet the evolving challenges of the future. This strategic investment not only strengthens individual capabilities but also contributes to the overall success and innovation of FREITAG as a forward-thinking organisation to implement circular practices. Furthermore, they engage their customers, partners and stakeholders in their circular journey. According to Oliver, it's about 'inspiring and encouraging our ecosystem to embrace circular practices'.

FREITAG's approach to product and service design is equally inspiring. They don't just create bags and accessories; they design with the end of a product's life in mind. Brunschwiler mentioned how they strive to make products and services that are easily repairable, refurbishable or recyclable. But it's not just about materials; it's about creating unique, robust products that also significantly reduce waste. Quality and durability are paramount, ensuring that their products have a longer lifespan and align with the core principles of circularity.

Beyond their products, FREITAG offers a range of circular services, for example by encouraging customers to have their bags and accessories repaired rather than replaced when issues arise. Their innovative bag exchange programme promotes product reuse, extending the lifespan of their products in a culture where disposability is common. FREITAG stands out as a company that has transformed an ambitious vision into practical, actionable steps that permeate every aspect of their self-organisation. Oliver's advice is clear: Trust, purpose and a well-defined roadmap are the key to a circular and sustainable future. In a world marked by disruption and distance, trust in others is the first step. Then find your purpose, align your strategy and become a leader in sustainability. Finally create a roadmap that guides your journey to shape a meaningful circular future.

Rethinking your business model and crafting your transition pathway towards your circular and regenerative vision is the next key step (Chapter 4). Reinventing your business models can turn emerging challenges into opportunities that help to reach your future ambition levels. Thereby your articulated vision serves as your north star, helping you better explore and prioritise various circular business opportunities. To effectively prioritise these business model opportunities, having a clear understanding of your destination and theory of change is crucial. You must shift away from isolated initiatives that lack integration into your overall strategy. While stand-alone projects may keep you occupied and create the illusion of progress, many of them often lack the scalability and impact needed to drive significant change. Therefore, having a clear understanding of your future horizon serves as a cohesive and interconnected approach to sustainable transformation.

The power of vision backcasting also lies in its ability to steer your organisation towards this ambitious goal by unveiling the key elements necessary to *prepare* for this future. You should proactively shape your organisational readiness. Chapter 5 will guide you in adopting this approach, helping you identify what is required for your circular business model from an early stage and preparing for potential challenges along the way. This approach thoroughly examines the gaps between your current state and your envisioned future. It forces you to ask critical questions about what needs to change, what innovative strategies must be deployed and what specific actions are required to reverse engineer those gaps.

As we close this chapter, let's reflect on the transformative journey we've undertaken. Throughout Chapter 3, we've delved deep into your emerging future to understand its potential and articulate an impactful and actionable vision. These visionary perspectives, though sometimes unconventional, may have already sparked creative ideas that can bring about change. With these insights, you are now prepared to turn this bold vision into reality through concrete circular business model opportunities. As we transition from the realm of opportunity ideas to practical implementation, the forthcoming chapters will guide you on how to bridge the gap between aspiration and realisation. Every bold dream starts with a vision and theory of change, and the courage to chase that vision sets the stage for a more circular and sustainable future.

Chapter 3 – In a nutshell

- **The circular economy aims to decouple economic growth and associated prosperity from resource extraction as a key answer to the sustainability challenges of our time.** The key principles include eliminating waste and pollution, circulating products and materials at their highest value and regenerating nature. This new economic model aims to be regenerative and restorative by design.

- **Crafting a circular and regenerative vision serves as your guiding north star.** This vision should combine your future environmental ambition (e.g. net zero, circularity principles, regenerative outcomes for nature) with your business impact aspirations (e.g. business development, resilience). Why and how is the world better off because your company is in it?

- **To develop an ambitious vision and theory of change, it's crucial to break free from the constraints of the past and present.** A powerful tool for envisioning a desirable future is 'backcasting', which starts with the desired future and works backwards to bring that vision to life. This approach empowers you to be an active agent of change rather than a passive observer of the future.

CIRCULAR BUSINESS MODELS

MONETISE EXTENDED PRODUCT LIFE

VALORISE WASTE

SERVITISE PRODUCTS

OPTIMISE RESOURCE USE

CAPITALISE REGENERATION & RESTORATION

TRANSFORMING INNOVATION

TRANSITION OPPORTUNITIES

QUICK WINS

START

Circular business
model opportunities

4

Exploring, developing and scaling commercially viable, circular business models describes a company's strategic journey to drive transformational change. Essentially, these are winning business models that capture economic value by prioritising resource productivity, circularity and regenerative design. From an environmental perspective, these business models have the power to decarbonise, dematerialise and regenerate. Yet, to be commercially viable, they also need to contribute to profitability and resilience. This can be achieved through better customer experience and loyalty, tapping into new value pools, commanding price premiums, achieving cost competitiveness or bolstering overall supply chain resilience and risk reduction. The convergence of environmental and business impact encapsulates what we term 'net impact'. This chapter will shed light on five circular business model archetypes, in which a set of 15 business model patterns are embedded. These patterns span the spectrum from supply side– to demand side–focused business models, offering a comprehensive lens to examine new and emerging opportunities for your organisation.

Five business model archetypes

To simultaneously generate both economic value and environmental benefits, change must materialise in your business models. This means either advancing or transforming your existing business model(s) or developing new ones to seize emerging opportunities. But before delving further, let's revisit the fundamental concept of a business model.

Business models, as described by Alexander Osterwalder and colleagues, typically deliver a business case and are composed of the following core elements: the value proposition, value creation and delivery, and value capture and retention. In their renowned Business Model Canvas, they emphasise that a value proposition must articulate a concrete value and offering to a specific customer segment.[1] Subsequently, value creation centres around how a company internally organises key activities, allocates resources, forges partnerships and manages external aspects such as distribution channels and relationships to deliver the value to the customer segments. Lastly, value capture revolves around establishing a revenue model and optimising associated costs to retain profits. This framework applies to circular business models, where these elements must synergise to delineate 'how a company creates, captures, and delivers value with the value creation logic designed to improve resource efficiency.'[2]

Circular business models hold the promise of delivering an impact case. They may address a specific environmental challenge or inefficiency in your current value chain. They serve as a catalyst for implementing some of the circular R-strategies introduced in the previous chapter as mechanisms through which environmental benefits are realised. However, embracing circular R-strategies alone does not automatically result in a circular business model. This poses a critical challenge that many companies face when they embark on their journey to incorporate the circular R-levers into their operations: how to align their environmental goals with their core business practices. Real circular business model innovation requires a thorough re-evaluation of the value proposition, value creation and value capture mechanisms, all with a focus on achieving both economic value and environmental benefits. Environmental value should be additional, durable and long-lasting. Business models are the key to practically activating the R-strategies and unlocking their full impact potential. The focus on building commercially viable, scalable, circular business models embodies what we refer to as a company's 'license to innovate'.

To support your exploration process, we have developed five circular business model archetypes, in each of which is embedded a set of distinct business model patterns (Figure 4.1). Transitioning from a linear to circular value creation systems requires business models that radically optimise resource productivity on both the supply side and demand side.

Meet a business model expert

Alexander Osterwalder: 'Explore, experiment, learn, adapt'

We had the chance to talk to Alexander Osterwalder, the co-creator of the Business Model Canvas and the founder of Strategyzer, about the importance of aligning environmental ambitions with a clear business case in developing circular business models. Alexander is a leading author, speaker and consultant on innovation and strategy, and has helped many organisations around the world to design and implement innovative business models. He emphasised that circular business models have the potential to combine benefits for the planet with successful business practices as they can reduce the ecological footprint, save costs, create new revenue streams and gain a competitive edge: 'Circular business models are not a trade-off between profitability and sustainability, but a win-win situation. But you need a clear business case that shows how you create and capture value in a viable and scalable way.'

He then stressed that the toolkit of business model thinking is a crucial skill for developing circular business models as it helps to clarify and communicate the value proposition, the value creation and the value capture mechanisms. 'Many sustainable business models fail because they don't consider the core business aspects, such as who are the customers, what are their needs and pains, how to reach them, how to make money and how to scale. Business model thinking helps to address these questions and to design a circular business model that creates value for customers and stakeholders.'

However, Alexander also warned that such radically new business models are not easy, as they require experimentation, learning and adaptation. 'Circular business models are more complex and uncertain than linear ones as they involve multiple actors, feedback loops and system dynamics. You need to test your assumptions, measure your impact and iterate your business model until you find the best fit.' Finally, he pointed out that circular business models are not only a matter of technology, but also of culture and mindset that require a shift from a linear to a circular logic, from a product-centric to a service-centric view, from a transactional to a relational approach. They also require collaboration across the value chain to create a circular ecosystem. 'You need to change the way you think, the way you work and the way you interact with others.'

Figure 4.1. Circular business model patterns

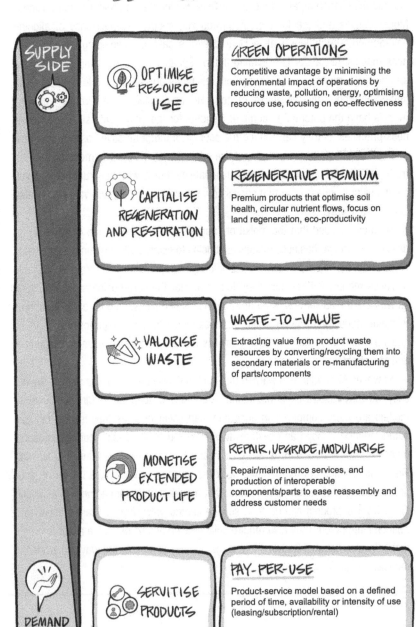

BUSINESS MODEL PATTERNS

SUPPLY SIDE

OPTIMISE RESOURCE USE

GREEN OPERATIONS
Competitive advantage by minimising the environmental impact of operations by reducing waste, pollution, energy, optimising resource use, focusing on eco-effectiveness

CAPITALISE REGENERATION AND RESTORATION

REGENERATIVE PREMIUM
Premium products that optimise soil health, circular nutrient flows, focus on land regeneration, eco-productivity

VALORISE WASTE

WASTE-TO-VALUE
Extracting value from product waste resources by converting/recycling them into secondary materials or re-manufacturing of parts/components

MONETISE EXTENDED PRODUCT LIFE

REPAIR, UPGRADE, MODULARISE
Repair/maintenance services, and production of interoperable components/parts to ease reassembly and address customer needs

SERVITISE PRODUCTS

PAY-PER-USE
Product-service model based on a defined period of time, availability or intensity of use (leasing/subscription/rental)

DEMAND SIDE

SECONDARY & DECARBONISED MATERIALS

Resilience through secondary/recycled and recyclable materials, and sustainable, decarbonized sourcing practices

BIO-BASED MATERIALS

Differentiation through materials (partially) made from biomass that can safely reenter the environment, derived from renewable, biological processes

ECOSYSTEM SERVICE SOLUTIONS

Value creation through ecosystem services based on carbon sequestration, land restoration and preservation, land resilience (carbon or biodiversity credits, insetting)

REGENERATIVE INFRASTRUCTURE

Increased space productivity through additional renewable energy generation and storage, space utilization, urban forests and farming, eco-tourism

BY-PRODUCT UTILISATION

Resource utilisation of by-products from production or use phase as inputs for new products or processes

SECONDARY MATERIAL MARKET PLATFORMS

Actively facilitating the exchange of secondary raw materials via platforms, external or internal marketplaces

RECOMMERCE

Actively steer recommerce by recovering products for resale, potentially including refurbishment of components or products for resale

REUSE AND REVERSE LOGISTICS ECOSYSTEM

Ecosystem model supporting resource recovery and extended product life through take back, reverse logistics and reuse solutions

PAY-PER-OUTCOME

Product-service model based on the achievement of pre-determined operational/ financial outcomes for customers (results, performance)

SHARING/ POOLING

Service model in which a product is used by a number of users through co-access or co-ownership, often platform-based model or multi-brand

Figure 4.2. Circular business model archetypes

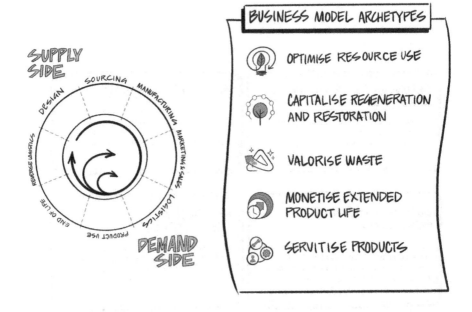

These business models enable circular practices not only in how products are produced, and the materials applied, but also in how products are marketed, used and valued by customers. Circular business models, therefore, hold the potential to foster sustainable production and consumption patterns. They capture economic value through resource productivity and circular and regenerative design. These are the business models with the transformative power to decarbonise, dematerialise and regenerate. They aim to move the mindset from merely 'doing less bad' to actively 'doing good' as a new norm, intentionally contributing to restoring and preserving nature. Let's take a moment to acquaint ourselves with these diverse archetypes (Figure 4.2).

1. **Business models that optimise resource use and supply to strengthen the competitive edge and offering.** Circular business model patterns within this archetype focus on greening operations and the integration of secondary, decarbonised or bio-based materials. These business models can lead to cost savings, increased resilience, improved reputation or enable superior product positioning. For example, Interface (provider of modular flooring such as carpet tiles), Philips (global healthcare technologies) or Ecoalf (sustainable and recycled clothing) have established holistic approaches to circular resource use as integral elements into their business models.

2. **Business models that focus on capitalising regeneration and restoration.** These business models may integrate regenerative production principles at the core of their product and operating model. They often involve regenerative agricultural practices, such as

agroforestry and soil health initiatives, as well as activating ecosystem services provided by natural resources, treating nature as a valuable asset. This increasingly relevant model aligns with land restoration and preservation efforts and ties into emerging (voluntary) credit schemes. Circular infrastructure development allows for increasing resource productivity via additional revenue streams, often linked to energy or mobility. Examples include Dr. Bronner's (regenerative organic agriculture as basis for products), or Slow Forest Coffee (agroforestry-based coffee integrated into direct-to-business-customers model) or VEJA (shoe company establishing ecosystem services agreements).

3. **Circular business models that valorise waste into economic value through material recovery strategies.** In this archetype business model patterns centre around extracting value from resources that would otherwise go to waste, as well as efficiently utilising by-products. Another pattern involves creating secondary marketplaces for the efficient exchange of secondary raw materials at scale. For example, BASF (launched a partnership to recover monomers from old mattresses), FREITAG (creates bags from old truck tarps) or Schwarz Gruppe (retailer that is vertically integrating into waste and resource management).

4. **Business models that monetise extended product life cycles.** Circular business model patterns in this category revolve around providing maintenance and repair services, as well as offering product upgrades and modularisation. More advanced models focus on refurbishing or reselling products, thereby adopting a more active role in secondary markets, and guiding products (and customers) through multiple sales cycles. Another approach is the development of takeback and reuse ecosystems, where companies establish partnership models with their customers. Examples include Patagonia (building a successful programme to trade in used gear and buy refurbished items via their WornWear platform), Walmart (piloting their Walmart Restored programme) or RECUP (reuse system for cups and bowls).

5. **The final business model archetype centres around the servitisation of products and delivering better business outcomes to customers.** Companies may choose to offer a service based on a usage or outcome-performance rate, often resulting in increased utilisation and improved unit economics. Products may also be offered in sharing or pooling solutions. Business model patterns within this archetype essentially emphasise the transition from product ownership to access, changing incentives of producers towards prioritising quality and repairability, to ensure that products run successfully in the service-based model. For example, Swapfiets (offering bike-as-a-service solutions in urban spaces), Hilti (providing a leading tool-fleets-as-a-service offering) or Decathlon (testing a rental and subscription model).

Business model exploration – Get started right now!

Strategically exploring these archetypes and patterns will help to identify your opportunity set. This exploration is a dynamic process that involves creative ideation and the generation of diverse opportunity scenarios. Potentially attractive business models may span from incremental adjustments of existing business models to groundbreaking innovations with the potential to shape a 'circular business revolution'. Some business models might have the character of sustaining the 'business-as-usual' scenario while others hold truly transformative potential. Your emerging opportunity set can become a valuable asset for your organisation. The exploration process to get there may reveal that combining certain archetypes and patterns can yield the highest net impact potential. To maximise effectiveness focus your exploration on the most relevant archetypes first. The following worksheet (Figure 4.3) can help you to get an initial perspective on those archetypes that may be most relevant for you.

Your creative journey should then take a more granular view by exploring specific patterns and identifying opportunities. The objective is to develop a deeper understanding of how these specific patterns can unlock both economic value creation and environmental benefits. The following chapters will guide you through the different business model patterns.

Figure 4.3. Taking stock of initial ideas and thoughts

TAKING STOCK: NOTE YOUR INITIAL IDEAS AND THOUGHTS

	PARTICULARLY RELEVANT IF...	INITIAL IDEAS
OPTIMISE RESOURCE USE	• High, costly, unsustainable resource use • Strong supplier relationships, integration, or value chain transparency • Good access to secondary, low-carbon or bio-based resources ○-○-○-○-○	
CAPITALISE REGENERATION AND RESTORATION	• Direct land use • Indirect impact on land or sea use • Large own infrastructure and buildings • Customers value premium quality and sustainability ○-○-○-○-○	
VALORISE WASTE	• Waste as potentially valuable resource • Access to potentially valuable by-products • Ability to influence waste segregation • Currently significant waste generation in the value chain directly or indirectly ○-○-○-○-○	
MONETISE EXTENDED PRODUCT LIFE	• High-quality brand and products • Design can support long product lifecycles • High value retention of used products • Products often underutilised over lifetime • Opportunity to take back used products ○-○-○-○-○	
SERVITISE PRODUCTS	• Good customer relationships and direct interaction • High customer value add through services • Underutilised capacities and productivity • High degree of digitalisation ○-○-○-○-○	

Relevance

Very low ⊗○○○○   *Low* ○⊗○○○   *Neutral* ○○⊗○○   *High* ○○○⊗○   *Very High* ○○○○⊗

4.1 Optimise resource use

In the heart of the Japanese culture lies the concept of *Mottainai* – a profound word embodying a sense of regret over wasted intrinsic value in objects or resources. Rooted in Buddhist teachings that recognise the spirit in all things, *Mottainai*, tracing back to the thirteenth century, promotes the efficient and effective use of resources while minimising waste. Today, it still affects daily Japanese life, particularly among children, who learn from parents and teachers not to waste food, water, energy or any resource. Environmentalists have used *Mottainai* as a call to action for sustainability. In 1982 a campaign featured the *Mottainai* Ghost, haunting those who wasted resources. But the principles of *Mottainai* also hold profound implications for companies. By minimising resource use and adopting efficient operational practices, companies enhance their operational resource productivity and bottom line. The exclamation *Mottainai!* – translating as 'What a waste!' – becomes a strong reminder for businesses to reconsider their processes, reduce unnecessary resource use and explore innovative ways to repurpose and recycle precious materials. Is your company haunted by the *Mottainai* Ghost? If so, get yourself some inspiration for how to get rid of this ghost by zooming into the first business model archetype.

Decisions regarding resource use represent a core business model strategy that can determine whether your company emerges from a crisis in a position of strength. Embracing a circular and eco-effective approach to resource management can address the underlying issues behind many supply chain crises and foster the creation of low-carbon products. A fundamental step involves rethinking how you design, source and produce goods. While resource optimisation is commonly pursued in tandem with decarbonisation endeavours, adopting this approach as a business model necessitates that your refined resource management confers a distinct competitive edge. This advantage might empower your company to achieve premium pricing, captivate novel customer segments, solidify its standing within a specific industry or embed cost benefits and resilience into your business model.

(a) Green operations

Greening operations involves diminishing the ecological footprint of your business model through waste reduction, pollution mitigation or eliminating harmful substances. It encompasses measures such as sustainable energy supply, energy efficiency and integrating energy recovery methods into the offering. It extends to efficient resource use in product design (e.g. light weight, material complexity) as well as process innovations for decarbonisation. This has the potential to reduce the environmental impact while concurrently enhancing the resource productivity of your business model. It might result in a better cost base, ensure compliance, bolster your brand's sustainability reputation and attract both consumers and B2B customers seeking sustainable alternatives.

Impact case	Business case
• **Refuse:** Eliminate hazardous materials or chemicals (e.g. asbestos, lead or mercury) and opt against using unsustainably sourced materials, such as those from non-renewable resources, endangered species or obtained through harmful practices • **Reduce:** Minimise waste, energy and water consumption through measures like adopting renewable energy, water-saving technologies and optimising packaging and transportation logistics • **Regenerate:** Support biodiversity, soil health and watersheds by implementing practices like conserving natural habitats and reducing pesticide and fertiliser use.	• **Cost savings:** Establish more effective resource utilisation, energy efficiency, process optimisation or workflow efficiency to achieve substantial long-term cost savings. Automation and supply chain optimisation can further reduce operational costs • **Supply chain resilience:** Enhance overall business efficiency and strengthen resilience against external price volatilities and uncertainties • **Differentiation and reputation:** Integrate ambitious sustainable practices to distinguish your business from competitors and attract B2C as well as B2B customers prioritising sustainability in purchasing decisions

Industry relevance

Greening operations is generally relevant for all industries, but it is particularly relevant for sectors that are resource- and carbon-intensive or generate a significant amount of waste and pollution. Examples of industries where greening operations can become a relevant market differentiator include:

- **Manufacturing:** The manufacturing sector holds the potential to optimise a significant share of CO_2 emissions, with energy-intensive industrial emissions contributing more than 20 per cent of emissions in regions like the EU.[3] This sector is often driven by small and medium-sized enterprises. Manufacturers adopting resource-efficient operations can capitalise a cost benefit and cater to a growing market seeking environmentally responsible options.

Case example: Interface, a global manufacturer of modular carpet tiles, focuses on reducing energy consumption, water usage and waste generation throughout their entire production process. They have pioneered innovations in sustainable materials, such as using recycled materials and implementing closed-loop recycling systems.

- **Energy and utilities:** The transition to renewable energy sources is gaining momentum as governments and consumers prioritise clean energy. Greener operations in this sector can attract investments and customers demanding low-carbon solutions.

  Case example: Ørsted has transformed itself from a fossil fuel–based energy provider to a global leader in renewable energy. Focusing on scaling offshore/onshore wind and solar energy while phasing out coal-fired power plants, Ørsted stands out as a front runner in the renewable energy sector.

- **Construction and real estate:** Sustainable building practices are becoming mainstream due to environmental regulations and consumer demand. Companies greening their operations are ahead of the curve in terms of upcoming regulation and can offer higher standards to environmentally conscious clients seeking energy-efficient and sustainable properties.

  Case example: Baufritz is an award-winning German company that specialises in sustainable buildings. They emphasise eco-friendly wood-based construction, decarbonisation, modularity, energy efficiency and material health. The brand is known for is premium, high-quality and health-focused solutions.

- **Mobility and transportation:** The paradigm shift towards electric vehicles and sustainable mobility solutions is happening across most regions, especially in urban areas. Manufacturers and providers of mobility or logistics solutions need to embrace green operations to enable a sustainable mobility product offering.

  Case example: Swisspod's innovative Hyperloop technology utilises low-pressure tubes and levitated capsules propelled by electromagnetic propulsion. This approach significantly reduces energy consumption and CO_2 emissions while achieving high travel speeds. With a vision to establish sustainable, carbon-neutral and high-speed transportation solutions between major cities, Swisspod aims to make Hyperloop technology scalable and more accessible.

- **Textiles:** The textile industry is known for its significant environmental impact due to the use of hazardous chemicals, high water consumption, energy-intensive processes and end-of-life waste problem. Adopting green operations, such as reducing water consumption, using non-toxic dyes and chemicals and cleaner production processes can help companies reduce their environmental impact and gain a competitive edge.

  Case example: DyeCoo has developed a unique dyeing process called DryDye, which uses supercritical carbon dioxide ($scCO_2$) instead of water to dye fabrics. This process uses no water, produces no waste, consumes 50 per cent lesser energy than conventional dyeing methods and eliminates the need for chemical additives. The $scCO_2$ used in the process is recycled, making it a closed-loop system.

- **Food:** Growing consumer concerns over the environmental impact of food production highlights the need for sustainable practices. Companies embracing green operations practices, such as optimising on-site water and nutrient cycles, enhance their resilience and appeal to a market segment valuing sustainably produced food.

  Case example: Danone has developed a robust water stewardship approach as part of its comprehensive impact programme. This approach includes promoting water circularity within and around production sites, conserving water resources in agriculture and watersheds and ensuring access to safe drinking water for communities.

Additional case examples: Impossible Foods (plant-based meat alternatives with about 89 per cent lesser global warming potential versus a typical beef burger); Deutsche Post DHL (decarbonising logistics operations and enabling business through circular supply chain operations); Solidia Technologies (reduces the carbon footprint of concrete by up to 50 per cent compared with traditional methods); Veolia (holistic approach to green operations and developing circular solutions for waste water).

Pitfalls to avoid

- Don't focus on the low-hanging fruit only. While immediate opportunities are valuable a truly impactful green operations strategy should include transformative changes for significant environmental benefits.
- Avoid making exaggerated or misleading claims about environmental efforts. An authentic, holistic approach is crucial for maintaining trust among customers and stakeholders.
- Ensure that environmental initiatives don't inadvertently lead to negative outcomes in other areas, such as increased resource consumption outside of your organisation's boundaries or impacts on employee well-being.

Keep an eye on

The evolving green hydrogen market!

- **What it is:** Green hydrogen, produced through renewable energy electrolysis, has the potential to substitute fossil fuels particularly for transportation, energy generation and manufacturing. This shift reduces carbon emissions and supports hard-to-abate industry decarbonisation. It can be used as a means of energy storage and optimise grid balancing.

- **Companies to have on your radar:** Linde, Air Liquide, Reliance Industries, First Hydrogen, Plug Power.

(b) Secondary and decarbonised materials

The integration of secondary and decarbonised materials into the circular economy business model involves embracing sustainable product design and procurement practices and opting for materials primarily composed of recycled (and recyclable) and decarbonised resources. This strategic approach offers the chance to optimise resource use and significantly reduce the environmental footprint of your production inputs and purchased goods. Incorporating secondary materials can therefore not only reduce reliance on virgin materials, but also drive decarbonisation and unlock new value streams to gain a competitive edge in the market. Of course, this business model pattern should be combined with a mindset of designing the products for recycling as well. Some companies may build a closed-loop model where they recover their own material (e.g. from post-industrial waste or post-consumer waste) to be reused as recycled input for new products (see Section 4.3 for the waste-to-value business model pattern).

Impact case	Business case
● **Reduce:** Utilise recycled and decarbonised materials to replace virgin resources, reducing the environmental impact associated with extraction and processing of resources ● **Reuse:** Extend the lifespan of resources by incorporating secondary materials into production processes, preventing the continuous production of new materials and diverting resources from landfills or incineration ● **Recycle:** Encourage resource recycling by designing products to be recycled at the end of life. This supports a system where resources are continuously reintroduced into production cycles thereby minimising downcycling and waste.	● **Cost savings:** Utilising secondary materials can yield cost savings (though market dynamics may impact recycled material prices). Long-term contracts or an independent recovery strategy can secure a favourable cost advantage ● **Supply chain resilience:** Enhance supply chain resilience by reducing vulnerability to shortages and disruptions in virgin resource supply, ensuring more stable processes and planning ● **Differentiation and reputation:** Adopt secondary and decarbonised materials to foster innovation in product design, providing a competitive edge and opening up new market avenues beyond average industry recycled content targets

Industry relevance

Using secondary and decarbonised materials is generally relevant for all industries. It is particularly interesting for sectors that heavily depend on primary resources, especially for products with short lifetimes and those that generate a significant amount of waste. Some examples of industries where secondary and decarbonised materials can become a strategic differentiator include:

● **Packaging:** The packaging industry faces increasing scrutiny for its contribution to plastic waste and pollution (e.g. ocean plastics, microplastics). Adopting secondary materials in packaging not only aligns with consumer preferences for more eco-friendly products, but also anticipates increasing regulatory pressure. Leading companies combine the use of recycled materials with a design-for-recycling approach to enable recycling.

Case example: Frosch, a German eco-pioneer backed by Werner & Mertz, embraces a holistic environmental strategy. Their commitment extends from natural, plant-based products to sustainable manufacturing and water treatment. Notably, the bottles are made from 100 per cent recycled plastics and they aim to follow closed-loop principles by collaborating with industry partners to obtain high-quality recyclates.

- **Textiles:** The challenges in the textile industry in terms of pollution and waste, largely driven by the fast fashion phenomenon, have led to a growing interest in sustainable fashion. Incorporating recycled fibres beyond industry standards addresses concerns related to resource consumption and waste production. An ambitious approach speaks to a growing market that prioritises environmentally friendly choices and potentially allows to develop a premium product positioning and brand loyalty.

Case example: Ecoalf, a Spanish company dedicated to sustainable fashion and lifestyle products, strives to minimise its reliance on natural resources across materials, energy and transport. Renowned for its commitment to using recycled materials, Ecoalf crafts high-quality clothing and accessories through post-consumer waste and fibre-to-fibre recycling. Beyond that, Ecoalf tries to activate and promote environmental awareness.

- **Furniture:** The furniture industry uses a significant amount of resources (e.g. wood, energy, water, metals, plastics) and several companies have been criticised for reduced product quality, lack of repairability or substantial waste generation. Using secondary materials in combination with an ambitious circularity vision presents an opportunity to cater towards more sustainable alternatives and evolving customer demand.

Case example: IKEA has articulated its strategic commitment to transition to a circular business. For example, the company has taken a pioneering stance in innovating recycling processes for fibreboard, traditionally a challenging material to recycle. Leveraging R&D and collaborating with partners, IKEA has developed a method that reintegrates recycled fibre into its products, ensuring material performance and quality.

- **Automotive:** The automotive industry contributes to a significant amount of CO_2 emissions and natural resources consumption. Ambitiously utilising secondary and decarbonised materials in vehicle production supports climate action commitments and resilience and may help to set companies apart in a competitive market.

Case example: BMW is committed to enhancing energy and raw material efficiency. Their 'secondary first' approach seeks to elevate the use of recycled and reused materials in their cars. Additionally, BMW operates a dismantling and recycling centre in Unterschleißheim near Munich.

- **Construction and real estate:** Sustainable construction practices are gaining traction as the industry needs to decarbonise and regulations are becoming more stringent. Integrating secondary materials, such as recycled concrete, steel, glass or insulation materials, aligns with the industry's move towards more eco-friendly building solutions. Companies that embrace these materials are ahead of the curve.

Case example: Holcim's ECOCycle circular technology platform pioneers circular construction, recycling up to 100 per cent of construction materials. With a focus on cement, concrete and aggregates, Holcim aims to reduce natural resource use and minimise the environmental footprint of building solutions.

Additional case examples: BASF (aims to significantly increase recycled and waste-based raw materials to replace fossil raw materials); Steelcase (committed to responsible material use combined with design for circularity and decarbonisation); PepsiCo (pushing for recycled content, design for recycling and investing into recycling infrastructure); HP (developing electronic products and ink/toner cartridges using recycled content).

Pitfalls to avoid

- Ensure that secondary or decarbonised materials meet the required quality and performance standards for the intended application. Subpar materials could compromise product functionality and durability. Be open to adjusting technical specifications and product design to optimise for secondary material use.
- Adopt a holistic approach to recycled content and recycling. Your product should not only use recycled material but also be recyclable at the end of its life. It is key to take a systems perspective to ensure that materials stay in the loop at their highest value and are not downcycled. Also, while using secondary materials can reduce environmental impact, ensure that sourcing these materials does not inadvertently cause negative ecological consequences.
- Communicate transparently with customers about the use of secondary materials. Some consumers may have concerns about the quality or origin of these materials, so addressing these concerns can help build trust.

Keep an eye on

The emerging waste-to-plastic market!

- **What it is:** This growing sector transforms various types of waste, especially hard-to-recycle plastics, into valuable recycled plastic feedstocks. Technologies like mechanical recycling reshape plastics for new applications without altering their chemical composition. Innovative methods in chemical recycling, such as pyrolysis and depolymerisation, break down plastics into reusable components for creating new materials.

- **Companies to have on your radar:** UBQ Materials, Eastman, Loop Industries, Carbios, Axens, Plastic Energy, Enerkem, DePoly, Topsoe, or Gr3N.

(c) Bio-based materials

This business model involves utilising materials made (partially) from biomass, sourced from renewable resources or biological processes, that can safely re-enter the environment and that can be continuously regenerated or replenished. These materials, derived from plants or organic waste, can either be biodegradable or non-biodegradable. Examples include cellulose fibres, bioplastics and wood. It is crucial that you ensure that the production and sourcing of bio-based materials are done in an environmentally and socially responsible manner, avoiding impacts on food production and security, natural ecosystems or local communities. Additionally, considering competition for land and the actual end-of-life scenarios is vital as this emerging field presents various applications, evolving technologies and complex trade-offs.

Impact case	Business case
• **Reduce:** Integrate bio-based materials to decrease carbon emissions, offering a renewable alternative to fossil fuels and contributing to carbon sequestration • **Reuse:** Biodegradable materials return to the biocycle through composting while non-biodegradable ones should be recycled or repurposed across applications, enhancing resource efficiency and reducing waste • **Regenerate:** Ensure sustainable agricultural practices and optimise design choices to actively support natural resource regeneration	• **Resource efficiency and cost savings:** Achieve cost benefits and heightened resource efficiency by applying renewable, bio-based materials that often come with better footprint, energy and water profiles • **Supply chain resilience:** Reduce dependence on finite and costly non-renewable resources like fossil fuels to bolster supply chain resilience. Mitigate risks associated with resource scarcity and meet the demand for responsibly sourced materials • **Differentiation and reputation:** Distinguish your company by catering to sustainability-conscious customers, actively driving innovation and enhancing brand reputation

Industry relevance

Relevant across various industries, bio-based materials play a crucial role in supporting decarbonisation, especially in sectors with short product lifetimes and substantial waste generation. Industries where bio-based materials can serve as a market differentiator include:

- **Energy:** Bio-based materials provide sustainable alternatives to fossil fuels. This includes utilising biofuels and biomass in transportation, power generation and heating applications. However, to ensure the environmental benefits it's crucial to align these practices with sustainable land use principles, such as avoiding land conversion and implementing regenerative agricultural practices that consider impacts on water and biodiversity. This approach has the potential to significantly reduce carbon emissions and meet the growing demand for renewable energy sources.

Case example: Neste, a Finnish oil refining company, has pioneered the development of a range of renewable fuels and bio-based chemicals. Their portfolio includes renewable diesel and renewable jet fuel, as well as various bio-based chemicals applicable to a wide range of industries.

- **Chemicals:** On the search for alternatives to fossil-based feedstocks, bio-based materials find applications in lubricants, solvents and additives. These chemicals can be derived from various feedstocks like corn, sugar or lignocellulosic biomass. Investments and innovation in the field of green chemistry are needed to advance solutions for renewable feedstocks, paired with sustainable sourcing principles.

Case example: Bloom Biorenewables has implemented a bio-based materials business model providing a viable alternative to petroleum by transforming natural biomass materials. Their aldehyde-assisted fractionation (AAF) technology efficiently harnesses the potential of cellulose, lignin and hemicellulose, opening up new possibilities for sustainable materials production.

- **Packaging:** Bioplastics or plant-based fibres offer a sustainable alternative for traditional plastic-based packaging materials. These materials can possess characteristics such as biodegradability, compostability or recyclability. Their impact on waste reduction and environmental considerations varies based on the respective solution.

Case example: Notpla, a UK-based innovator, is leading the way towards nature-based packaging solutions to replace fossil-based packaging. Utilising seaweed, the company has crafted a portfolio of products that are both biodegradable (within 4–6 weeks) and home-compostable. Importantly, the material remains unaltered (i.e. without chemical modifications).

- **Textiles:** Fashion items based on bio-based materials, such as organic cotton, bamboo or hemp, offer sustainable alternatives for the textile industry. When cultivated with sustainable land use practices, these materials, requiring less water and fewer pesticides, contribute to reduced environmental impact. The fashion industry, faced with the need for transparent supply chains, fair labour practices and minimised environmental footprint, can benefit from such alternatives.

Case example: Bolt Threads utilises yeast to create spider silk, a strong and elastic material. The primary input is plant-based sugar. They've also introduced a bio-based leather alternative, known as Mylo, derived from rapidly grown mycelium, providing an alternative to traditional leather production.

- **Toys and childcare:** Bio-based materials offer sustainable options for toys and childcare products. Examples include wood, organic pigments and bio-based adhesives, providing safer and more eco-friendly alternatives to traditional petroleum-based counterparts. Prioritising child safety builds trust and loyalty among parents seeking sustainable choices for their children.

  Case example: PlanToys makes award-winning, environmentally friendly, natural toys (e.g. from rubber wood). They use plant-based ink and chemical-free wood, non-formaldehyde glue, organic colour pigments and water-based dyes. PlanToys also introduced a programme called PlayCycle, a community-based approach to pass on toys to the next kids, to ensure active use and long product life.

Additional case examples: Lenzing (produces materials like TENCEL from renewable wood fibres); Stora Enso (various types of wood-based packaging materials, including paperboard, corrugated packaging and moulded fibre packaging); Solvay (various bio-based, renewable feedstocks, e.g. bio-based solvents that can be applied in fragrances, paints, inks or cleaners).

Pitfalls to avoid

- Not all bio-based products are circular! Challenge the resource basis and end-of-life reality to shape an informed opinion about the impact potential of your product. Are biodegradable solutions being returned to the biocycle? For example, assess the recyclability of your bioplastics application within the existing recycling systems.
- Consider competition for land! To prevent shortages and rising costs in the food sector, carefully select feedstocks that do not directly compete with essential food crops. Prioritise materials derived from marginal or underutilised lands to minimise any negative impact on food production (e.g. seaweed). Or choose materials that require less water for cultivation and processing and emphasise effective water management practices throughout your supply chain. Opt for suppliers committed to sustainable land use practices.
- Be careful with respect to resource competition and price volatility by avoiding reliance on a single bio-based feedstock. Implement diversified sourcing strategies to maintain supply chain stability.

Keep an eye on

The emerging mycelium market!

- **What it is:** Mycelium, a multicellular fungus like yeast, grows into macro-size structures like mushrooms. It assembles small molecules precisely and can be guided to create predictable structures through temperature and airflow control, enabling rapid growth within days to form sheets and structures. Applications span across diverse industries, including packaging, construction, food or textiles.

- **Companies to have on your radar:** Ecovative, MycoWorks, BIOHM or Mogu.

Taking Stock

Now, let's take a moment to reflect using the following worksheet (Figure 4.4.). Have these business model patterns sparked initial opportunity ideas for you? Are there specific initiatives in your business that, if scaled, could represent significant opportunities? Broaden your thinking and note down these opportunities.

Next, select one of these opportunities and explore it further. Examine how the classic business model elements manifest, including the value proposition to the customer, operational delivery and high-level economics for value retention. Outline a preliminary business case for scaling this business model, estimating the potential size of the opportunity from low to very high. Additionally, assess the environmental impact potential of the opportunity – do you anticipate the benefits as low or high?

Figure 4.4. Taking stock of identified opportunities

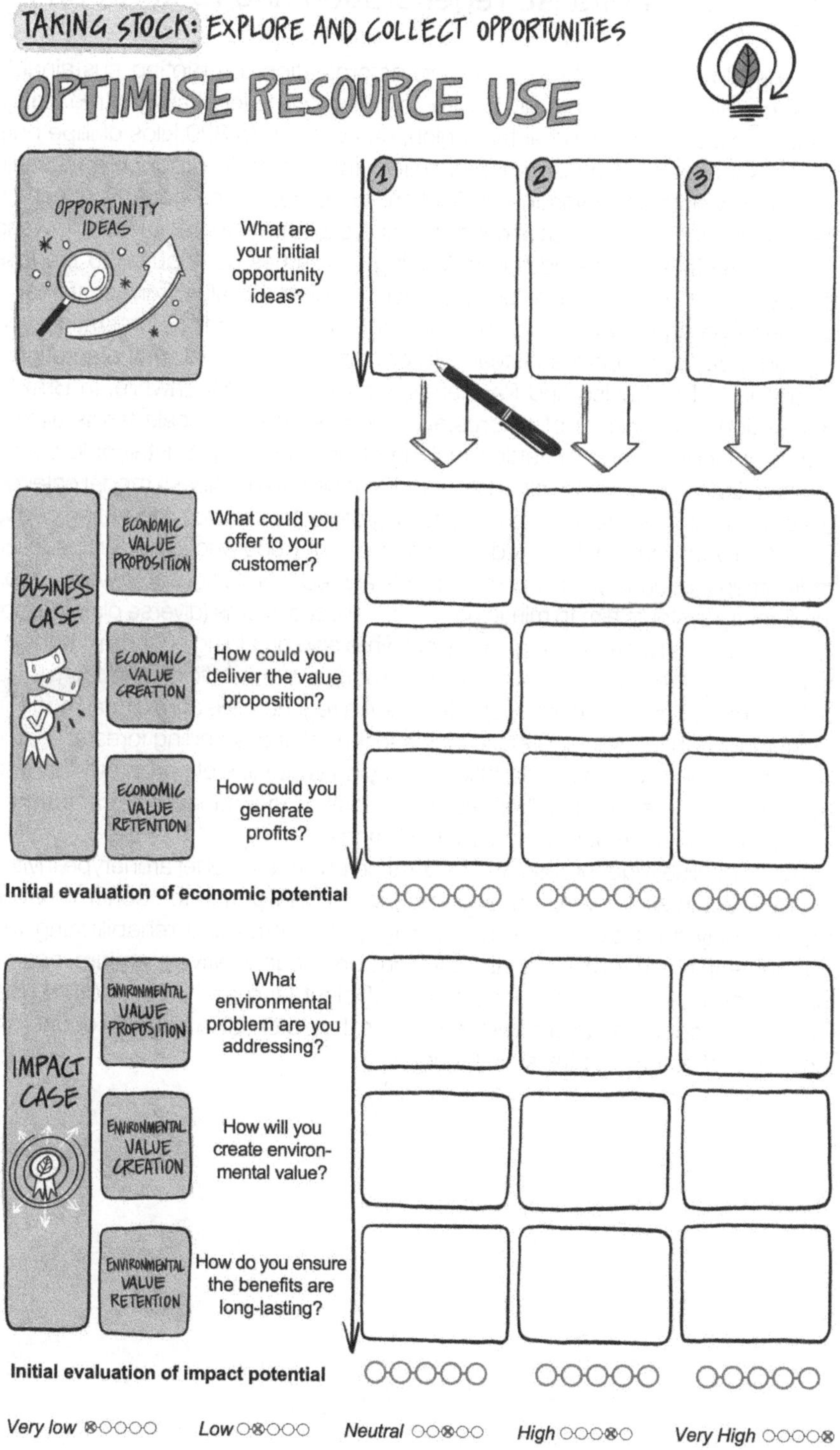

TAKING STOCK: EXPLORE AND COLLECT OPPORTUNITIES

OPTIMISE RESOURCE USE

OPPORTUNITY IDEAS

What are your initial opportunity ideas?

① ② ③

BUSINESS CASE

ECONOMIC VALUE PROPOSITION	What could you offer to your customer?	
ECONOMIC VALUE CREATION	How could you deliver the value proposition?	
ECONOMIC VALUE RETENTION	How could you generate profits?	

Initial evaluation of economic potential ○○○○○○   ○○○○○○   ○○○○○○

IMPACT CASE

ENVIRONMENTAL VALUE PROPOSITION	What environmental problem are you addressing?	
ENVIRONMENTAL VALUE CREATION	How will you create environmental value?	
ENVIRONMENTAL VALUE RETENTION	How do you ensure the benefits are long-lasting?	

Initial evaluation of impact potential ○○○○○○   ○○○○○○   ○○○○○○

Very low ⊗○○○○   *Low* ○⊗○○○   **Neutral** ○○⊗○○   *High* ○○○⊗○   *Very High* ○○○○⊗

4.2 Capitalise regeneration and restoration

Can the illipe nut contribute to halting deforestation, promoting sustainable resource utilisation and combating climate change? The tengkawang tree, native to Indonesia's Borneo/Kalimantan region, can yield up to 800 kilos of illipe nuts per season. Local communities can collect these nuts to produce a versatile butter highly suitable for various applications in the cosmetics industry, offering a sustainable alternative to shea or cocoa butter. Despite its potential, the tengkawang tree is currently endangered due to logging, which has contributed to the loss of 50 per cent of Borneo's forests. Creating economic value from sustainably sourced illipe nuts can protect the standing forest, prevent deforestation and support local communities instead of converting land to palm oil plantations, according to Forestwise and Partnerships for Forests.[4] Meanwhile, in Brazil's Pará region, 40 per cent of deforestation occurs on small-scale farms aiming to bolster income through cattle ranching or crop farming. Sustainable cocoa agroforestry can present an alternative and regenerative business model catering to the demand for sustainable chocolate.[5] Agroforestry involves integrating cocoa cultivation with the planting and management of trees and other crops in an environmentally friendly, socially responsible and economically viable way. Cocoa agroforestry systems aim to mimic natural forest ecosystems (diverse planting, soil health, biodiversity, carbon sequestration) while also providing economic benefits to farmers. There are many other forest products like medicinal plants, resins, rubber, honey, bamboo, fruits or seeds, where a regenerative agricultural model in partnership with forests can help to increase the value of standing forests, enable land restoration and support ambitious sourcing strategies of corporates around the word. These examples illustrate a business model capable of capturing a regenerative premium for producers and brands.

The capitalise regeneration and restoration business model archetype invites you to invest in and champion projects that not only generate economic value but also play an active role in revitalising ecosystems and rehabilitating the environment. Underlying patterns may focus on a regenerative premium, enable valuable ecosystem services or promote efficient land and infrastructure use. Capitalising regeneration and restoration has the potential to improve economic success and natural capital simultaneously.

(a) Regenerative premium

The regenerative premium business model pattern provides an opportunity to actively contribute to environmental restoration and preservation while offering high-quality, sustainable products to customers. Regenerative production systems and interventions on land should prioritise soil health, circular nutrient flows, biodiversity and the wholesome enhancement of ecological conditions. More and more customers are willing to pay a premium for products knowing their purchase directly supports crucial regenerative efforts. Imagine premium coffee or chocolate cultivated through agroforestry practices, cosmetics crafted in collaboration with local communities, furniture sourced from revitalised timber lands or sneakers built upon a sustainable natural rubber supply chain.

Impact case	Business case
● **Rethink/regenerate:** Design products or services to actively support natural ecosystems, contributing to regenerative land use practices, land restoration and preservation	● **Premium pricing:** Achieve a premium quality, positioning and pricing based on regenerative products or services. Build value chain partnerships to manage potential investments for regenerative projects
● **Reduce:** Regenerative practices aim to minimise land use footprint through increased productivity or switch to less land-intensive resources. They may reduce water consumption and other inputs, ideally lowering overall resource demand	● **Differentiation and reputation:** Demonstrate a commitment to regeneration and responsible business practices to differentiate from competitors, create a unique proposition and strengthen reputation
● **Refuse:** Avoid harmful chemicals or pesticides to prevent adverse effects on ecosystems, biodiversity and general well-being	● **Increase resilience:** Fortify against environmental risks and regulatory uncertainties in the supply chain. Verifiable regenerative practices increase transparency, efficiency in reporting and may boost yield

Industry relevance

Relevant across various industries, with a pronounced impact in sectors highly reliant on natural resources, notably the agricultural and food industries, and also technical products that directly rely on land use, such as fashion and construction. Several examples illustrate how a regenerative premium can emerge as a market differentiator:

● **Agriculture and food:** Farmers and food companies directly influence ecosystem health and biodiversity. Developing premium products that are cultivated through regenerative practices and ecological restoration principles appeals to environmentally conscious consumers and also fosters the wider adoption of the respective farming techniques.

Case example: Slow Forest Coffee combines sustainable, agroforestry-based coffee production with a B2B business model supplying the artisanal coffee to companies directly (farm-to-fork). Their agroforestry models aim to maximise regenerative impact over conventional industrial farming methods like monoculture. They integrate trees and crops in a way that enhances biodiversity, soil health and ecosystem resilience. This circular system relies on trees to provide shade for coffee plants, reduce erosion and foster wildlife habitats.

- **Fashion and textiles:** The fashion industry's environmental footprint calls for a circular and regenerative transformation. Companies can spearhead this change by offering clothing crafted from sustainable materials that endorse regenerative practices. Pioneering approaches are needed to drive a positive industry shift.

  Case example: EILEEN FISHER is a fashion brand known for its commitment to circular design and regenerative practices. They focus on using organic and regeneratively sourced fibres like organic cotton and TENCEL in their clothing lines. More recently, they introduced an innovation called 'regenerative wool', a fibre that is restoring grasslands in Patagonia.

- **Beauty and personal care:** The beauty industry can embrace the regenerative premium model to provide consumers with eco-friendly products while ambitiously supporting regeneration. More and more consumers seek ethical and responsible personal care choices. It is also an opportunity to nudge more sustainable consumption behaviour.

  Case example: Dr. Bronner's, known for its organic and fair-trade personal care products, has applied a regenerative business model that aligns with its commitment to sustainability. They work with farmers who implement regenerative agriculture practices, such as cover cropping, composting and crop rotations, to promote soil health, biodiversity and carbon sequestration. In addition, Dr. Bronner's allocates a portion of its profits to support various regenerative projects and organisations dedicated to ecological restoration, such as agriculture research and soil health initiatives.

Additional case examples: Natura (cosmetics company with strategic focus to circularity and regeneration, established a network and collaboration with more than 2000 Brazilian farming communities); Carpe Diem (producing organic grapes and raisins in South Africa based on regenerative practices and tracking its impact).

Pitfalls to avoid

- Do not make unsubstantiated claims about regenerative practices. Be transparent about your initiatives and ensure they are backed by credible certifications or technology-enabled measurement, reporting and verification solutions. Partner with leading organisations to learn about regenerative practices (e.g. Science Based Targets for Nature, SBTN) and how to optimise supply chains.

- Regenerative practices might initially involve higher costs due to sustainable sourcing and production. Passing on these costs directly to customers may deter them. A better way might be to gradually introduce the regenerative premium model and communicate the long-term benefits it offers. You may partner with specialised investors who aim to invest in nature's potential.

- Customers may want to see tangible and measurable results from their support of regenerative initiatives or restoration projects. If you can't demonstrate the positive impact, the business model loses credibility. Provide regular updates and reports showcasing the environmental and social outcomes achieved through your efforts.

Keep an eye on

The booming LOHAS market!

- **What it is:** LOHAS (Lifestyles of Health and Sustainability) represents a consumer segment characterised by a strong commitment to personal well-being and environmental sustainability. These consumers prioritise products and services that align with their values, showing a willingness to pay a premium for items that are ethically sourced, eco-friendly and contribute to social and environmental regeneration. This segment's conscious purchasing decisions drive demand for sustainable and regenerative products across various industries.

(b) Ecosystem service solutions

Nature delivers valuable services to humanity, such as providing resources and regulating the ecosystem (e.g. climate, pollination) or supporting functions (e.g. photosynthesis, nutrient cycling) and providing cultural value.[6] Measuring, reporting and verifying ecosystem services present an innovative strategy for enhancing nature restoration and conservation. The 'ecosystem service solutions' business model offers an opportunity to engage in activities aimed at restoring and preserving ecosystems while pursuing your business objectives. This involves creating a model where these services are manageable or tradeable, incentivising land stewards (e.g. implementing regenerative practices) by beneficiaries (e.g. society or businesses benefiting from carbon sequestration, biodiversity conservation). Incentives include investments, subsidies or market-based payments facilitated by mechanisms like credit systems to capture measurable benefits. For instance, restoring degraded peatlands can create measurable climate mitigation benefits, certified in credits for carbon trading schemes or voluntary markets. Another mechanism could be the increasingly important practice of 'insetting', where companies actively engage and invest in nature-based solutions within their supply chain. For instance, agrifood companies managing upstream emissions via regenerative sourcing, or co-producing ecosystem services to reduce risks and strengthen resilience.

Impact case	Business case
• **Rethink/regenerate:** Actively engage in restoring and preserving ecosystems, contributing to critical ecosystem services through projects such as habitat restoration, biodiversity enhancement and carbon sequestration	• **Differentiation and reputation:** Ambitiously adopting ecosystem service solutions can competitively differentiate your business by driving a regenerative impact agenda across the value chain, fostering long-term value increase and potentially creating new income streams
• **Refuse:** Regenerative practices avoid harmful inputs, such as chemicals or pesticides, preventing negative impacts on biodiversity and ecosystem health	• **Resource efficiency and cost savings:** Investing in ecosystem service solutions may allow for long-term cost savings and increased efficiency, and offers a cost-efficient pathway for decarbonisation and sustainable sourcing
• **Reduce:** Integrate the value of ecosystem services into decision-making processes across value chain partners to reduce negative externalities and risks, supporting the long-term health of ecosystems	• **Increase resilience:** Engage in ecosystem service solutions in the value chain to reduce impairment and other risks, especially climate and nature-related risks. Strengthen resilience of regional land use ecosystems and value chain infrastructure

Industry relevance

Actively integrating ecosystem service solutions into a business model holds relevance across various industries with particular significance for sectors heavily reliant on natural resources and respective land use. Some exemplary industries and cases include:

- **Agriculture and food:** The agriculture industry depends on ecosystem services such as pollination, soil fertility and water availability. Actively embracing regenerative practices and supporting land restoration can improve soil health, reduce water usage and foster biodiversity, ensuring more sustainable and resilient food production systems. Agricultural companies should take the lead in promoting regenerative practices and strengthening natural cycles for long-term food security.

  Case example: Perrier, a French mineral water company under Nestlé, pioneered a range of payment mechanisms as early as the 1990s to change land use around its water catchment areas. The goal was to secure long-term water quality and reduce the nitrates and pesticides entering the springs in France. They achieved this through engaging with upstream landowners, establishing long-term contracts for improved agricultural practices and reforestation of sensitive filtration zones. This is an example for direct company-financed deals for ecosystem services.

- **Fashion and textiles:** Brands can advance the sustainability transformation in the fashion sector by thinking beyond sustainable operational practices. Downstream, they can play a proactive role in addressing the waste problem in the sector. Upstream, they can ensure sustainable supply chains and foster ecosystem services.

  Case example: VEJA Shoes, founded in the early 2000s, aims to create the most sustainable trainers. They've established a profitable natural rubber value chain in Brazil, protecting forests by buying native rubber from Acre's tappers. Traditionally, rubber tapping is an economic activity in the Amazon, but demand has waned due to low prices and competition from plantations. VEJA pays above-market prices and initiated a Payment for Social Environmental Services (PSES) for producers adhering to environmental standards, discouraging deforestation and promoting forest protection.

- **Beauty and personal care:** The beauty and personal care industry can address environmental and social impacts throughout the consumer interface and value chain. This can include ingredient sourcing, production and packaging. By promoting regenerative practices and ecosystem services, brands can align with their identity, mitigate carbon footprints, regenerate soil health and support local communities.

Case example: Weleda, a leading producer of organic beauty products and pharmaceuticals, actively invests in nurturing soil health and employs carbon insetting strategies to enhance ecosystem services. For example, partnering with SEKEM Farm in Egypt, they cultivate jojoba plants in the desert, strategically planting trees to green the area and sequester CO_2.

- **Forestry and land habitats:** Forest ecosystems play a crucial role in carbon sequestration and biodiversity conservation. Implementing regenerative practices in forestry can support sustainable timber harvesting, especially when combined with reforestation and ecosystem restoration from degraded land.

  Case example: Terrasos, a Colombian specialist company, structures environmental investments into conservation and restoration projects. Their approach involves creating 'habitat banks' and biodiversity credits through 30-year conservation projects. This aligns with emerging regulations, like in Colombia, where businesses offset biodiversity damages. Terrasos not only addresses mandatory offsets but also extends its reach into voluntary initiatives.

- **Marine:** Marine industries play a crucial role in scaling regenerative business models focused on ecosystem services. Seaweed farming, sustainable fishing (e.g. scallops, mussels, oysters), coastal tourism with sustainable practices and offshore renewable energy can collectively support marine ecosystem regeneration.

  Case example: GreenWave, a global network of regenerative ocean farmers, pioneers a sustainable blue economy through innovative polyculture farming. They cultivate diverse seaweeds and shellfish, offering training and support for market development and commercial scaling. This approach provides ecosystem services, enhances biodiversity and sequesters carbon.

Additional case examples: followfood (tracks the impact of regenerative practices across suppliers as basis for creating outcome-based payments); Ecosia (Internet search engine that uses its profits to plant trees, invest in reforestation projects to restore ecosystems, combat deforestation and promote biodiversity).

Pitfalls to avoid

- Implementing ecosystem service solutions requires specialised knowledge of ecology, biodiversity and restoration techniques. Collaborate with experts, environmental organisations and scientists to ensure your projects are scientifically sound and yield the desired outcomes.

- From a company lens, broaden your perspective on ecosystem services, moving beyond avoidance and reduction efforts. Reject the 'offsetting mindset'; instead, integrate regeneration and preservation into the active collaboration with your supply chain partners. Ensure credibility and accountability by actively monitoring and reporting the progress and outcomes of your ecosystem service solutions.

- Ecosystem service solutions often have social and community dimensions. Neglecting to engage local communities and stakeholders can lead to resistance and hinder project success. Involve local communities, indigenous peoples and stakeholders from the outset to ensure buy-in and support.

Keep an eye on
Emerging standards and guidance on ecosystem services:

- **What it is:** Several developments aim to enhance the standardisation, harmonisation, assurance and scalability of ecosystem services. Beyond Value Chain Mitigation (BVCM), for instance, extends the scope by incorporating actions outside a company's direct control. For land areas not directly managed by your company, consider the emerging guidance on BVCM from leading initiatives like the Science-Based Targets initiative (SBTi). Also follow the guidance from the SBTN on target-setting for land, biodiversity, freshwater and ocean. Beyond that, note that the carbon market and carbon credits have matured, for instance through emission trading schemes. In contrast, biodiversity credits are still emerging. Scaling these requires guiding protocols ensuring common principles like additionality, permanence, traceability and verifiability. Ensuring adherence to the mitigation hierarchy is essential, preventing credits from being used solely for offsetting.

- **Organisations to have on your radar:** SBTi/SBTN, the World Resources Institute (WRI) and the World Business Council for Sustainable Development (WBCSD). As well as emerging innovators such as The Landbanking Group, Terrasos, goodcarbon, Revalue, Wilderlands, ValueNature, Orsa Besparingsskog, NCX or Restor.

(c) Regenerative infrastructure

Embracing regenerative infrastructure offers a unique circular business model avenue, allowing for the design of resource-productive spaces, effective infrastructure and sustainable built environments. Depending on your location(s), it helps to embed your organisation into a circular and regenerative ecosystem and explore related opportunities. This model encompasses strategies such as optimising space productivity through renewable energy generation and storage, promoting efficient building utilisation or integrating elements like urban forests and farming to enhance ecological health. Real estate and infrastructure play a direct role in influencing climate, biodiversity and landscape. Integrating a regenerative infrastructure into your business models can enable you to address environmental challenges, but you may also unlock innovative income streams associated with sustainable buildings, energy management and ecosystem regeneration.

Impact case	Business case
• **Rethink/regenerate:** Rethink how to incorporate regenerative infrastructure into your business, facilities and land use to enhance natural ecosystems, rejuvenate degraded lands and create symbiotic relationships between the built environment and nature • **Reduce:** Optimise space utilisation, minimise resource consumption (e.g. energy and water) and reduce waste generation to improve your environmental footprint and resource efficiency • **Reuse/repurpose/recycle:** Productively reuse materials, such as repurposing construction waste or upcycling materials in building projects, aligning with circular principles to lessen the demand for virgin resources	• **Increase resilience:** Embrace regenerative infrastructure to enhance business model resilience against climate-related risks and supply chain disruptions • **Cost savings:** Resource-efficient space use can improve energy efficiency, water conservation and waste reduction, unlocking significant operational benefits for a strengthened cost base • **Differentiation and reputation:** Investing in regenerative infrastructure emerges as a substantial differentiator in markets that are progressively prioritising genuine actions over mere claims. This positions your organisation at the forefront of an authentic commitment to sustainability

Industry relevance

Embracing regenerative infrastructure as a business model is particularly relevant for companies that rely on significant land use for buildings and operations and when the infrastructure can serve as a market differentiator:

- **Buildings and urban environment:** A circular and regenerative urban environment can seamlessly integrate renewable energy systems, green roofs and facades, biodiversity corridors or urban gardens or even watersheds. This strategy not only enhances land use efficiency but also presents a significant opportunity to address the increasing demand for sustainable living and working solutions. This approach is broadly applicable, ranging from integrated urban spaces to commercial real estate.

Case example: Schoonschip, an innovative floating neighbourhood in Amsterdam, integrates regenerative initiatives. Featuring sustainable elements like solar panels and a smart grid, the community fosters biodiversity with floating gardens and bee hotels, experiments with water-purifying plants, and promotes a circular and regenerative mindset through collaborative learning among residents. Thereby this neighbourhood contributes to a resilient, adaptive and environmentally harmonious urban living model.

- **Agriculture:** In rural areas, a regenerative infrastructure model may add to regenerative farming practices: water management systems like retention ponds and rainwater harvesting, on-site renewable energy, sustainable farm buildings constructed with eco-friendly materials, on-farm processing facilities to reduce transportation needs and others (e.g. beekeeping).

Case example: Sundrop Farms in Australia is an agricultural innovator that integrates solar power, hydroponics, freshwater conservation and desalination to grow crops and vegetables in degraded regions. The practice to combine agriculture with solar energy production is referred to as 'Agrisolar', an emerging integrated regenerative infrastructure approach that has significant potential across many regions.

- **Tourism:** With its reliance on the allure of natural surroundings, the tourism sector has a unique opportunity to prioritise regenerative practices. Businesses may stand out by curating premium experiences that actively contribute to the preservation of local ecosystems, catering to travellers who seek immersive and environmentally conscious travel options.

Case example: Inkaterra has pioneered regenerative tourism in Peru since 1975, restoring and conserving areas in the Andean cloud forest near Machu Picchu. Their holistic approach adds value to rural areas, promoting biodiversity conservation, education and sustainable community development. Inkaterra's efforts have transformed pastureland into a remarkably biodiverse environment.

Additional case examples: NREP (a real estate investor that sees itself as a change agent to drive decarbonisation in the urban environment); Triodos Bank (circular headquarters inspired by nature, including demountable structures and material passport); Home.Earth; (an urban development company that seeks to design, build and operate homes and spaces inspired by the Doughnut Economy); Indigo Ag (offers products and technologies that help farmers improve soil health, runs carbon sequestration programmes).

Pitfalls to avoid

- Don't rush into regenerative infrastructure projects without comprehensive planning and embeddedness with your business model. Think strategically how this may advance your opportunity space. Invest in feasibility studies, engage local communities, experienced architects, engineers, biomimicry experts and landscape designers to holistically consider the ecological, social and economic impact potential of your project.

- Regenerative projects need to be adapted to the specific ecological characteristics of each location. Avoid a one-size-fits-all approach; conduct site assessments to understand local ecosystems and tailor design and interventions.

- Infrastructure solutions can involve complex technologies, materials and construction methods. Collaborate with experienced contractors, suppliers and technology partners who specialise in circular and regenerative practices.

Keep an eye on
The emerging agrivoltaics market!

- **What it is:** Agrivoltaics combine agriculture with solar energy production by installing solar panels on agricultural lands. This dual-use scenario maximises land efficiency, provides renewable energy and offers multiple benefits such as increased crop yields, reduced water evaporation and improved microclimates for plant growth. For example, Australian farmers use this integrated regenerative infrastructure approach to farm on degraded land while European farmers apply these strategies to protect wine grapes from intense sun or other weather extremes (e.g. hail). Various technologies, including ground-mounted panels, elevated panels, photovoltaic (PV) rooftops and floating PV systems, are employed.

- **Companies to have on your radar:** AgroSolar Europe, Sundrop Farms, Sun'Agri, Susten.energy, Ciel & Terre, Pacifico Energy Partners, Fraunhofer ISE.

Taking Stock
Let's take a step back and reflect using the following worksheet (Figure 4.5). Did this business model archetype and its patterns spark initial opportunity ideas for you? Looking at your current business, are there already specific initiatives that could be scaled to capture significant opportunities? Please note down these opportunities.

Next, select one of these opportunities and explore it further. Examine how the classic business model elements manifest, including the value proposition to the customer, operational delivery and high-level economics for value retention. Outline a preliminary business case for scaling this business model, estimating the potential size of the opportunity from low to very high. Additionally, assess the environmental impact potential of the opportunity – do you anticipate the benefits as low or high?

Figure 4.5. Taking stock of identified opportunities

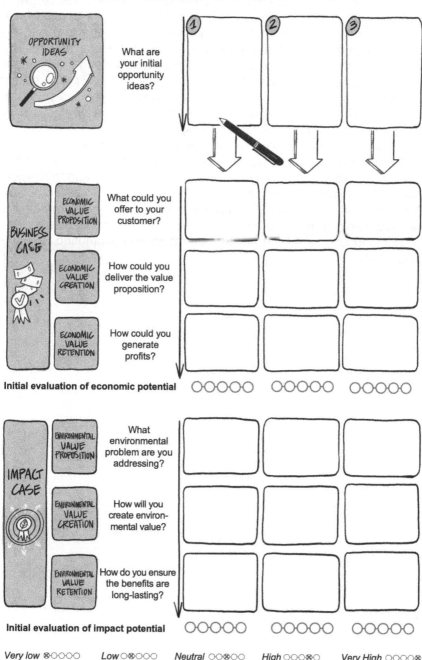

4.3 Valorise waste

For centuries, bread has been a vital food source for many people. Particularly during and after World War II people in Europe suffered from food shortages and had to be creative in utilising the few food items that were available. When food could not be used for its original purpose any longer, for example bread had become too hard to eat, they would find creative ways to use it as a precious ingredient in different recipes, such as *Panzanella* (bread salad), *Açorda* (bread soup), bread pudding or *Arme Ritter* (French toast). Today, around 17 per cent (931 million tonnes) of all food available is wasted, according to UNEP.[7] Bread is often among the most wasted food item in the developed world. How can we unlearn to waste stuff and instead find creative ways to use it as a valuable input resource for something else?

The business model archetype 'valorise waste' represents a commitment to reclaim and repurpose waste materials and integrate them into new production cycles. Embracing the 'close the loop' principle and 'zero-waste mindset' is a fundamental premise of this business model archetype. Resources are consistently regenerated within biological cycles and restored within technical production processes, diminishing reliance on virgin resources, curtailing waste generation and promoting resource productivity.

(a) Waste-to-value

In the realm of this business model pattern, you engage in the strategic endeavour of repurposing precious resources that might otherwise be discarded within conventional linear value chains. By adeptly capturing and extracting valuable materials from waste streams, these resources are reintegrated into the production cycle through methods like reuse or recycling, effectively breathing new life into what was once considered waste.

Impact case	Business case
• **Repurpose:** Transform wasted products, parts or resources into new items, contributing to a circular system that maintains resources at high value	• **Cost savings:** Achieve cost savings or capture resource value, whether by reusing resources in a closed loop or capturing the monetary value of products and embedded resources through resource recovery
• **Reuse/remanufacture:** Waste-to-value recovery involves reintroducing parts or materials into the production cycle, reducing the need for new materials and supporting energy and resource savings in manufacturing	• **Unexploited business opportunities:** Uncover new business development horizons, enabling innovation in products and services based on reclaimed materials and supporting brand differentiation or expansion into new customer segments
• **Recycle/recover:** Opt for recycling to convert wasted materials into secondary resources, establishing a closed-loop system that reduces the demand for virgin resources and raw material extraction	• **Increase supply chain resilience:** A closed-loop material system strengthens resilience by mitigating the impact of price fluctuations and supply chain disruptions, safeguarding operations against resource scarcity or geopolitical uncertainties

Industry relevance

The business model holds significance for a range of industries, especially those that generate substantial waste streams or where the value retention of the resources is relatively high. Examples where resource recovery can emerge as a business opportunity:

- **Construction:** The construction sector, a major contributor to global waste, presents a promising opportunity space for resource recovery. Through reclaiming and repurposing materials like concrete, metal, wood and glass, businesses can reduce waste and tap into a valuable source of reusable resources.

  Case example: Concular, a platform for resource-efficient construction, digitises materials in existing buildings. It facilitates matching architectural needs with available materials, transporting them from deconstruction to new construction sites. Restado, their linked secondary material market platform, innovatively connects companies and individuals with surplus materials to those in need, fostering resource exchange in construction.

- **Manufacturing:** Resource recovery holds significant potential in the manufacturing sector. With a substantial reliance on materials like steel, aluminium, copper or critical metals, manufacturers can strategically recover and recycle these resources. This approach promotes closed-material loops, thereby mitigating resource depletion.

  Case example: Northvolt, the Scandinavian battery manufacturer, is innovating circular practices in the battery industry. As they are scaling battery manufacturing, they concurrently advance their battery recycling programme called Revolt. This in-house programme aims to close the loop on batteries, offering environmental benefits alongside strategic advantages such as sourcing and supply security for critical raw materials in new battery production.

- **Electronics:** Addressing the mounting challenge of electronic waste offers a strategic foothold for resource recovery. If designed well, a resource recovery programme can serve as a market differentiator and drive loyalty while generating better knowledge about the user journey and product performance. In turn, this can support innovation in electronic product life cycles.

  Case example: Closing the Loop (CTL) is a company that specialises in recovering valuable materials from discarded mobile phones in developing countries, where electronic waste is a significant issue. Partnering with local waste collectors and recycling centres, CTL extracts valuable materials like gold, silver and rare earth metals from discarded phones, integrating them back into the supply chain.

- **Fashion and textiles:** The textile industry is known for its resource-intensive processes and high levels of waste generation. Companies implementing resource recovery practices, such as recycling and repurposing textile waste, can reduce environmental impact, lower material costs and tap into new revenue streams. Outputs could be recycled feedstock, new textiles applications or upcycled products.

  Case example: FREITAG's ingenious concept of crafting individual bags from discarded truck tarpaulins not only resonates with eco-conscious consumers seeking sustainable options but also appeals to fashion enthusiasts looking for distinctive, unique pieces (each bag's one-of-a-kind design originates from varied tarpaulins). This approach allowed FREITAG to build a pioneering circularity brand that is pushing the boundaries of the textile industry.

- **Food and agriculture:** The food and agriculture industry grapples with significant waste issues, including food waste and associated by-products. Businesses can transform organic waste into valuable resources such as compost, biogas or alternative food products.

  Case Example: Toast Ale is a UK-based brewery that uses surplus bread to make beer. They take unsold bread from bakeries and sandwich makers, which would otherwise be wasted, and turn it into a key ingredient for their beer. This process reduces food waste while also creating a unique and flavourful product.

Additional case examples: ArcelorMittal (implemented a number of resource recovery initiatives across its steel operations); Dell (commitment to circularity across packaging, takeback and material use, e.g. also offering trade-in and recycling services); Re-Match (recycling system for artificial turf); ROCKWOOL (takeback and recycling of stone wool insulation); Concepts Plásticos (Colombian company converting plastic waste into sustainable construction materials); Too Good To Go (mobile platform app that connects users with local businesses to rescue surplus food).

Pitfalls to avoid

- The costs associated with collecting, sorting and processing waste might outweigh the estimated value of the reclaimed resources. To overcome this challenge, design products with resource recovery in mind, carefully assess optimisation levers and explore collaborative partnerships in your ecosystem.
- Be vigilant about unintended outcomes or trade-offs that could counteract the environmental gains of resource recovery, such as increased water or energy consumption, emissions or expanded land use. Mitigate these risks by conducting comprehensive life cycle assessments that account for the entire process, from collection to reuse, to ensure the overall impact is positive.
- Beware of potential regulatory hurdles and compliance challenges related to waste management and resource recovery. Failing to adhere to local, regional or international regulations could lead to legal liabilities, fines or reputational damage. Sometimes the regulations set unexpected challenges (e.g. waste declaration and handling duties). To navigate this challenge, ensure a thorough understanding of the relevant regulations and seek expert guidance.

Keep an eye on
Advanced waste-to-energy solutions.

- **What it is:** The waste-to-energy market involves converting various types of waste, particularly non-recyclable and non-compostable waste, into usable forms of energy, such as electricity, heat or fuels. It is important that this approach follows the logic of the waste hierarchy principles (prevention first, then reuse, then recycling at high material value, then recovery or energy conversion). This process utilises technologies such as incineration, pyrolysis, gasification and anaerobic digestion to extract energy from waste materials, while also reducing the volume of waste disposed in landfills. Emerging solutions may include carbon capture storage and utilisation solutions (CCUS).

- **Companies to have on your radar:** Veolia, Enerkem, Suez, Varme, Borealis.

(b) By-product utilisation

You can explore by-product utilisation as a business model that encourages collaborative resource exchange between organisations and industries. Repurposing resources generated as by-products in one industry's production can serve as valuable inputs in another application. This approach builds a business model from symbiotic relationships, embracing a collaborative 'open loop' approach where waste from one becomes a valuable input for someone else, fostering a more interconnected and sustainable industrial ecosystem.

Impact case	Business case
• **Rethink:** Challenge the linear mindset and rethink waste as a resource, driving innovation in finding new purposes, markets and partnerships within a 'zero waste' paradigm shift • **Repurpose:** Transform by-products into valuable inputs, extending the life cycle of materials and promoting more efficient resource use • **Recycle/recover:** Convert by-products into valuable resources (or energy) to actively contribute to waste reduction, minimising environmental impact associated with disposal and raw material extraction	• **Revenue diversification:** Transform surplus materials into a new revenue stream by selling by-products, fostering innovation through collaborations with other industries • **Cost savings:** Gain a competitive advantage by buying by-products at a lower cost than traditional raw materials, impacting your bottom line and showcasing a commitment to sustainability • **Increased innovativeness:** Incorporate by-products into processes to reduce environmental impact and fuel ingenuity, leading to the development of new products, services and operational approaches

Industry relevance

By-product utilisation is relevant across industries, especially those with significant processing waste. This approach offers unique opportunities for collaborative exchange, unlocking latent value in materials that might otherwise go to waste. Compelling examples of collaborative industry exchanges include:

• **Food and beverage:** Leveraging by-product utilisation is essential for reducing food waste and unlocking additional value creation. Repurposing food by-products as ingredients for other food, animal feed, bioenergy production or other inputs presents a strategic opportunity. This not only helps to reduce costs, such as waste disposal expenses, but also opens avenues for generating additional income through symbiotic benefits.

Case example: At McDonald's, a major waste source is cooking oil. In a collaboration with Neste, this used cooking oil is converted into

Neste MY Renewable Diesel. McDonald's employs this eco-friendly fuel to power its delivery trucks, achieving a 90 per cent reduction in greenhouse gas emissions compared to fossil diesel.

- **Manufacturing and industrial processes:** In industries such as steel, chemicals and paper manufacturing, by-products are frequently generated. Converting these by-products into valuable inputs not only enhances operational efficiency but also reduces the need for and reliance on virgin resources. This leads to cost savings and can elevate the company's overall sustainability performance.

  Case example: CarbonCure Technologies has developed a technology that captures carbon dioxide (CO_2) emissions from industrial sources and injects them into concrete during the mixing process. The CO_2 chemically reacts with the concrete to form a mineral, enhancing the strength and performance of the concrete.

- **Energy:** By-products from energy production, such as heat or waste gases, can be used for energy recovery or in industrial applications. Repurposing these by-products for energy generation or industrial processes can lead to reduced energy costs, improved resource utilisation and a decreased ecological footprint.

  Case example: ElectraTherm has developed a technology that captures waste heat from industrial processes or power generation and converts it into electricity using organic Rankine cycle (ORC) systems. This technology enables industry partners to generate additional power from what was once considered a waste stream and supports decarbonisation and overall process efficiency.

- **Agriculture:** The synergy between agricultural and industrial sectors facilitates the effective utilisation of waste products for innovative applications. This collaboration offers an opportunity to enhance agricultural practices and promote sustainable resource management, contributing to higher yields and cost savings.

  Case example: Studio Tjeerd Veenhoven has innovatively extracted value from discarded tulip flower heads by extracting pigments through a mechanical and biochemical process. These pigments, derived from the flower petals, have found diverse applications ranging from colouring biological plastics to finger paint, transforming the aesthetic value of the petals into economic benefits.

- **Fashion and textiles:** The fashion industry can transform textile waste into various applications while also incorporating by-product resources from other industries for textile fibre production. This not only reduces waste but also presents an opportunity to offer sustainable products that resonate with environmentally conscious consumers.

Case example: Orange Fiber transforms citrus fruit waste into circular fabrics, utilising the 'pastazzo'. This is a by-product of citrus juice production, which constitutes 60 per cent of the fruit's weight. The company extracts cellulose from citrus pulp at its production sites in Sicily to create the circular textile fibre TENCEL.

Additional case examples: Stora Enso (repurposes by-products from pulp and paper production to create renewable chemicals, materials, biofuels and battery materials); Phoenix Fibers (collaborates with Levi Strauss & Co. and other affiliated companies to repurpose denim scraps from their jeans production as insulation material for homes).

Pitfalls to avoid

- By-product utilisation often requires collaboration between industries or organisations. Failing to establish strong partnerships can impede resource exchange. Adopt an ecosystem and partnership mindset.

- By-products may vary in quality and consistency, making it challenging to incorporate them into other processes. Work closely with partners to establish quality standards and implement processes for testing, treatment or refinement to meet desired specifications.

- Compliance with regulations and standards related to by-product utilisation can be complex. Failure to address regulatory aspects can lead to legal issues. Consult legal experts and regulatory authorities to ensure that your by-product utilisation processes comply with environmental and safety regulations.

Keep an eye on
Creative upcycling opportunities!

- **What it is:** Upcycling is a repurposing process in which discarded materials or products are transformed into new items of higher value, functionality or quality. Unlike traditional recycling, which often involves breaking down materials, upcycling creatively repurposes them without significant degradation or even value added. In fashion, designers upcycle old textiles or even ocean plastic waste into unique garments. In the furniture industry, discarded wood or metal materials are transformed into stylish, functional pieces. Beyond these examples, upcycling has gained traction across sectors, contributing to waste reduction and promoting a more environmentally conscious approach to production and consumption.

- **Companies to have on your radar:** Looptworks, Bureo, ecoBirdy or Uncommon Goods.

(c) Secondary material market platforms

Incorporating secondary material market platforms into your business model strategy allows you to facilitate a transaction where surplus resources find new life. By connecting those with excess products or recyclates to those who can reuse or repurpose them, you enable a more circular economy that promotes resource productivity. This approach reduces waste and fosters a more resilient ecosystem across industries.

Impact case	Business case
• **Reuse:** Platforms facilitate finding new users for surplus materials, scaling sustainable reuse within a collaborative ecosystem • **Reduce:** Actively contribute to waste reduction by diverting materials from landfills or incineration, minimising environmental impacts and reducing the need for virgin resources and associated emissions • **Recycle:** Platforms scale recycling efforts, reducing transaction costs and enabling a more eco-effective use of resources across industries through closing material loops	• **Cost savings:** Platform providers generate revenue and reduce waste disposal costs by selling or exchanging surplus materials. Buyers gain access to cost-effective materials, optimising procurement costs • **Increased innovativeness:** Platforms foster creative problem solving leading to product innovation and differentiation. They also enable entry into a pure digital, asset-light business model • **Unexploited business opportunities:** Platform management or participation links you to potential partners (suppliers, customers) and broadens your business network and revenue opportunities

Industry relevance

Secondary material market platforms are relevant across various industries, especially in sectors characterised by high resource consumption and waste generation, and those with a high demand for secondary materials. Examples where these platforms can be highly relevant include:

- **Metals and manufacturing:** The metal processing and manufacturing industry often generates significant production waste. Secondary material market platforms offer a strategic opportunity to exchange unused materials, reduce transaction and scrap disposal costs, while fostering resource efficient practices.

  Case example: Metalshub operates as a digital marketplace and procurement solution that connects metal producers, traders and consumers. It allows participants to buy and sell a variety of metals, including non-ferrous and ferrous metals, alloys or scrap across different categories.

- **Construction and buildings:** The construction industry, often challenged for its considerable construction and demolition waste, can harness the power of platforms to unlock substantial benefits. Facilitating the reuse of materials like wood, steel, concrete and insulation through secondary market platforms not only cuts down on waste, but also enables more cost-effective and sustainable construction projects.

Case example: Oogstkaart is an urban mining platform (owned by New Horizon Urban Mining, founded by the architect collective Superuse Studios). The platform works with architects, design professionals, builders and project developers to enable searching, finding and dismantling reusable building materials.

- **Plastics and packaging:** Many plastics and consumer goods companies are committing to secondary material quotas, leading to increasing demand. The markets for recyclate are developing, but they are fragmented and require new technological solutions to scale (e.g. chemical recycling).

  Case Example: Cirplus operates as a B2B digital marketplace that connects buyers and sellers of plastic waste feedstock and recyclates. The platform reduces transaction costs by aggregating data and standardising recyclates as a tradable commodity.

Additional case examples: Recykal (marketplace that connect buyers and sellers of scrap material across metals, plastics, paper and e-waste in India); Sparetech (provides a platform for collaborative spare part management between original equipment manufacturers and machine operators across companies); METYCLE (platform for international secondary metal trade); Cyrkl (marketplace for industrial waste, by-products or secondary raw materials).

Pitfalls to avoid

- Failure to establish quality standards for materials and resources traded on the platform can result in subpar products and dissatisfaction among users. Implement rigorous quality control measures, robust security measures, verification processes and user reviews to maintain high-quality standards and trust.
- A viable monetisation strategy requires scale on the platform. Strategically leverage (regional) network effects. Explore revenue models such as subscription fees, transaction commissions, or premium features to ensure the platform's viability early on.
- Challenge your value creation potential regularly. Pure platform models might not be enough to secure a strong position in the long run. Explore features that improve your vertical integration and add customer value (e.g. sourcing management, track and trace, reporting).

Keep an eye on
Advanced technology developments around (circular) platforms!

- **What it is:** In addition to the immediate benefits of resource exchange, an exciting trend within the secondary material market platforms is the proliferation and professionalisation of cloud technologies and advanced artificial intelligence. These technologies enhance transparency, traceability, automation and efficiency in material transactions, providing a real-time, data-driven approach to resource management. These technologies allow platforms to quickly morph into global networks, connecting businesses across borders to create a more extensive and dynamic secondary material ecosystem. Embracing these innovations not only streamlines resource utilisation but also positions businesses at the forefront of a rapidly evolving and interconnected circular economy.

- **Companies to have on your radar:** AWS, Google, Microsoft, Mirakl, McFadyen.

Taking Stock
Now, let's take a moment to reflect on this business model archetype using the following worksheet (Figure 4.6). Have these patterns sparked initial opportunity ideas? Have you heard of any specific initiatives in your business that could represent significant opportunities, if scaled? Please take stock of these opportunities.

Next, select one of these opportunities and explore it further. Examine how the classic business model elements manifest, including the value proposition to the customer, operational delivery and high-level economics for value retention. Outline a preliminary business case for scaling this business model, estimating the potential size of the opportunity from low to very high. Additionally, assess the environmental impact potential of the opportunity – do you anticipate the benefits as low or high?

Figure 4.6. Taking stock of identified opportunities

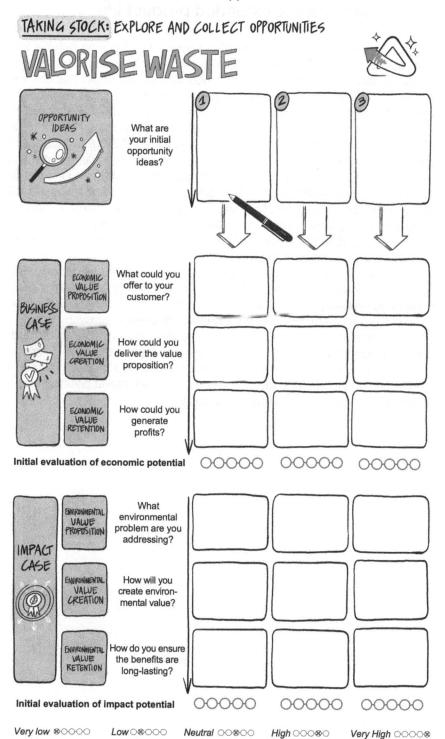

TAKING STOCK: EXPLORE AND COLLECT OPPORTUNITIES

VALORISE WASTE

OPPORTUNITY IDEAS

What are your initial opportunity ideas?

① ② ③

BUSINESS CASE

ECONOMIC VALUE PROPOSITION — What could you offer to your customer?

ECONOMIC VALUE CREATION — How could you deliver the value proposition?

ECONOMIC VALUE RETENTION — How could you generate profits?

Initial evaluation of economic potential ○○○○○ ○○○○○ ○○○○○

IMPACT CASE

ENVIRONMENTAL VALUE PROPOSITION — What environmental problem are you addressing?

ENVIRONMENTAL VALUE CREATION — How will you create environmental value?

ENVIRONMENTAL VALUE RETENTION — How do you ensure the benefits are long-lasting?

Initial evaluation of impact potential ○○○○○ ○○○○○ ○○○○○

Very low ⊗○○○○   *Low* ○⊗○○○   *Neutral* ○○⊗○○   *High* ○○○⊗○   *Very High* ○○○○⊗

4.4 Monetise extended product life

Did you like playing with trains as a kid? Is somebody still playing with the toys that you used? If yes, chances are high that you might know the BRIO wooden railway system. The system consists of modular wooden tracks that children can use to create custom layouts by snapping the tracks together. Wooden trains with magnetic couplings can be attached to one another and moved on the tracks. The Swedish brand for simple wooden toys launched its first toy in 1907 (a wooden, locally produced horse), and then in 1958 they introduced the wooden railway toy set. Over time, the company went international and expanded its toy set, always relying on modular, high-quality and long-lasting designs. In many families, especially in Europe, the tracks and trains are still actively used in the third generation, old and new modules are mixed. These toys trade very actively on secondary marketplaces beyond the control of the brand. What is the suitable business model for such a high-quality, timeless product that strikes a chord across many generations?

Focusing on monetising extended product life cycles opens up opportunities to generate additional revenue by offering repair solutions, replacement parts and upgrade accessories that extend the usefulness of your products. Embracing concepts like recommerce, sharing, take-back and reuse ecosystems allows you to explore innovative avenues for increasing product value. Catering to changing customer needs and preferences may lead to stronger customer loyalty and connections. Ultimately, monetising extended product life cycles has the potential to enhance revenue streams, improve market positioning and generate more value over the entire product life.

(a) Repair, upgrade and modularise

This business model pattern offers the opportunity to provide repair and maintenance services that extend product lifespans. Alongside this, modular interoperable components and parts can ease reassembly, add functionality and cater to changing customer preferences. This approach can directly contribute to waste reduction and better resource use by emphasising product durability and reusability. Such a product and service ecosystem can support the transition from a linear to a circular design and consumption model.

Impact case	Business case
• **Repair:** Adopt a 'repair first' mentality to extend product lifespan, reducing the need for new purchases and inherent resource use • **Reuse:** Design products for high value retention, incentivising repair and modular replacement of components to promote the continuous reuse of the product or functional elements • **Reduce:** Facilitate product upgrades and customer loyalty to decrease the need for new products and materials, and reduce overall waste generation	• **Unexploited business opportunities:** Repair services or modular components enable new revenue streams, increasing short-term profitability and strengthening long-term value creation • **Customer loyalty and engagement:** Providing repair services and upgrade options may enhance customer experiences and allow for adaptability, fostering brand loyalty and regular interactions • **Increased innovativeness:** Modular components and upgrade options can drive innovation through better intelligence based on product and customer data

Industry relevance

Relevant across various industries, particularly in sectors where the business model can address fast consumption and waste generation, or for products that are characterised by high quality and value retention. Illustrative examples include:

- **Electronics:** In the electronics sector, rapid technological advancements often result in product obsolescence. Offering modular upgrades and repairs appeals to eco-conscious customers but also tech enthusiasts seeking to stay current without discarding entire devices. Companies may focus on repair, upgrade packages and component sales.

   Case example: Fairphone designs and produces smartphones with modularity in mind. Their phones feature easy-to-replace modular components, such as the camera module and battery, allowing users to repair and upgrade specific parts rather than replacing the entire device.

- **Mobility and transport:** Modular parts and upgrades may allow customers to enhance their vehicles and equipment over time. Companies may guide their products over multiple product use cycles and customers. This model also appeals to fleet owners seeking operational efficiency and minimising downtime and costs.

Case example: Caterpillar is running an advanced service ecosystem that includes repairs, rebuilding, remanufacturing and retrofitting. This is already considered in the design decisions for their excavators, loaders or trucks. For example, the Certified Rebuild programme returns end-of-life machines into a like-new condition (offered for single components to complete machines).

- **Machinery and manufacturing:** Industrial equipment downtime can be costly. Repair services and modular components ensure continuous operations, appealing to businesses focused on efficiency and minimising disruptions, which offers cost savings over extended lifespans.

Case example: BigRep employs an innovative approach to repair, upgrade and modularisation using large-scale 3D printers. This technology is capable of producing customised parts and components for industrial machinery and enables businesses to fabricate complex components on-demand, reducing lead times and costs associated with sourcing and shipping traditional replacement parts.

- **Construction and real estate:** Modularity in construction streamlines project timelines, cost efficiency, and allows for easy adaptations. This minimises material waste and construction risks, making it appealing to stakeholders across construction and real estate who seek sustainable and efficient building solutions.

Case example: Blokable is a modular building approach that relies on designing and manufacturing low cost, modular housing units that can be easily assembled on-site. Their modular building approach allows for quicker construction, less waste and more efficient resource utilisation.

- **Fashion and textiles:** More than 70 per cent of materials used to produce fashion are landfilled or incinerated at the end of life. Increasing textile-to-textile recycling is important to improve material recovery and supply. But the system also requires turning around the fast fashion trend and a more structurally emphasising on high quality, repairability and durability.

Case example: Houdini is a Swedish outdoor clothing brand that focuses on the design philosophy to provide products that last. Through a take-back programme and a circular hub in Stockholm, they emphasise repairability, offer a product lifetime warranty and provide reuse and rental options, aligning with their design philosophy.

Additional case examples: Lorenz (water meters designed to be reused over multiple product life cycles); Tesla (electric vehicles feature over-the-air software updates that enhance vehicle performance and introduce new features); Liebherr (remanufacturing programme for repair of engines, gearing or hydraulic systems).

Pitfalls to avoid

- If repair costs surpass the price of new products, customers may opt for replacement. Offer competitive pricing and incentivise repair. Work on optimising repair costs (e.g. design-enablers, or consolidated logistics and operations).
- Design is key! Products not designed for modularity may hinder component replacement or upgrades. Incorporate modular design principles from the early stages of product development, enabling easy disassembly and reassembly.
- A shortage of skilled technicians for repair and maintenance services can limit your business model's success. Invest in training programmes for staff or collaborate with certified repair partners to ensure qualified professionals are available.

Keep an eye on
Repair and support communities.

- **What it is:** Repair and support communities are grassroots networks of individuals with shared interests in repairing and maintaining products, often collaborating through online platforms or local gatherings. These communities contribute to product longevity, reduce waste and promote a circular economy by extending the life of items. Beyond the environmental impact, these communities create social connections, sharing knowledge and skills related to repair. For businesses, engaging with these communities can provide valuable insights into product performance, user needs and design improvements. This drives innovation by tapping into the collective expertise of the community.
- **Companies/organisations to have on your radar:** FixFirst, iFixit, AfB social & green, The Restart project, or fixez, among others. Numerous local repair cafes.

(b) Recommerce

Resale, reuse, renewed, vintage, pre-owned, pre-loved, re-loved, second-hand, revived or wornwear? There are various terms for recommerce offerings. Circular recommerce presents a distinctive business model opportunity, focusing on the strategic recovery, refurbishment and resale of used products. This enables reusing products over multiple life cycles, creating value from unused or discarded goods. It may unlock revenue streams with new customer segments, notably Gen-Z. When designed effectively, this business model can also enable you to improve the loyalty of your customer base.

Impact case	Business case
● **Reuse:** Managing active resale of pre-owned items in the market allows products to continue fulfilling their original function, increasing resource productivity and utilisation over their lifetime ● **Reduce:** Extend product life cycles to reduce uncontrolled waste and mitigate the demand for new production, thereby helping to decrease primary resources use ● **Repair/refurbish/recycle:** Offer take-back tied to recommerce to structurally support repairing, remanufacturing, refurbishing or upgrading products. It enables building a circular infrastructure and managing circular processes including recycling	● **Revenue diversification:** Access a market segment valuing sustainability or better price points. Combining resale with a trade-in programme can strengthen customer loyalty ● **Cost savings:** Remanufacturing and refurbishing reduces production costs compared to manufacturing anew, requiring fewer raw materials. A strategic intake approach can optimise cost effects and reduce risks during supply chain disruptions ● **Steering secondary markets:** Strategically control secondary markets to maintain pricing standards, quality control and brand reputation. Prevent counterfeiting and capture value in the resale market. Generate data and learnings for improvements

Industry relevance

This business model is relevant across various industries, particularly in segments characterised by high quality and value retention. Luxury goods, for instance, experience a robust resale market, and if brands don't engage in reselling their own used products, third parties often do. Additionally, recommerce is significant in segments with short use cycles, such as kids' products and seasonal items. Industry examples include:

● **Fashion and textiles:** Fashion industries, both B2C and B2B, can leverage recommerce to extend the life of clothing and accessories, addressing the fast fashion challenge and global waste problem. Brands and retailers benefit from the growing demand for sustainable fashion choices. Fashion recommerce necessitates enabling services and operations, including fulfilment, reverse logistics, grading and repair.

Case example: Patagonia's WornWear programme focuses on repairing and reselling used clothing and gear. What sets them apart is the holistic approach to sustainability ingrained in their heritage. Emphasising a commitment to quality, the brand ensures that products meet high standards before resale, and they invest in a robust repair infrastructure. Patagonia has partnered with Trove, a technology platform facilitating resale through enabling services, including omnichannel trade-in and market insights.

- **Consumer electronics:** Recommerce is highly relevant for consumer electronics as it allows customers to access affordable and refurbished devices, catering to budget-conscious consumers and businesses. It presents an opportunity to recapture value from returned or outdated electronics.

Case example: Walmart's Restored programme refurbishes and resells pre-owned electronics and appliances. Leveraging its wide reach and brand recognition, Walmart makes sustainable and budget-friendly alternatives accessible to a broad customer base. It strategically partners with original manufacturers or authorised sellers/suppliers.

- **Machinery and manufacturing:** B2B sectors like manufacturing and heavy machinery can harness recommerce to offer refurbished equipment and components. In the professional B2B space, where emotional attachment to brand-new products is often much lower, this approach caters to businesses seeking reliable machinery, reducing procurement costs and fostering sustainable practices.

Case example: Voith, a global technology company specialising in drive systems, hydropower and papermaking, integrates circularity principles into its strategy and sustainability programme. As part of this initiative, Voith has established a second-hand marketplace for refurbished machines and key spare parts.

- **Medical equipment:** The healthcare sector can strategically leverage recommerce to optimise the utilisation of medical equipment. The refurbishment and resale of medical devices offers dual benefits: it reduces costs for healthcare providers, making quality equipment more accessible, while simultaneously extending the lifespan of valuable assets.

Case example: Siemens Healthineers employs recommerce for medical equipment through its 'ecoline' offer. This initiative provides a comprehensive portfolio of refurbished medical systems, ensuring the equipment meets rigorous standards and performs like new. Additionally, customers have the option for a trade-in.

- **Furniture:** Furniture is integral to daily life, with its environmental footprint (e.g. natural resources, waste generation) depending a lot on the respective design choices regarding material use, modularity and durability. High quality and timeless design can enable premium pricing and contribute to long-term brand value.

  Case example: USM, a Swiss modular furniture system, is renowned for its timeless design and modularity. The minimalistic design of the items (shelves, desks, etc.) uses durable materials and is optimised for adaptability and extended product life. The system uses steel tubes and connectors that allow for customisation and adaptation of the standardised modules. With circularity at its core, USM operates a network of certified 'Second Hand Partners,' contributing to high-value retention on the secondary market.

Additional case examples: Rebuy (an online platform matching sellers of consumer electronics such as phones, consoles, headphones or cameras with buyers); Foxway (offers a suite of circular solutions for life cycle services, recovery and remarketing); ThredUP (offers resale-as-a-service to support brands); ReTuna Återbruksgalleria (the world's first recycling mall based in Sweden, gives products a new life through repair and upcycling).

Pitfalls to avoid

- If the return-logistics and refurbishment process is intricate and time consuming, it can impact efficiency and economic feasibility. Streamline refurbishment workflows, automate processes where possible and optimise (e.g. speed, scale, consolidation). Proactively steering the quality of your incoming goods through trade-in programmes or incentives can significantly impact the success of the operating model. Designing and scaling assortments effectively is essential to create a compelling offer.

- Implement rigorous quality control processes to ensure that all refurbished products meet high standards. Inform and educate customers about the refurbishment process and warranty offered for refurbished items, emphasising the cost savings and evidence for better environmental impact. Brand your recommence offering beyond 'second hand' and consider lifetime warranty offerings.

- Adopt design choices that support durability and long-lasting product life. Enable the recommerce offering to replace new products in the market at scale and facilitate sustainable consumer choices.

Keep an eye on
Digital identity technologies for authentication and traceability!

- **What it is:** Digital identity technologies play a crucial role in recommerce business models by enabling reliable verification of pre-owned products (and sellers) and buyers through secure authentication. Traceability technologies add another layer of trust and confidence. Being able to follow your products along their life on a product level and user level may unlock huge potential to optimise the business model. This includes accessing information about the product's condition, handling and location. Efficient communication with customers, potentially enabled by direct-to-consumer channels, can foster loyalty and be a strong advantage.

- **Technological solutions to have on your radar:** Operating systems (e.g. Trove, reverse.supply, Lizee), advanced data intelligence (e.g. twig, Faircado), or digital product passports and track and trace solutions (e.g. Circularise, Circulor).

(c) Reuse and reverse logistics ecosystem

The business model for establishing a take-back, reuse and reverse logistics ecosystem revolves around creating an efficient infrastructure and logistics framework that facilitates the return and recovery of used products, components or materials. For example, a popular use case is reusable packaging ecosystems. By developing an ecosystem, your company actively manages the life cycle of its products in circulation. This proactive approach minimises waste, improves resource productivity and promotes sustainable consumption patterns, and also offers the potential for cost savings and enhanced customer loyalty.

Impact case	Business case
• **Reuse:** Collect and recirculate used products, components or materials to extend their lifespan through multiple product cycles • **Reduce:** Implement a take-back and reuse ecosystem to actively decrease the consumption of virgin resources and reduce waste, directly increasing utilisation and cutting the demand for new production • **Rethink:** Operating a reuse ecosystem and infrastructure challenges the traditional linear mindset, reimagining how products partner with customers over an extended product life rather than just how they are used	• **Unexploited business opportunities:** A streamlined take-back and reuse ecosystem addresses B2C/B2B demands for affordable, eco-friendly products and can evolve into a systemic solution with strong network effects • **Regulatory compliance:** Mitigate legal liabilities and reputational risks by engaging in a comprehensive reuse and logistics ecosystem that adheres to stricter regulations on unsustainable material use (e.g. single use bans) • **Differentiation and reputation:** Demonstrate dedication to sustainability, fostering long-term partnerships, loyalty and differentiation as a leader in a competitive market

Industry relevance

This business strategy holds value across various industries, with notable impact in sectors characterised by extensive 'single-use' consumption patterns or fast consumption. The concept of reuse ecosystems is particularly vital in industries such as:

- **Food and consumer goods:** Food and grocery offerings are often burdened by extensive packaging and many consumer goods come with single-use packaging. A reuse business model can address such sustainability concerns and may be smartly integrated into the regular shopping routine. Reusable alternatives like cups and containers may reduce waste and lower procurement costs. A return system for these items offers businesses the opportunity to establish a closed-loop system.

  Case example: Algramo provides a refill system, where consumers can bring their containers to the refill stations in supermarkets. The company from Chile partners with globally operating retailers. The system uses smart technology and RFID-tagged reusable packaging, aiming to minimise plastic waste and encouraging an easy reuse experience for customers.

- **Plastics and packaging:** Both B2C and B2B packaging sectors can benefit from a reuse ecosystem business model by innovating more sustainable packaging materials and embedding those into a closed loop system. Examples may include packaging solutions such as boxes, containers, bottles or pallets.

  Case example: Loop is an innovative platform that partners with major brands to deliver products in durable, reusable packaging. Consumers order products online, receive them in reusable containers and return the empties via Loop's reverse logistics system for cleaning and refill. By eliminating single-use packaging, Loop reduces waste and encourages a circular economy, offering a convenient and sustainable way for consumers to access everyday products.

- **Logistics and supply chain:** The reuse and reverse logistics ecosystem business model presents a compelling business opportunity for the logistics industry. By establishing an effective reverse logistics framework, companies can not only contribute to sustainability but also tap into new markets and operational efficiencies.

  Case example: IFCO has been redefining the fresh grocery supply chain through its B2B reusable packaging pooling system. The 'IFCO Smart-Cycle' involves delivering clean containers to growers and producers, collecting them from retailers and then cleaning and sanitising them before redistribution.

Additional case examples: CHEP (global supply chain solutions provider, contributes to a reverse logistics ecosystem by offering pallet and container pooling services); RePack (offers a reusable packaging solution for e-commerce shops, rental or take-back offerings or company internal shipments); Recup (pioneering a circular reuse ecosystem by facilitating the distribution of reusable coffee and food containers at the point of sale).

Pitfalls to avoid

- Complicated return procedures may discourage customer participation, yet such buy-in and collaboration are key to achieving high return rates. Prioritise convenience to ensure customers' willingness to engage. Develop a straightforward return process that minimises friction and optimises ease of use.
- Achieving feasible economics requires scale and partnerships. Consider partnerships that allow to create a shared infrastructure and manage

pooling intelligently. Poorly managed logistics can lead to delays, additional costs and inefficiencies. Optimise your reverse logistics network jointly to facilitate efficient product collection, refurbishment and distribution.

- Customise designs for reuse, especially with respect to standardisation. Insufficient quality in the reuse ecosystem can quickly disappoint your customers and impact economics. Sustainable material choices, standardisation and design for durability should be the fundamental principles of your approach.

Keep an eye on
Microfactories

- **What it is:** Microfactories represent a revolutionary shift in reverse logistics and remanufacturing. They establish compact production facilities or operations hubs near consumption points. This localised approach transforms urban waste into reusable materials, and minimises the need for long-distance transportation and complex logistics. For example, this may involve creating small-scale, flexible manufacturing set-ups that are strategically placed in urban centres allowing for efficient processing of discarded items into new, usable products. By shortening supply chains, microfactories reduce costs, carbon emissions and delivery times, fostering customer satisfaction and enhancing resilience.
- **Companies to have on your radar:** TerraCycle, Trashpresso by Miniwiz, Re-fresh Global, Tomra's reverse vending solutions.

Taking Stock
Now, let's take a moment to reflect on the following worksheet (Figure 4.7). Which of these business model patterns has sparked initial opportunity ideas? Are there any initiatives in your business that, if scaled, could represent significant opportunities? Please note down these opportunities.

Next, select one of these opportunities and explore it further. Examine how the classic business model elements manifest, including the value proposition to the customer, operational delivery and high-level economics for value retention. Outline a preliminary business case for scaling this business model, estimating the potential size of the opportunity from low to very high. Additionally, assess the environmental impact potential of the opportunity – do you anticipate the benefits as low or high?

Figure 4.7. Taking stock of identified opportunities

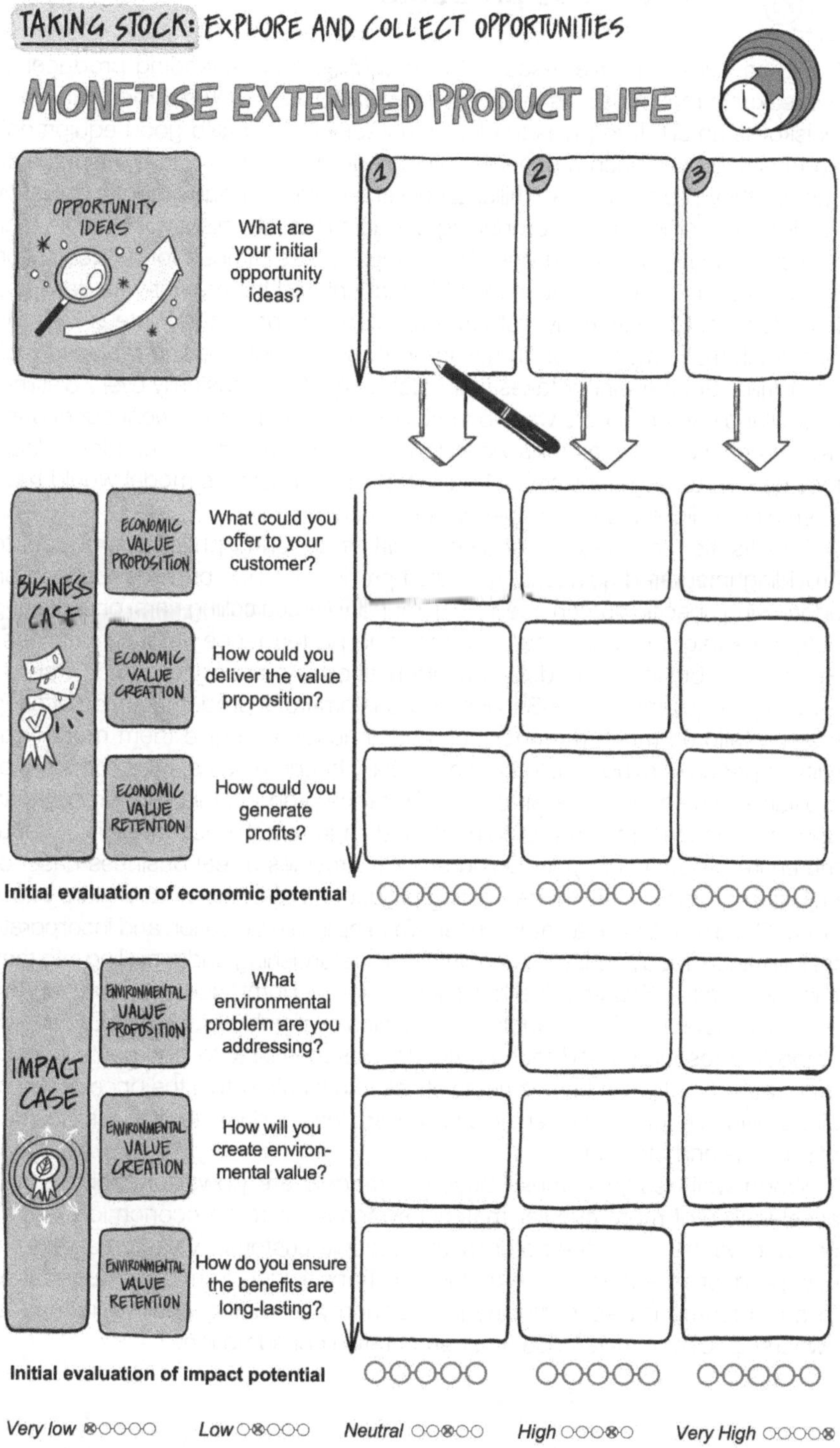

TAKING STOCK: EXPLORE AND COLLECT OPPORTUNITIES

MONETISE EXTENDED PRODUCT LIFE

OPPORTUNITY IDEAS

What are your initial opportunity ideas?

BUSINESS CASE

ECONOMIC VALUE PROPOSITION — What could you offer to your customer?

ECONOMIC VALUE CREATION — How could you deliver the value proposition?

ECONOMIC VALUE RETENTION — How could you generate profits?

Initial evaluation of economic potential

IMPACT CASE

ENVIRONMENTAL VALUE PROPOSITION — What environmental problem are you addressing?

ENVIRONMENTAL VALUE CREATION — How will you create environmental value?

ENVIRONMENTAL VALUE RETENTION — How do you ensure the benefits are long-lasting?

Initial evaluation of impact potential

Very low ⊗○○○○   *Low* ○⊗○○○   *Neutral* ○○⊗○○   *High* ○○○⊗○   *Very High* ○○○○⊗

4.5 Servitise products

Could servitisation have rescued Porteus Mills, once a leading producer of unbreakable malt mills? As every Whiskey enthusiast knows, producing good whiskey is an art. It requires the finest ingredients, and also good equipment. Porteus Mills was such a superior equipment manufacturer. In the nineteenth century they produced malt mills, an essential piece of equipment in whiskey production, particularly for producing certain types of whiskey like single malt Scotch or some craft bourbons. The company was famous for its dedication to their product, every Porteus Malt Mill that entered the market was designed to perfection. Quickly many distilleries realised how good the Porteus Malt Mill was, such that almost all distilleries in Scotland bought one and replaced their other mills. So, the winner takes it all? Not really. When basically every distillery in Scotland had one, there was no more business left. Porteus went out of business, because their malt mills were 'too good' and lasted for decades. Would they be still running a successful business if their business model would have been directly linked to their superior performance?

Servitisation involves the strategic shift from selling physical products to providing integrated solutions, so called product-service bundles focused on addressing specific human needs (e.g. mobility versus selling cars) or delivering outcomes (e.g. produced parts or machine performance versus machines). Respective business models are often titled 'As-a-Service' (e.g. Car-as-a-Service, Equipment-as-a-Service). For customers, a product-service offering may be tailored much more to their actual needs and give them more flexibility or peace of mind. Customers essentially become users. For producers or providers, who typically retain ownership of the product, this shift presents an opportunity to tap into new value pools and engage with customers throughout the entire product life cycle. Doing so also provides a real business case for high-quality design and longer lasting products that can be used more intensively. Companies have a natural incentive to optimise utilisation and incorporate maintenance, repair, reuse, remanufacturing, refurbishing and recycling into their thinking.[8] Walter Stahel, a leading figure in the performance economy, underscores its potential: 'The manufacturer retains ownership of the product and its embodied resources and thus carries the responsibility for the costs of risks and waste. [. . .] Covering the costs of risk and waste within the price of use or hire provides economic incentives to prevent loss and waste over the lifetimes of systems and products.'[9]

When well-designed these business models are powerful enablers and accelerators of more circular material systems. From an economic systems perspective they have the potential to decouple customer value creation from new production and resource extraction. Transitioning from a product-based to an outcome-based performance economy, enabling access instead of ownership, can dematerialise and democratise consumption.

(a) Pay-per-use

Pay-per-use is a product-service model that provides customers with the opportunity to utilise a product or service for a specified duration, based on availability or usage intensity. Instead of making an upfront purchase, customers pay for the value they derive from the product on a temporary basis. The pricing structure can be tailored and dynamically adjusted according to factors such as usage patterns, demand and specific customer needs. As the product manufacturer, you would typically handle maintenance, repairs and end-of-life management, contributing to product longevity and waste reduction.

Impact case	Business case
• **Rethink:** Create incentives for more intensive product use. Customers consciously engage only when needed. Manufacturers ensure a functional product. Altogether this supports replacing new production through higher utilisation and eventually fewer products	• **Revenue diversification:** Rental or subscription models establish a recurring revenue stream, potentially with a price premium due to enhanced service. This model can attract new customer segments, surpassing traditional one-off product sales revenue
• **Reuse, repair and refurbish:** Actively enable reusing products and integrating repair and refurbishment practices to improve the business and impact case. Expedite the re-entry of products into active use cycles	• **Cost savings and increased efficiency:** Optimise utilisation by increasing active-in-use time or allowing more customers to access, leading to efficiency gains. Extend product lifetime through repair or refurbishment for better total cost of ownership, offering cost benefits to users or improve pricing strategy.
• **Recycle:** Take back used products for remanufacturing or recycling and integrate this process into your product design. Optimise designs to facilitate repair and recycling, enabling an end-to-end circular approach	• **Differentiation and reputation:** Enhance customer insights and data intelligence, fostering deep partnerships and a competitive edge, boosting differentiation and reputation

Industry relevance

Pay-per-use models can be strategically relevant for many product-driven industries. These business models tend to be more effective for products that are capital-intensive, easily transportable or used infrequently. Illustrative examples include:

- **Mobility:** Mobility-as-a-Service (MaaS) business models are already widely adopted globally, especially in urban areas for various solutions such as bicycles, scooters or cars. Providers need to optimise operational efficiency and availability, and design plays an important role to ensure these solutions contribute to a more sustainable urban mobility ecosystem. Classic leasing or short-term car rentals have been industry standards in the automotive sector for many years. However, service levels have evolved over time towards more full-service models (e.g. subscription models). These may include long-term or flexible designs that go beyond leasing and cover repair and maintenance, taxes, insurance, tyre renewal and potentially even seasonal vehicle exchange.

Case example: Swapfiets, a Dutch bicycling innovator, provides a subscription model for a fully functional bicycle at a fixed monthly fee. The core benefit is the hassle-free and convenient service package for a sustainable urban mobility solution, including maintenance and repair. Bikes, easily identifiable by their 'iconic blue front tyre' are quickly fixed or replaced within 48 hours in case of issues.

- **Equipment and retail:** Some equipment manufacturers and retailers are in an attractive position to run 'As-a-Service' business models, especially if they have a strong brand, have a high-quality product portfolio and operate physical stores. A physical infrastructure can provide collection and drop-off points for a wide range of products, including electronics, toys, furniture, equipment, tools, books, media and others.

Case example: Decathlon, the French sporting goods retailer, operates a global network of stores. The company is experimenting with multiple circular business models across regions. For example, in Belgium, Decathlon launched the 'We Play Circular' initiative, an offering particularly tailored to families to rent sports items from their local store for a monthly budget. In the UK, Decathlon has introduced a short-term, local rental model for items such as bicycles, kayaks, paddle boards and tennis racquets.

- **Aerospace:** Service-based business models can enhance operational efficiency and performance in capital-intensive industries. For instance, in aviation, services like charter options and aircraft leasing enable flexible fleet management. Additionally, maintenance and overhaul services that prioritise performance outcomes contribute to efficiency improvements.

Case example: Rolls-Royce pioneered the 'power by the hour' business model in 1962, applying it to aircraft engines like the de Havilland/Hawker Siddeley 125 business jet. This model entailed the airline paying a fixed 'all inclusive' rate for engine operation, aiming to eliminate risks associated with downtime and maintenance, providing cost predictability. Rolls-Royce has expanded its service offerings over the years through further corporate care programmes.

- **Construction equipment:** Heavy machinery and construction equipment is investment intense and only needed for specific phases of a construction project. A pay-per-use model that focuses on actual user needs may improve cost efficiency and flexibility for the users, while having access to the latest technology and reducing downtime risks.

  Case example: Liebherr introduced a pay-per-use programme for heavy construction machinery and equipment such as mobile excavators, telescopic handlers, or tower cranes. The offering aims to increase the flexibility for customers to rent equipment on a daily or annual basis, according to their needs. They also offer complementary circular solutions such as used machines and spare parts.

Additional case examples: Volvo (Care by Volvo is the subscription model offered by the Swedish automotive brand, represents an all-inclusive service offer for a fixed monthly fee); ON (subscription programme for a recyclable running shoe within their circularity programme Cyclon); Ahrend (Furniture-as-a-Service to adapt work environment for a fixed monthly fee); Porsche (Porsche Drive exemplifies a vehicle subscription and rental model available in the US); RUBBLE MASTER (offers heavy crusher equipment also in rental programme).

Pitfalls to avoid

- Don't be gentle, it's a rental! Keep in mind that users who don't own the product may not treat it with comparable care. This can be addressed through design adjustments or incorporating features that encourage careful behaviour, such as incentives for cleaning, reminder cards, community benefits or low-carbon usage.

- Tailor design choices to suit specific use case as this is crucial for impact. This means prioritising quality and repairability, while also avoiding unintended negative effects. For example, a product unfit for its designated use breaking after a single use cycle might be less environmentally friendly due to premature disposal and waste.

- Evaluate the systemic role and impact of your service offering. For example, e-scooter rentals face scrutiny over whether they genuinely support sustainable micro-mobility or merely replace more sustainable transport modes like walking, cycling or public transport.

Keep an eye on
Enabling software services

- **What it is:** Transitioning to pay-per-use models is challenging. It may require solutions for complex billing and pricing calculations, data security and seamless integration with existing systems. Other examples may require tracking and monitoring software using IoT technology to capture real-time data accurately. Or advanced data analytics and reporting tools, aiding in forecasting demand, optimising pricing strategies and enhancing decision-making. To overcome such challenges, companies may rely on innovative software solutions tailored to support this transition.

- **Companies to have on your radar:** circuly, Relayr, Zuora, Nitrobox, CashOnLedger, Findustrial, Twist, Lizee.

(b) Pay-per-outcome

The pay-per-outcome model is a distinctive product-service approach where the producer commits to delivering predetermined operational or financial outcomes to customers. This approach focuses on delivering precise results, performance or solutions that cater to customers' needs. Instead of buying a product, your customers engage in contracts or agreements where you ensure the attainment of their desired outcomes. The pricing structure is formulated around the successful delivery of these outcomes, which can be assessed through factors like product performance units, energy savings, waste reduction, cost optimisation as well as other performance metrics or customer satisfaction.

Similar to pay-per-use, the pay-per-outcome business model shifts from the transactional (one-time) sales of products to building longer relationships between customers and producers, typically original equipment manufacturers (OEMs). The key distinction lies in the payment structure: pay-per-use involves customers paying based on usage (e.g. time-bound rental of a tool, leasing of a machine, subscription to a car), whereas the pay-per-outcome model centres on delivering specific outcomes, results or performance (e.g. performance of a tool fleet, parts that a machine produces).

Impact case	Business case
• **Refuse:** Seek opportunities to fulfil agreed outcomes or functions more effectively, with different, more sustainable products. Design and optimise for reusable alternatives, eliminate packaging or transition from physical to digital solutions • **Rethink:** Transform your approach to product use by prioritising higher utilisation, enabling to replace new production and resource consumption. Actively reconsider how products are employed, emphasising efficiency and intensification as key success factors • **Reuse, repair, refurbish, recycle:** Retain ownership to control maintenance, repair, reuse, refurbishment and end-of-life material recovery. Optimise these processes and consider them in design to enhance both the business and impact cases. Maintenance ensures functionality, while remanufacturing and refurbishment enable quick product reuse. Recycling can create closed-loop flows, driving sustainability and less waste	• **Customer satisfaction:** Optimise customer value by focusing on specific end results, addressing their problems and pain points. Allow for continuous learning and improvement based on customer usage data and preferences, in order to enhance features, service components or processes • **Revenue diversification:** Transform revenue generation through long-term contracts and recurring streams, shifting away from a product-cost-focused legacy model. The emphasis on service elements provides an opportunity to increase customer lifetime value and flexibly expanding service offerings • **Cost savings:** Achieve better product utilisation as a key driver for total cost of ownership reduction. This creates value for customers and enhances the pricing position for providers. Enhanced usage can result from increased productive-in-use time, efficient capacity utilisation and extended product lifetimes

Industry relevance

Pay-per-outcome models can be relevant for manufacturers of products across various industries. The business models require measurable outcome units or utility as basis for the transaction. Customer benefits may be particularly high for products that are investment intensive.

- **Machinery and manufacturing:** Machinery and Equipment-as-a-Service (EaaS) business models challenge a traditional industry to rethink. EaaS can help OEMs to build deep customer relationships while providing a higher degree of flexibility. When designed for circularity, they can enable a more resource-efficient manufacturing industry. Given that machines play a crucial role in the processing of nearly all products across industries, embracing EaaS represents a critical intervention point.

  Case example: TRUMPF, a renowned German machinery company, innovatively introduced a pay-per-part business model for their TruLaser Center 7030 premium metal laser cutting machine. Instead of purchasing the machine, customers pay solely for the produced metal parts. The model aims to fully align incentives with customers by improving their performance, flexibility and transparency. The 100-year-old family business developed the business model together with innovation partners by applying an iterative, customer-centric design process.

- **Chemicals:** Outcome-oriented business models in the chemical industry often manifest in chemical leasing. In this model, payment and optimisation are based on the functions performed by a chemical. Chemical providers collaborate with customers to optimise chemical use, focusing on fulfilling specific functions. This approach also facilitates closed-loop systems for refining chemicals.

  Case Example: SAFECHEM offers COMPLEASE, a precision cleaning solution for metals in a chemical leasing model. Customers don't buy volumes of solvent, but a tailored performance package for a fixed monthly rate. This model incentivises optimising performance with fewer resources, as the solvent is considered a cost factor. Additional enabling services, such as lab services and waste management, support the offering.

- **Tools:** Especially for B2C use cases, the high initial costs of tools compared to often low usage frequency could make renting more attractive than buying. In B2B use cases, it is important for customers to access high-quality equipment at predictable cost while minimising the risk of downtime. From a sustainability perspective, circularity performance can be optimised when producers retain ownership and optimise product design and operations for the fleet of tools.

Case example: Hilti offers a fleet management solution for their construction tools. Construction businesses pay a monthly fee for access to a customised tool fleet that's optimised for uptime, inclusive of maintenance, repairs and replacements. The fleet can be adjusted to specific needs and short-term peak demand. At the end of the product life, Hilti assesses the tools and batteries for reuse, remanufacturing, spare part use or recycling.

- **Facility management:** The use phase of buildings involves a significant footprint (e.g. energy and waste) and costs. Outcome-based business models customised for energy efficiency, space utilisation, smart equipment and asset usage, water savings or waste (cost) reduction can yield significant improvement potential.

Case example: CWS is an innovative provider of workplace solutions around hygiene, dust control mats, workwear or fire protection. CWS focuses on sustainable and digital rental solutions for B2B customers such as offices and gastronomy. The Hygiene-as-a-Service model, for example, provides solutions for washrooms, from soap dispensers to cotton towels, in a full-service model. This focuses on tailoring the solution to customer needs and includes all operations related to cleaning, refilling or logistics.

Additional case examples: Hewlett Packard (HP Instant Ink is a subscription based monthly programme that provides customers with replacement ink, covering involved services and also the proper recycling of the used cartridges); Siemens (offering Energy-Efficiency-as-a-Service solutions); Kaeser Compressors (offering compressed Air-as-a-Service); SKF (integrated solutions offering for rotating equipment based on a performance agreement).

Pitfalls to avoid

- Consider the risk shift! While this business model may significantly increase customer value, the liability of risks can be significant for the manufacturer, ranging from operational risks (technical failures, handling) and capital financing risks (asset value, capital cost) to information risks (credit and payment default, economic developments). Carefully evaluate these risks together with your customer and experts (e.g. bank, legal, insurance). Adjust the legal terms and structures of your agreement to manage the risks.
- Producing products versus providing outcomes might change your complete operating model. An integrated service design should centre on customer needs. However, an outcome-focused model also requires adjusting the product design and operational excellence.

- Check your digital readiness. Some say servitisation is the next evolution stage after digitalisation. Pay-per-outcome models are enabled by data and digital technologies. You may benefit from solutions for asset monitoring, remote maintenance, automation, advanced analytics, AI-driven optimisation of utilisation, digital product passports, or intelligent ERP, billing and CRM systems.

Keep an eye on
The capex-to-opex shift

- **What it is:** How to manage the balance sheet dilemma? If the manufacturer retains the asset ownership in an 'As-a-Service' business model, this may significantly extend the balance sheet and funding requirements. For the user/customer, the asset-light balance sheet and flexibility (capex-to-opex shift) is of course an important benefit. Manufacturers should practice careful planning to manage the financing, balance sheet and cash-flow implications (see Chapter 5).

- **Companies to have on your radar:** Banks such as BNP Paribas Leasing Solutions, Intesa San Paulo or Deutsche Bank are developing tailored offerings for Asset-as-a-Service.

(c) Sharing/pooling platforms

Sharing or pooling is a service model in which a product is made accessible to multiple users through co-access or co-ownership arrangements. These product-service bundles are often established by third-party providers, not the manufacturers directly, which act as platforms that enable access across various brands. Co-access is a form of collaborative consumption and involves users having access to a shared product for a specific period or under certain conditions without full ownership. Pooling is a particular form of collaborative sharing that involves aggregating participants, while co-ownership entails multiple individuals jointly owning a product or resource and sharing associated costs and benefits. These business models are typically facilitated through platforms that connect providers with users (B2C) or users with each other (C2C, B2B, peer-to-peer).

Impact case	Business case
• **Refuse:** Shift consumption patterns to more conscious consumption and encourage sharing/pooling. Replace individual ownership with more eco-friendly choices – opting for access over ownership can lead to reduced consumption • **Rethink:** Prioritise access over ownership in sharing/pooling models, optimising for intensive use and resource efficiency. This includes maximising the productivity of assets like fleets or shared equipment. Efficiency considerations encompass material resources, energy and infrastructure • **Reuse:** Embrace sharing/pooling to avoid single-use items and new product consumption. Reuse can lower environmental impact compared to new production, potentially reducing demand for new products at scale. High-quality products and effective maintenance or refurbishment practices are essential for maximising this effect	• **Unexploited business opportunities:** Leverage structural advantages to enter the sharing/pooling market opportunities. Companies with inherent strengths, such as marketplaces, online communities, infrastructure firms, or logistics operators, can navigate this territory better than traditional manufacturers • **Ecosystem innovation:** Actively participate in a growing partner network and customer ecosystem. This engagement broadens your business network and unlocks opportunities for secondary value creation, such as cross-selling services, brand value, loyalty and valuable data • **Utilisation:** Sharpen your focus on optimising utilisation and efficiency. Intensify utilisation benefits from economies of scale and a robust digital platform. Platforms can navigate the dual-sided approach (providers and users) and leverage network effects, whereby value increases as the user base grows

Industry relevance

Sharing and pooling models are effective across diverse industries, particularly for products that are easily transportable, infrequently used or have lower emotional attachment, making users more willing to share. The success of such models often hinges on the practicality and ease of shared access to these products.

- **Mobility:** Sustainable mobility is a popular use case for sharing and pooling business models. This is enabled by consumer trends that shift towards flexibility and convenience, as well as city-based policy support towards sustainable urban spaces, reduced congestion and efficient resource use.

  Case example: Via is a mobility and technology company specialising in on-demand transportation solutions. Their TransitTech platform, designed specifically for operators of public transportation, multimodal transport, schools and corporate mobility, empowers them to operate Mobility-as-a-Service. This includes features such as dynamic route optimisation and pooling intelligence.

- **Fashion and textiles:** Sustainability challenges in global fashion accelerated significantly since 2000. The surge in production and decrease in utilisation, largely propelled by the rise of fast fashion, have contributed to a steep increase of waste and pollution. Scaling new business models that tackle the demand side and foster a systemic push for quality and durability is critical. Business models that centre around actual fashion use are one way to potentially reduce the absolute demand for new clothing.

  Case example: Rent the Runway operates a fashion rental platform. The company is active in the United States with a focus on designer clothing and accessories from a variety of brands. Users have the flexibility to rent items for a specific duration. Their offer is structured around a membership model, complemented by a concierge service, providing members access to a designated number of items each month, thereby eliminating the necessity to purchase new clothing.

- **Consumer electronics:** Rapid technological advancements in various electronics segments increase the e-waste problem and call for solutions to keep devices in circulation and at high utilisation. This business model revolves around providing access, rather than ownership. It demonstrates the potential to cater to new customer segments, such as users with short-term device needs.

  Case example: Grover, a German consumer electronic marketplace, operates a flexible subscription model for multiple products and brands. Customers enjoy flexible access (between 1 and 24 months) to smartphones, laptops, tablets, gaming consoles or wearables and further products, all for a monthly fee. The devices are regularly refurbished, ensuring they remain in active use.

- **Equipment and consumer goods:** Several home appliances and many other household products are infrequently used by tenants. Items like sports, leisure or party equipment may be only needed seasonally. With students often residing in apartments for short durations, owning expensive appliances becomes impractical. Additionally, some consumer groups prefer a minimalistic lifestyle. Sharing products with neighbours in the same building or community offers a resource-efficient alternative to ownership.

  Case example: TULU provides an infrastructure for buildings that enables tenants to rent household appliances and other products required at home. Tenants can avoid purchasing items such as vacuum cleaners, projectors or printers; instead, they share these resources with fellow occupants.

- **Furniture:** Like fashion, furniture is an integral part of everyone's life. It is similarly subject to consumer trends, and comes with sustainability challenges (e.g. fast furniture with low quality and waste issues). In urban areas, where young people often relocate, lifestyles evolve and flexibility is preferred, the concept of access over ownership can align with these changing preferences.

  Case example: Feather is a New York City-based platform offering flexible furniture subscriptions. It allows residential as well as business customers to rent high-quality furniture from a variety of brands on a monthly, quarterly and yearly basis, providing a sustainable alternative to traditional furniture ownership.

Additional case examples: Peerby (enables neighbours to borrow and lend diverse products within their regional community, e.g. tents, bicycles, tools, clothing); Uber (ride hailing solution that connects drivers with passengers, expanded to features like Uber Pool that enables multiple passengers to share their ride); Klarx (platform to rent construction equipment).

Pitfalls to avoid

- Beware of unintended consequences! Use insights into consumer behaviour for optimising a sharing/pooling model and avoiding potential negative side effects. These may include issues like overconsumption due to low costs, or systemic challenges (e.g. people choosing shared ride-hailing over public transport, leading to traffic congestion and emissions). For peer-to-peer platforms, conflicts among consumers may arise due to the less regulated nature of the sharing economy.
- Circular product design and portfolio choices are essential to ensure that the products perform well in the sharing/pooling business model.

Consider complementing sustainable product portfolio and design choices with consumer nudging elements and incentive strategies. This may encourage users to adopt more responsible behaviours, for instance through offering discounts or rewards for returning items in good condition, promoting proper handling and care.

- Consider the environmental implications of delivery and collection transport logistics in your sharing or pooling business model. Depending on the model's design and the sharing frequency, significant emissions and logistical efforts may be associated with operations. These operations impact the overall viability of the business case and impact case. Finding the sweet spot for your potential sharing/pooling business model involves balancing factors like product holding periods, exchange frequency and logistics intensity to achieve economically viable and environmentally sustainable outcomes.

Keep an eye on
Sustainable urban spaces – such as 15-minute cities!

- **What it is:** Many cities are actively designing urban spaces to enhance well-being, resilience and climate mitigation. Urban environments are intricate systems where the built environment, infrastructure, waste management, mobility, energy, nature and the social system must synergise to create a sustainable urban space. The concept of 15-minute cities exemplifies this vision, where residents can meet most of their daily needs locally through sustainable and shared mobility, community engagement, local consumption, sharing economy practices, better social equity and nature integration.

- **Organisations to have on your radar:** C40 and city examples (e.g. Barcelona's Superblocks programme; Paris' Collective for Climate Project in La Porte de Montreuil; Milan's L'Innesto aims to be the first Zero Carbon 'Housing Sociale').

Taking stock
Now, let's take a moment to reflect on the following worksheet (Figure 4.8). What are your initial opportunity ideas based on these business model patterns? Are there already any initiatives in your business that, if scaled, could represent significant opportunities? Broaden your thinking and note down these opportunities.

Next, select one of these opportunities and explore it further. Examine how the classic business model elements manifest, including the value proposition to the customer, operational delivery and high-level economics for value retention. Outline a preliminary business case for scaling this business model, estimating the potential size of the opportunity from low to very high. Additionally, assess the environmental impact potential of the opportunity – do you anticipate the impact as low or high?

Figure 4.8. Taking stock of identified opportunities

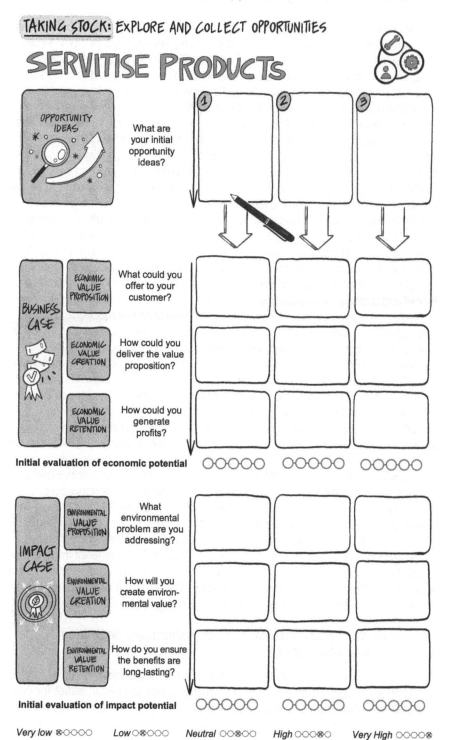

4.6 Embarking on your business model revolution

Ray Anderson, the visionary founder of Interface, a global carpet tile company, had an environmental awakening in 1994 after reading *The Ecology of Commerce* by Paul Hawken. Realising his company's role in environmental degradation, he formulated an ambitious vision known as 'Mission Zero', which aspired to eliminate all negative environmental impacts by 2020. To achieve this mission, Anderson devised a strategy using a mountain analogy, breaking down the vision into seven 'fronts'.

He started with the fronts that could be implemented relatively easily and quickly and had immediate benefits for the company and the environment. These were the fronts of eliminating waste and benign emissions. He challenged his employees to find ways to reduce or eliminate any material that did not add value to the product or the customer, and to eliminate any harmful emissions or substances from the production process. He then moved on to the fronts that required more investment and time, like renewable energy, closing the loop and resource-efficient transportation. He invested in solar panels, wind turbines and biomass boilers to power his operations with renewable sources of energy. He also redesigned his products to make them more recyclable or reusable and used recycled or bio-based materials as inputs. He finally tackled the fronts that required radical changes in his business model and system, including sensitising stakeholders and redesigning commerce.

Besides engaging all stakeholders, he created new business models and systems that supported and rewarded sustainability, such as leasing, service or performance-based contracts. Although Ray Anderson passed away in 2011, his legacy lives on through Interface. The company achieved Mission Zero in 2019, a year ahead of the 2020 target, reaching net-zero emissions across their product life cycle. Their new mission, 'Climate Take Back', aims to become a carbon-negative company by 2040, for example by developing processes that create value from waste carbon. As you embark on your own transformative journey, let yourself get inspired by Interface's remarkable story. Draw insights from their achievements in Mission Zero. How can these lessons guide you in realising your ambitions and making a meaningful impact? Your journey begins with thoughtful consideration and purposeful action. Reflect on the path you will carve to shape a legacy that resonates with your aspirations.

As you envision your circular business future, the key lies in building and scaling commercially viable, circular business models. These models shape the path towards achieving your circular vision and possess the transformative power to decarbonise, dematerialise and regenerate. They shift the mindset from merely 'doing less bad' to actively 'doing good' as a new norm, intentionally contributing to the restoration and preservation of nature. With this mindset, we will guide you in 'thinking back' from your vision and build your business model pathway.

Your opportunity set – quick wins, transition opportunities or transformative innovation?

Synthesise your business model exploration process and ideas to arrive at your comprehensive opportunity set. This opportunity set itself is an asset for your organisation. Building on the previous chapters, summarise your opportunity ideas in the next worksheet (Figure 4.9). Given your initial rating of economic and environmental impact potential, which opportunity ideas would you consider as most relevant to take into the set?

The nature of your business model opportunities will typically range from quick wins to transition opportunities to truly transformational innovation.

- **Quick wins** are strong tools for swiftly mitigating negative externalities in the short term. They predominantly involve incremental adjustments with a focus on the current context, sustaining the existing model and ensuring your continued 'license to operate'.

- **Transition opportunities** extend beyond the present focus and yield impact in the mid-term. They often centre around more ambitious changes that shape emerging circular norms and practices. These opportunities not only address negative externalities but also pave the way for positive externalities to thrive.

- **Transformative innovations** aim to manifest your future vision of a circular and regenerative world. They may necessitate radical transformation, emphasising a future-oriented approach and serving as your 'license to innovate'. The aspiration here is to unlock transformative power and foster positive externalities.

Your opportunity set might already show some patterns. This can have both positive and negative implications. On the positive side, patterns may show interconnectedness and the mutually reinforcing nature of your circular business models. You will have realised that these business models are also not mutually exclusive; they offer strong synergies. However, there is a downside to this as well. If your opportunity set is heavily skewed towards quick wins, the danger might be that you are only *sustaining* the existing linear economy. Although it serves the purpose of securing your 'license to operate', it falls short of making substantial contributions for real change. This might be unintentional and a result of the prevailing short-term pressures that dominate many companies. Consider the example of a car manufacturer: the most relevant identified opportunities may focus on replacing virgin materials (e.g. aluminium, steel, plastics) with secondary materials, thereby contributing to less extraction of raw materials. However, if the systemic challenge of extensive individual mobility through the ever-increasing sale of new cars is not addressed and the future of intermodal urban mobility is not considered, it merely sustains the current linear business model and makes only incremental progress towards sustainability.

Conversely, if your opportunity set is full of transformational ideas, it's essential to challenge yourself about what should be prioritised in alignment with your future vision. While pursuing multiple transformative opportunities reflects a commendable ambition for genuine transformation, it also carries the risk of overwhelming your organisation due to the complexity of the task and the extensive changes required. Returning to our car manufacturer example: imagine they are contemplating addressing the root causes of their

Figure 4.9. Worksheet to synthesise opportunities and plan the pathway

WORKSHEET 3: SYNTHESISE YOUR IDEAS AND DRAFT
YOUR BUSINESS MODEL REVOLUTION PATHWAY

OPPORTUNITY SET

BUSINESS MODEL REVOLUTION

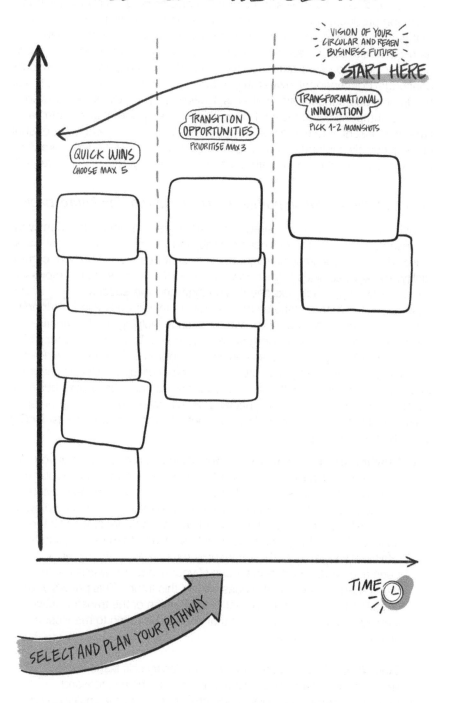

VISION OF YOUR CIRCULAR AND REGEN BUSINESS FUTURE

START HERE

TRANSFORMATIONAL INNOVATION

PICK 1-2 MOONSHOTS

TRANSITION OPPORTUNITIES

PRIORITISE MAX 3

QUICK WINS

CHOOSE MAX 5

TIME

SELECT AND PLAN YOUR PATHWAY

product's issues, leading to the consideration of a shift from merely selling cars to offering them as-a-service. They recognise the potential in providing a mobility service that seamlessly integrates a diverse range of alternative transportation products such as e-bikes and scooters. Effectively running a fleet that is also a material bank. Another moonshot might be offering Batteries-as-a-Service in combination with advanced energy storage solutions. These opportunities represent authentic transformational prospects that radically challenge conventional ownership models and aspire to foster circular production and consumption patterns. However, it is crucial to acknowledge that the company cannot feasibly pursue all these opportunities at the same time. It is essential to make well-informed decisions about which moonshot ideas genuinely contribute to your vision and influence your strategic direction. Employing the backcasting method can be immensely helpful in this regard.

Your circular revolution pathway – Thinking from the future-back

Revisit your vision of the desired future as a starting point and then work backwards to embed the business models and the steps to bring that vision to life. The future you imagine might be significantly different from your current reality. The key headlines of your news article in 10–15 years might emphasise a net-positive approach, exponential change and the success of a circular business model that contributes more to nature than it consumes. Your articulated vision serves as your north star for change, helping you to prioritise the various circular business opportunities in your set. To transform your vision into reality, let's employ a reverse engineering approach. This process, known as backcasting, encourages a 'future-back' perspective. Embark on a journey through time, starting from the vision of your circular and regenerative business 10–15 years ahead and moving backwards, ultimately reaching the present. Let's look at this step by step and take a hypothetical fashion brand *(FashionCo)* as an illustrative example:

- **Starting from your future vision:** Begin by articulating what you will have achieved in the future – building on the vision for your circular and regenerative business future that you have developed in the previous chapter. Remember to be ambitious yet also realistic. When employing backcasting, the crucial step is to articulate the future state as if the desired change has already been achieved, and then to ask yourself: 'How did we get there?'. By framing the future as if it has already been achieved, you shift the focus of your mindset towards the 'how' rather than questioning the possibility of this future. This primes your cognitive processes for a reflective exploration of the transformative journey and the strategic steps that need to be taken to manifest the envisioned future state.

    Example FashionCo: We have led a revolutionary shift in the textiles sector towards generating positive outcomes for both nature and society. Embracing a circular design philosophy, we have implemented innovative processes to maintain materials at their highest value; zero waste and zero pollution are now the norm for our entire product range. We have ensured safe, living-wage working conditions in the entire ecosystem (up and downstream).

- **Exploring your transformational innovation opportunities:** Remaining in that distant future, zero in on the transformative innovation opportunities that align closely with your articulated circular future. Delve into your opportunity set and seek to incorporate the most impactful, groundbreaking ideas. If you were to choose just one or two moonshot initiatives, which ones would they be? These business models will be at the heart of turning your ambitious vision into tangible reality.

  Example FashionCo: (1) Pioneering a recommerce ecosystem where high-quality products are recirculated through sale, trade-in and resale, (2) establishing pay-per-use business models for short-term fashion rentals. Both business models work in sync and create an ecosystem of advanced customer value from every garment made, while enabling us to establish fully circular technical and biological cycles.

- **Bridging the gap with transition opportunities:** Next, shift your focus to the transition opportunities which act as a bridge connecting your aspirational future with your current business reality. They may either present substantial advancements to your current business model or serve as the initial steps in realising your future vision, ensuring seamless operations during the transition phase. It's advisable to focus on no more than three transition opportunities, with each playing a pivotal role as an intermediate step between your company's present and future.

  Example FashionCo: (1) Achieving a premium for a new product line based on next generation materials (e.g. consisting of 100 per cent regenerative wool) that supports nature-positive local land use practices; (2) actively recycling materials from textile-to-textile, thereby capturing value from what was once textile waste. This is enabled by design choices for value retention as well as fully traceable, clean, green supply chains operating at highest standards of efficiency.

- **Arriving in the present:** Lastly, bring your journey to the present moment. Here, you can introduce the quick-win opportunities that you've identified. These represent critical adjustments to your business model that help maintain your 'license to operate'. While these opportunities are usually easier to implement, it's essential to limit your focus to a maximum of five to avoid becoming overly reliant on quick fixes. How can your quick wins also plant the seed for the transformational business model opportunities or shape the preconditions?

Example FashionCo: (1) Optimising resource use through green operations (energy, water, materials, chemicals), not only in own operations but also by actively reducing resource intensity throughout the supply chain (paired with ensuring safe, living-wage working conditions); (2) extending fashion repairing options by partnering with local sewers to extend product life; (3) establishing 100 per cent sustainably sourced raw materials (e.g. introducing a fully organic cotton product line) that also allows to trace textiles from 'seed-to-sew'.

Successfully navigating this business model pathway requires proactive leadership, not just passive management. This is crucial when venturing into the realm of circular business models known for their revolutionary nature. When embarking on this journey, it's vital to consider how existing business models can lay the groundwork for the successful development and scaling of your revolutionary circular business models. Similarly, ambitious ideas can greatly benefit from envisioning a minimum viable version – a simplified iteration that can be introduced to the market to initiate your transformation.

An experimentation mindset becomes pivotal in this context. By starting in a smaller, trusted space, you can rigorously test and refine your concepts before expanding them further. However, as we have often experienced in our work with companies that have embarked on this journey, you must shift away from isolated initiatives and a wave of pilot projects that lack alignment with your overall strategy. These initiatives can mobilise only limited commitment and pose challenges in terms of scalability. While they may keep you busy and create the illusion of progress, many of them ultimately lack the scale and impact required to drive substantial change. Therefore, implement a 'kill or scale' strategy, ensuring that you have a well-defined method for selecting the most promising concepts and scaling them. At the same time, this approach equips you with the courage to discontinue initiatives that lack the potential for scalability. By doing so, you maintain focus, efficiency and a clear trajectory towards your circular and regenerative business vision.

Moving on to the implementation stage, it's crucial to recognise that each business model pathway will have its own challenges, highly dependent on the specific characteristics of your organisation. In the following chapter we will delve into the practical aspects of adopting this approach. This chapter aims to assist you in identifying the early stage requirements for your circular business model and in preparing for the potential challenges that may arise throughout the journey. We will once again rely on the power of backcasting. By aligning your actions with your long-term vision and strategy, you can harness its potential to steer your organisation towards ambitious goals while unveiling the key elements necessary for preparing for this future. Effective execution of the business model should not only be focused on implementing the product and operating model, but also strengthening the organisational readiness and wider integration. Most importantly, it should empower and support a leadership mindset that encourages and enables your people to drive the transformation. This comprehensive approach ensures that your organisation is fully prepared and equipped to embark on the path towards a circular and regenerative business model.

Chapter 4 – In a nutshell

- **Building commercially viable, circular business models serves as the central engine for your transformation towards a sustainable future.** Essentially, these are winning business models that capture economic value through resource productivity and circular and regenerative design with the power to decarbonise, dematerialise and regenerate. They aim to move the mindset from 'doing less bad' to 'doing good' as a new norm, intentionally giving back to nature.

- **There are five circular business model archetypes, within which a total of 15 business model patterns are embedded.** These patterns span from supply side– to demand side–focused business models. First, business models that optimise resource use/supply to strengthen the competitive edge and focus on greening operations as well as using secondary, decarbonised materials, or bio-based materials. Second, business models that create value through regeneration and restoration. Third, valorising waste into economic value via material recovery strategies or new service offerings. Fourth, monetising extended product lives through maintenance and repair services, upgrades and modularisable options as well as refurbishing or reselling products. Finally, business models that move from ownership to access by servitising products and delivering business outcomes to customers.

- **Circular and regenerative business model innovation aims to improve both business impact and environmental benefits by radically optimising for the highest 'net impact'.** Environmental impact describes climate-related factors (i.e. carbon emissions) and also regenerative nature-focused aspects (i.e. biodiversity, freshwater). Business impact, such as long-term profitability, is often characterised by increased customer experience, new value pools, price premiums, cost competitiveness, reduced risks or better supply chain resilience.

- **A strategic exploration of these business models archetypes and patterns will help to identify your comprehensive opportunity set.** This is a process of creative ideation and exploration, translating the relevant patterns into concrete business model opportunities. Potentially attractive business models may range from quick wins to transitional opportunities, to new activities that can be completely transformational and 'revolutionary'. This opportunity set is an asset in itself for your organisation.

- **Shape your business model revolution pathway from the 'future back'.** This involves incorporating transformational innovation ideas, transition opportunities and quick wins that align with your vision. The emerging pathway will be entrepreneurial, driven by a lean, business model-focused strategic approach, serving as an alternative or complement to complex, top-down corporate transformation programmes.

FROM IDEA TO ACTION

LEADERSHIP

MINDSET

STRATEGY

BUSINESS MODEL IMPLEMENTATION

ORGANISATIONAL INTEGRATION

PEOPLE

From idea to action

5

Do you carry a Swiss Army Knife with you? If so, you understand that it's more than just an all-purpose tool; it's a symbol of adaptability, resilience and practicality. It is designed to help you in any situation, concealing a universe of solutions within its sleek design, ready for any challenge. Implementing your circular business pathway will hold a range of challenges. This chapter aims to help you prepare for the journey and navigate through its challenges. It equips you with valuable tips and best practices. In a way, it provides you the Swiss Army Knife that you want to take on your implementation journey. Just as the Swiss Army Knife seamlessly handles diverse tasks, we've designed a circular readiness framework to turn your vision into reality.

As you move from idea to action, you should strengthen your readiness for this journey on three dimensions – strategy, execution and people – encompassing a set of 10 factors (Figure 5.1). The strategy dimension provides direction and visionary alignment of *where to play* – in line with the vision of your circular and regenerative business future. The execution layer builds the operational backbone for your journey – *how to win*. The people foundation focuses on the foundational skill set and leadership mindset to drive change across the entire organisation – *how to empower*.

Embarking on your journey, consider the Swiss Army Knife's multifunctionality and its ability to adapt to unforeseen challenges. This mirrors your requirement for versatility and agility as you navigate the diversity of factors and unpredictable terrain of circular business implementation. As we unravel this narrative, discover a captivating twist: Victorinox, the maker of the Swiss

Figure 5.1. Circular readiness framework

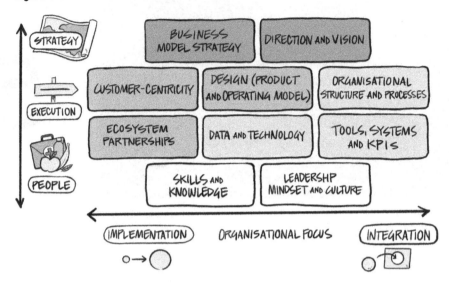

Army Knife since 1897, stands as a hidden champion in circularity. Victorinox, a family-owned company, divides its ownership uniquely between two foundations, the Victorinox Foundation (90 per cent) and the Carl and Elise Elsener-Gut Foundation (10 per cent), ensuring independence and alignment with its purpose. Their circular strategy is a testament to longevity, actively encouraging product durability and repair over replacement. Their knives withstand wear and tear, backed by lifetime warranties. The company prioritises renewable, recycled and highly recyclable inputs, minimising waste and optimising material usage. Sustainable supply chains ensure ethical and circular material sourcing and Victorinox embraces circular design thinking, ensuring easier disassembly and effective recycling.

Circular readiness scan

Now, much like how the Swiss Army Knife became a symbol for tackling any challenge, our circular readiness framework enables you to prepare for the unexpected and equips you with the essential tools to turn your ideas into reality. Engaging in a short survey will help you to scan through these factors and especially interpret your readiness in the context of your prioritised business model patterns.

Use the worksheet survey (Figure 5.2) to assess your readiness using a scale from 1 (strongly disagree) to 5 (strongly agree). The resulting picture will help you to navigate through the different elements of the circular readiness framework detailed throughout the remainder of this chapter.

Figure 5.2. Worksheet circular readiness scan

WORKSHEET 4: ASSESS YOUR READINESS AND ORGANISATIONAL ENABLERS

CIRCULAR READINESS SCAN

BUSINESS MODEL STRATEGY	1. We have systematically **assessed the most relevant circular business model opportunities** ○○○○○○
	2. We have **defined a strategy and roadmap** for the circular business models ○○○○○○
	3. We have calculated the **business cases** (e.g. revenue, profitability) for the key circular business models ○○○○○○
	4. We have analysed the **impact case** (e.g. environmental benefits) of the circular business models ○○○○○○
	5. We have a clear plan for **managing the funding requirements** and mitigating risks ○○○○○○
DIRECTION AND VISION	6. Our circular **business model strategy helps to deliver our sustainability goals** ○○○○○○
	7. The circular business strategy is **linked to the company strategy, vision and mission** ○○○○○○
	8. Our **internal communication** transports the circularity ambition and provides regular updates ○○○○○○
	9. Our **external communication** addresses our circular economy ambition ○○○○○○
CUSTOMER-CENTRICITY	10. We **refocus on the fundamental customer needs** for developing new circular products or services ○○○○○○
	11. The circular offering **creates superior customer value** (convenience, flexibility and economic benefits) ○○○○○○
	12. Our **value proposition finds a good balance** between customer value and environmental value focus ○○○○○○
DESIGN (PRODUCT AND OPERATING MODEL)	13. We generally **apply a full product life cycle perspective** from material origin over use phase to end-of-life ○○○○○○
	14. We **adjust the product design to the needs** of the circular business models ○○○○○○
	15. Clear **circular design principles guide our decisions on environmental, cost and technical performance** ○○○○○○
ECO-SYSTEMS	16. We **involve our suppliers or customers in creating and delivering** circular products and services ○○○○○○
	17. Our organisation **joins relevant ecosystems or coalitions** that drive circularity in our industry and beyond ○○○○○○

DATA AND TECHNOLOGY	18. We are applying **technology to support data transparency across our supply chain**	○○○○○○
	19. We regularly assess **new, green technology solutions** to advance our sustainability and circularity agenda	○○○○○○
ORGANISATIONAL STRUCTURES AND PROCESSES	20. We have **clear roles and responsibilities for implementing** our circular economy ambitions	○○○○○○
	21. We have allocated **specific financial resources and budget** to develop the business models	○○○○○○
	22. We **improve our end-to-end processes** based on the circular business model requirements	○○○○○○
TOOLS, SYSTEMS AND KPIs	23. We have **defined specific objectives, targets or key results** for the circular strategy	○○○○○○
	24. We are using **clear metrics to monitor the progress and impact** of our circular activities	○○○○○○
	25. Our **management steering systems/dashboards are linked to the circular business targets** and metrics	○○○○○○
	26. The company's **performance rewards and incentive systems** consider the circular business targets	○○○○○○
SKILLS AND KNOWLEDGE	27. Our **internal talent can dedicate sufficient working capacity** to the circularity agenda	○○○○○○
	28. Dedicated **learning programmes inform and help** all colleagues to understand and manage circularity	○○○○○○
	29. Our teams have **access to the relevant knowledge to develop** circular business models	○○○○○○
	30. We are able to **find and onboard relevant external talent** to build circular business models (if needed)	○○○○○○
	31. An **active internal community supports the exchange and best practice sharing** around circularity	○○○○○○
LEADERSHIP MINDSET AND CULTURE	32. Company **leaders explain and inspire a shared vision** on sustainability and circularity	○○○○○○
	33. Our leaders **adopt and support an agile mindset for long-term transformation** and the required changes	○○○○○○
	34. Our senior **management sponsors and backs** circular business model initiatives	○○○○○○

Strongly disagree ⊗○○○○   Disagree ○⊗○○○   Neutral ○○⊗○○   Agree ○○○⊗○   Strongly agree ○○○○⊗

5.1 Strategy

The strategy dimension encompasses a cohesive set of choices that deliver on a shared vision and goal. Your vision, outlined as your north star for a circular and regenerative business future in Chapter 3, serves as a guiding principle. Building on the opportunities you explored in Chapter 4, your strategy should describe such an integrated set of patterns that shapes your pathway towards that vision. Are you confident that your defined pathway will help you to reach the future state you have summarised in the news article looking 10–15 years ahead? Great! However, your readiness to implement your chosen circular pathway requires more than confidence; it demands strategic readiness for implementation.

Business model strategy

Your business model pathway should align seamlessly with compelling strategic planning and roadmapping, shaping both the business and impact case, as well as developing a funding strategy. This is not a one-off and isolated exercise, but an ongoing practice. As Dwight D. Eisenhower aptly expressed: 'Plans are worthless, but planning is everything.' The sentiment underscores the dynamic nature of effective strategic planning.

Business model exploration and roadmap
The process of exploring circular business model opportunities marks the initial step in your transformation journey. Whether your chosen business models focus on optimising resource supply, capitalising on regeneration and restoration, valorising waste, monetising extended product life or servitising products, it is key to approach your opportunity set with an open mind. Planning the prioritised opportunities towards your future horizons should consider quick wins, transition opportunities and transformational innovation. This shapes your circular revolution pathway and initial roadmap. As you move from exploration to action, your planning process will lead you to running initial pilots and generating learnings, while external conditions continue to change. Be ready to adapt your roadmap and re-prioritise.

Beyond that, exploring circular business models should become a real strategic *practice* linked to your strategic management, sustainability, R&D and organisational development processes. The methodology presented in this book guides you through that opportunity identification process, aiming to strengthen your 'license to innovate' muscle and to shift mindsets towards embracing the circular paradigm. Ensure a solid link to your company's key activities and identify change agents that are empowered to drive the innovation agenda for the highest net impact.

Philips serves as a compelling case for a company ambitiously adopting these elements in their large medical equipment business (diagnostic imaging, ultrasound, image guided therapy). Guided by the 'circular imperative' as a strategic framework, the team has systematically explored different circular business models. They established clear priorities and developed an end-to-end circular business model architecture that addresses both internal and external factors. This comprehensive approach includes a thorough assessment of the direct financial impact case, opportunity costs and environmental impact factors. By now, Philips has successfully implemented a range of business models spanning from refurbishment and parts recovery to remote circular services. This exemplifies how a strategic commitment to circular principles can lead to tangible and diverse business model innovations.

Business case and impact case

Successfully scaling circular business models relies on achieving commercial viability while delivering impact. It is essential to clearly assess the respective business case early on. First, this entails analysing the dynamics of the business model using not only classic performance indicators such as annual revenue and profit effects, but also measures that capture the full life cycle perspectives, like cumulative profits over product lifetime and total cost of ownership for the customer. Second, adopting a comprehensive economic view involves considering secondary drivers, including customer retention and the value of data. For example, a refurbishment and recommerce model may serve as the foundation for a wider loyalty programme, acting as a driver for cross-selling. It's also crucial to discuss the prospective development of key assumptions; increases in carbon pricing, for instance, may play a pivotal role in supporting circular business cases. Third, it is essential to think beyond the stand-alone circular business case and place it within the context of broader organisational and strategic benefits. Circular business models have the potential to radically reduce the price risks related to resource supply, especially critical resources. Embracing circular and regenerative farming practices in the supply chain can reduce nature-related risk costs and increase overall resilience. Furthermore, an ambitious and authentic circular business effort can positively impact brand equity.

The process of assessing the business case serves to significantly advance your business model idea. This typically involves the optimisation and validation of assumptions through expert interviews or customer insights. A practical tool can be to visualise an economic value creation waterfall and the different contributing elements (Figure 5.3). Another useful tool, especially in workshops, is a simple resource productivity metric or equation. Productivity metrics, like a long-term perspective on profit (numerator) over material use (denominator), facilitates discussions on optimising both the numerator and denominator.

Circular business models possess the unique capability to unite economic with environmental impact. Crafting an ambitious impact case can serve as a powerful motivator for an entire organisation. We recommend to always compute an impact case next to a business case. Even if preliminary and based

Figure 5.3. Illustrative example of a value creation waterfall for the recommerce business model

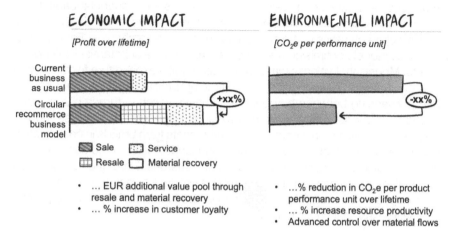

ECONOMIC IMPACT
[Profit over lifetime]

ENVIRONMENTAL IMPACT
[CO₂e per performance unit]

Current business as usual

Circular recommerce business model

+xx%

-xx%

▨ Sale   ▦ Service
▥ Resale ▯ Material recovery

- ... EUR additional value pool through resale and material recovery
- ... % increase in customer loyalty

- ...% reduction in CO₂e per product performance unit over lifetime
- ... % increase resource productivity
- Advanced control over material flows

on assumptions, an impact case significantly shapes the circular business model. Impact case dimensions need to be strongly tailored to the respective industry, product or regions, typically focusing on outcomes related to resource use (material consumption), climate (CO_2 emissions), pollution/waste or biodiversity (e.g. ecosystem services) and water. Consistent with the core principles of the circular economy, it is crucial to adopt a full life cycle perspective for this assessment. For example, drivers behind an impact case often relate to sustainable resource use (e.g. recyclate, closing material loops) or product utilisation (e.g. lifetime productivity, utilisation rates). More advanced companies may also include social outcomes in the assessment (e.g. community impact, health and safety). This comprehensive approach ensures that the circular business model is not only economically viable but also contributes positively to environmental goals.

Planet A Ventures, a venture capital investor based in Hamburg, stands out by consistently calculating the ecological impact potential alongside the business impact potential for their (potential) investments. The impact potential is an important factor in their investment decisions and the team adheres to science-based principles (e.g. LCA methodology) to arrive at quantified results.

Natura, the Brazilian cosmetics company, has embedded regenerative and circular practices (impact case) at the core of its premium product proposition (business case). The company is committed to supporting the 'standing rainforest economy', optimising packaging and actively participating in relevant networks (e.g. SBTN). Quantifying evidence for their impact proposition is deemed essential to Natura's approach, aligning their core business practices with their sustainability goals.

Funding model

The strategic design of funding models plays a pivotal role in the success of most circular business models, as it serves to secure financial capital and manage associated risks. Considerations for the financing model depend on the specific characteristics of the chosen business model archetype. For example, business models optimising resource use may require substantial R&D investments. Models that valorise waste may need capital expenditure for machinery and equipment. Those focusing on extending product lifetime might rely on bridge financing between buy-back and resale, which in turn is heavily influenced by the value retention of the products. Regenerative business models may demand investments or off-take commitments from brands in collaboration with regenerative supply chain partners and landowners. In the case of servitisation business models, a unique dynamic emerges. Here, the company, be it manufacturer or provider, typically retains product ownership, thereby tying up capital on their own balance sheet, to instead rent out the products or offer alternative servitisation arrangements.

Servitisation – Managing the 'balance sheet dilemma'

The concept of 'swallowing the fish', as coined by the Technology and Services Industry Association (TSIA) in 2016, aptly illustrates the challenges faced by established companies transitioning to servitisation business models (often called 'As-a-Service').[1] Figure 5.4 illustrates the typical revenues and cost developments for companies introducing As-a-Service models, spanning from the initial status quo (on the left) to a successfully transformed state (on the right). Usually, when a company shifts from an asset-based purchasing model to a subscription-based one, it may initially experience a decline in its top-line revenues. This occurs as former upfront payments are replaced by a steady stream of income generated through recurring revenue. While the long-term benefits have the potential to outperform the conventional model, the short-term

Figure 5.4. The fish model

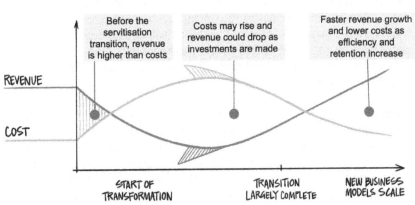

(building on TSIA Playbook)

impact demands careful cash management. Smart cash flow management becomes essential, often requiring additional funding capital to finance the transition. So, the question arises: how thick can you afford your fish to be? Of course, a thinner fish and thus a leaner financial approach is preferable.

Beyond addressing immediate cash flow challenges, companies adopting a servitisation model often encounter the 'balance sheet dilemma'. This dilemma arises from the shift in financial dynamics where the asset user or customer benefits from a lighter balance sheet (capex-to-opex shift), while the manufacturer or provider experiences an extension of the balance sheet and increased funding requirements. To effectively manage this balance sheet dilemma, manufacturers and providers have a range of strategic options and solutions involving financial engineering and contractual set-ups. Simplified archetypes of solutions include:

1. **Ownership retention and refinancing:** The company retains the ownership of the asset on its own balance sheet. This model is typically suitable in the early stages of As-a-Service models or when the capital requirements are relatively low. Financing can be achieved through debt/loan instruments (potentially a flexible financing scheme), equity-based financing or public funding via grants or subsidies (e.g. EU grants).

2. **Sale and leaseback arrangement:** The producer collaborates with a financing partner or bank to sell the asset to the partner, and then leases it back. The As-a-Service model is offered to the customer as a full-service contract, including hardware, software and services. The contractual design then provides the surrender of use to the customer. If designed right, this arrangement can allow the provider to operate asset light while offering the customer an integrated contract.

3. **Special purpose vehicle (SPV) creation:** For larger servitisation projects, the company may create a separate legal entity (the SPV) to own and operate the assets required for the As-a-Service model. By transferring the ownership of the assets to the SPV, it has its own balance sheet and can attract capital from investors or lenders. This can be achieved through various means, such as equity investments, debt financing or a combination of both. The manufacturer should have a stake in the new SPV, but the assets and associated debt are separate from the manufacturer's balance sheet. The company may loop in additional partners into the SPV (e.g. for risk monitoring).

4. **Adjusted traditional financing:** To keep assets off the producer's balance sheet while enabling an As-a-Service model for the customer, traditional financing instruments or leasing models can be adjusted. The customer may lease the asset (i.e. additional financing partners can be relevant) and receive a service contract, or the asset is transferred to the customer with a flexible refinancing scheme (such as flexible debt financing fees or pay-per-use credit). However, this approach does not fully qualify as an As-a-Service model, as it doesn't apply a use/outcome-based approach and is typically not off balance sheet for the customer, but can still provide flexibility.

In addition to the financing risks discussed here, there may be further shifts in risk profiles. As companies proactively take a perspective on the full life cycle, including the use phase and end-of-life, certain operational risks – such as technical failures, downtimes, and misbehaviour – come to the forefront. Additionally, there are information risks, including track and trace information and asset monitoring, which demand active management.

Direction and vision

Your business model pathway should have a reinforcing link with the vision of your circular and regenerative business future, as well as the broader business ambitions. Focus and simplicity are important to channel energy effectively towards your strategic aspirations. It is also critical to articulate internally and externally how the circular business strategy serves as a mechanism to deliver on the company vision/mission and how it helps to progress towards your strategic priorities and sustainability goals.

Strategic embeddedness

Linking circular business model activities explicitly to the company's general strategic priorities and sustainability goals is essential. This sounds like a no-brainer, but in practice this is often not the case – or not well-communicated. While there may be passionate teams driving new business model initiatives initially, the strategic embeddedness becomes critical, especially when scaling successful pilots. Ensuring everyone recognises the strategic priority of the circular business models is therefore key to overcoming intra-organisational barriers and securing sufficient resources. By employing the methodology of vision backcasting (see Chapter 3) you can ensure that your crafted business model pathway is anchored in your future circular vision and long-term priorities. A complementary strategic tool can be to define a clear system of objectives and the supporting key results to progress towards each objective (see OKR methodology by John Doerr).[2] This method ensures a clear direction for everyone involved, serving as a continuous reminder of the link between activities and higher level strategic priorities. If there is no link, the activity should be challenged.

> **Bosch**, a pioneering German tech leader, has strategically defined circular product and business model priorities related to material efficiency, recycled materials, reuse and remanufacturing. The priorities are intricately linked to Bosch's overarching company strategy, reflecting their ambition to design products and services that 'spark enthusiasm, improve quality of life and help conserve natural resources'.

> **SAP**, a global enterprise software giant, is guided by a commitment to 'help the world run better and improve people's lives' with an aspirational vision for a world with zero emissions, zero waste and zero inequality. This vision shapes SAP's sustainability ambition, leveraging its core business and extensive network of partners and data to explore inno-

vative opportunities. For example, the SAP team has recently launched Responsible Design and Production, a software suite that helps to compute extended producer responsibility (EPR) obligations and respective circular optimisation levers for more sustainable products and packaging.

Communication

Active and authentic communication is key to increase transparency, and also to signal commitment. Commitment from the teams in the driver seat, commitment from supporters and commitment from the leadership team. Communicating specific goals helps to maintain clarity on priorities and key results that underpin achieving them. Internal communication should facilitate transparency, collaborative engagement and celebrate successes (and failures!). Externally, communication is crucial for managing stakeholders, engaging customers with new solutions, acquiring talent and ensuring compliance. Your communication strategy should authentically reflect your actual achievements and activities to avoid falling into the greenwashing trap. Conversely, its lesser known counterpart, greenhushing, where a company refrains from communicating about its sustainability journey, can be just as damaging. It creates the impression of inactivity and reservedness, risking negative perceptions among stakeholders. Therefore, it is crucial to both: 'walk the talk' and 'talk the walk' and actively involve your stakeholders by taking them on board your sustainability journey.

A powerful tool for communicating your circular business ambitions and activities is to 'start with the Why', as advocated by Simon Sinek.[3] This approach emphasises the critical importance of clarity regarding purpose and deeper beliefs to guide the 'What' and 'How' of your initiatives. Ensure that every strategic priority is anchored in the overarching 'Why'. For example, explore the link to the foundations of your organisation, including shared purpose, values, guiding vision and mission. Reflect on your organisation's heritage – did it reinvent its business model in the past, and is the courage behind such radical innovation a driver of current success? Visualise the link between your circular business model pathway and the DNA of your company.

> **Lego** Replay embodies Lego's commitment to creating a positive impact beyond play. Rooted in the belief that every child deserves access to education and creativity, the company invites its customers to donate their used Lego bricks. Cleaned and redistributed to underserved classrooms and communities, these bricks become valuable educational resources. The programme's communication emphasises the shared journey with customers, inviting them to be active contributors to a more sustainable and inclusive world.

Another effective communication tool is to specify impact objectives and provide examples. You may explain how your circular business models support the 'net-zero' roadmap of your organisation. In the context of climate action, emphasise how optimising resource use and increasing resource productivity align with the core of addressing 'embedded emissions' and driving supply chain decarbonisation. Additionally, highlight the connection between your circular practices and the Sustainable Development Goals, with particularly strong relationships existing with SDG 6 (Clean Water and Sanitation), SDG 7 (Affordable and Clean Energy), SDG 8 (Decent Work and Economic Growth), SDG 12 (Responsible Consumption and Production) and SDG 15 (Life on Land).

Ecosia, a search engine engaged in ecosystem restoration, plants a tree for every 45th search query. As a user, you can always see how many trees you have already planted through your searches. This not only gives you the feeling of doing something good, but also playfully raises awareness of the issue of digital environmental pollution since each search query has an environmental impact.

Bring circularity to life through storytelling, putting a personal face on abstract concepts. Craft stories and narratives from employees, customers or communities experiencing positive change to appeal to your stakeholders. For example, sharing a real, impact story about how a circular business initiative directly impacted a community can make the abstract concept of circularity more relatable and tangible. Authentic storytelling builds trust by showcasing tangible impacts, thereby fostering credibility. Encourage participation by inviting stakeholders into the narrative, turning them into advocates for positive change. Highlighting progress, stories share achievements, celebrate milestones and outline future goals, ensuring stakeholders are informed and involved in the evolving narrative of circularity. This narrative-driven approach enhances engagement, fostering a deeper connection to your circular business initiatives.

Nespresso's 'Second Life' campaign communicates the ambition behind its dedicated recycling system for aluminium capsules. By collaborating with renowned Swiss brands like Victorinox, Zena and Caran d'Ache, Nespresso communicated a compelling narrative showcasing how recycled aluminium capsules were transformed into new items, thereby building trust and engaging customers in a visually impactful way. The communication emphasised transparency, personal connection and reciprocal engagement, making the rather impersonal recycling journey more relatable and inspiring for Nespresso's audience.

5.2 Execution

Execution builds the operational backbone of your business model pathway. It describes the key enablers required for implementing a circular business model and ensuring seamless organisational integration. Are you strongly committed to a user-centric value proposition and – this is particularly important – also adjusting your product design and operating model to align with the principles of the circular business model? Are you actively cultivating relevant partnerships to realise circular solutions and engaging your ecosystem of suppliers, customers and specialists? Furthermore, do you possess the relevant data and techno-logical backbone to effectively implement the business model? As you aspire to scale your business model, its integration into the organisational structure becomes paramount. Are resources and well-defined processes in place to support the initiative? Particularly within larger organisations, it is essential to scrutinise whether business steering and performance management tools are tailored to align with circular business targets. Let's delve into the intricacies of these factors.

Customer-centricity

Maintaining a strong focus on the customer is undeniably crucial for all businesses. So, why highlight its relevance in this context? Let's illustrate it with an example: Consider a company contemplating a circular rental business model for their product, such as a bicycle. The temptation might be to initiate one by simply incorporating a subscription model into their existing product and observing its reception among current customers. This often fails. The service models might be relevant only for specific customer segments, such as B2B, or Gen-Z. Moreover, the success of pay-per-use models often lies in their ability to create value through additional services beyond the product, such as flexible mobility or insurance. It's also possible that the product design may need adjustments to align with the subscription model, addressing potential concerns like a 'don't be gentle, it's a rental' mindset. Fine-tuning a circular business model necessitates a high level of customer-centricity. What are the underlying customer needs to be addressed? What is the value proposition for the key persona? Does the circular offering deliver superior convenience, flexibility and engagement? These are critical questions to explore in order to tailor the circular business model effectively to the customer's expectations and demands.

Customer needs focus

Developing a circular business model requires a strong focus on the human (or societal) need that the offering seeks to address. This means gaining a deep understanding of the problem, identifying pain points and addressing specific needs. The emphasis on needs extends beyond the initial business model design, playing a crucial role in consistently meeting these (evolving) needs throughout the entire product life cycle. Circular business models aim to guide customers through the complete product journey, optimising both product use phase and the end of use/life phases. This focus on fundamental customer needs becomes particularly evident in the servitisation archetype, where business models prioritise outcomes, performance and utility over traditional product sales. Examples include providing mobility instead of selling cars, offering a running tool-fleet as a service instead of selling individual machines or focusing on yield and crop protection instead of selling high volumes of fertiliser or pesticides. Innovators behind these business models need to push the reset button and return to a deeper understanding of customer needs.

CWS is a perfect case example. The company headquartered in Duisburg, Germany, operates a leading circular rental model for workwear in a B2B setting. The model's success lies in its incorporation of full-service cleaning operations and logistics, delivering 'hassle-free' solutions tailored to the specific operational needs of their customers. Beyond offering quality apparel products, the product design is optimised for long product life and repairability. In turn, the business model positions CWS as close partners to their customers, enabling continuous improvements and portfolio expansions. A 'circular advantage' study by CWS revealed that the rental service (including transport) reduces emissions by approximately 50 per cent compared to a purchase model.

User-centric value proposition

Customer-centricity involves gaining clarity on the essential drivers of customer value, including economic, functional and emotional considerations (Figure 5.5). Circular business models have the potential to reduce the total cost of ownership for customers. For example, they can eliminate the need for companies to purchase and maintain their own hardware and software infrastructure, thereby decreasing capital expenditures and enabling companies to allocate resources more effectively. Value can also be derived from the reduction of perceived risks, including financial, performance, social and psychological risks. From a functional value perspective, circular business models can offer greater flexibility, convenience, quality and an overall improved customer experience. For example, they allow for more customisable and configurable solutions tailored to specific needs. Circular solutions may include support services, technical

Figure 5.5. Exemplary value creation drivers

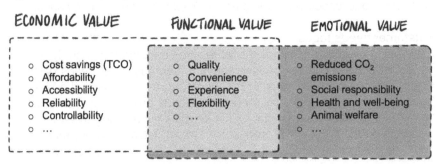

ECONOMIC VALUE	FUNCTIONAL VALUE	EMOTIONAL VALUE
o Cost savings (TCO)	o Quality	o Reduced CO$_2$ emissions
o Affordability	o Convenience	o Social responsibility
o Accessibility	o Experience	o Health and well-being
o Reliability	o Flexibility	o Animal welfare
o Controllability	o ...	o ...
o ...		

assistance and a commitment to enhanced communication and partnership with customers. Emotional value may derive from an ambitious environmental impact programme (e.g. reduced CO_2 emissions, animal welfare, chemical-/hazard-free products, health and well-being) or social impact agenda (e.g. social responsibility, personal fulfilment, empowerment, community).

In sum, a deep customer-needs focus and clarity on value drives should culminate in articulating the value proposition for the aspired circular business model. A practically helpful tool can be the value proposition canvas by Alexander Osterwalder and colleagues.[4] Designing a value proposition is a critical step that benefits from precisely defined ideal customer profiles, which can be achieved through tools such as persona descriptions or the jobs-to-be-done perspective. By identifying customer pain points, gains and points of delight, a comprehensive understanding of customer needs emerges. Subsequently, the economic, functional and emotional value drivers should align seamlessly with these customer needs, serving to either alleviate pains or create delightful experiences. Circular products and services must be built on a user-centric value proposition – typically linked to a higher environmental impact ambition. This approach ensures that the design and delivery of circular products and services resonate strongly with the target audience.

Design (product and operating model)

Many organisations underestimate the pivotal role of design in shaping a product's trajectory (e.g. footprint, handprint). Yet, in fact, design decisions have a substantial influence, accounting for a staggering 80 per cent or more of a product's environmental and social impact.[5] These decisions unfold early in the development process, shaping the entire product life cycle. Seen in this light, design emerges as the fundamental enabler of most circular business models. Tailoring both product and operating model design to align with the needs of the business model becomes a key driver for impact. Questions arise: Can the product be designed for quality and durability to endure multiple use cycles? What design tweaks contribute to the success of end-of-life material recovery business models? How can the operating model, encompassing aspects like reverse logistics or repair operations, be optimally designed? The implementation of regenerative and restorative circular economy principles must be enabled *by design*. This intentional role of design decisions sits right at the core, because 'with circular design, we can prevent the creation of waste and pollution right at the start'.[6]

Full life cycle perspective
Designers and decision makers must adopt a holistic perspective of the full product life cycle. This spans the 'build phase' (how materials are sourced and products manufactured) and the 'use phase' (how products and services are used and consumed), extending to the 'end-of-life/use phase' or ''loop phase' (how to recover materials and eliminate waste). An invaluable tool in this pursuit is the life cycle analysis (LCA), which provides insights into emissions throughout the product's entire life cycle. It's noteworthy that a significant portion of emissions often occurs during the use phase – for example, around 50 per cent for laptops,

20 per cent for smartphones and 60 per cent for battery electric vehicles, contingent on the energy mix. Despite this, many organisations predominantly focus solely on optimising processes related to the build phase, often lacking awareness of who the end consumer actually is (e.g. if you sell via retailers, or supply components) and what happens at the end-of-life stage. Conducting a thorough LCA becomes a cornerstone for enhancing transparency and providing decision makers with a fact-based foundation. While the LCA is a well-established methodology for comprehending a product's environmental footprint (PEF), a product carbon footprint (PCF) analysis is essentially an application of the LCA methodology with a specific focus on CO_2 emissions. The Cradle-to-Cradle (C2C) approach embraces a full life cycle mindset and goes a step further. It provides advanced methodological guidance to facilitate the circulation of materials and nutrients for closed loops. The full C2C philosophy has been developed by sustainability pioneers William McDonough and Michael Braungart.

Unilever has systematically employed LCA as a methodology to inform decision-making processes. This commitment expanded, especially following the launch of their Sustainable Living Plan, a strategic initiative aimed at positioning Unilever as a leader in sustainable business practices. Under this plan, Unilever conducted science-based assessments for more than 3000 products. Over the years they refined their methodological approach and developed advanced LCA versions, such as the Land Use Change Improvement (LUCI-LCA) dynamics.

Logitech has taken a proactive step by introducing carbon impact labelling across its product portfolio (e.g. mice, keyboards). The methodology employed is grounded in LCA, encompassing sourcing and manufacturing, transportation and storage, in-use and end-of-life. Notably, both the methodology and results are publicly accessible, encouraging other companies to adopt carbon labelling for improved 'carbon clarity'.

Megawood (NOVO-TECH) is a German innovator specialising in wood-based materials for outdoor applications such as terraces or facades. They have meticulously designed their products for extended lifetimes and sustainable recovery, aligned with C2C standards. Beyond that, Megawood has implemented a take-back system for its products and residual materials and has developed its own recycling process and reuse operations.

Circular design principles
Circular 'by design' entails adhering to a set of design principles outlined by the Ellen MacArthur Foundation. These central design principles revolve around eliminating waste and pollution, keeping products and materials in use at highest value and regenerating natural systems. Design, in this context, means intentionally shaping both the product design and operating model to optimise the environmental performance and economic performance – actively tailoring products and services for the respective business model in focus, rather than merely adapting

existing products. Applying circular design principles involves considering different levels and their interconnectedness (Figure 5.6). At the material level, design choices can significantly impact both upstream (e.g. designing for regenerative land use) and downstream in the value chain (e.g. ensuring full recyclability at the product's end of life). Product-level design decisions set the stage for the success of a circular business model over the full life cycle (e.g. determining if the product can efficiently function through multiple use cycles). Service-level design must start with addressing the actual customer problem and understanding the human needs behind the business model. Operating-level design choices determine whether the processes (e.g. reverse logistics, repair or refurbishment) efficiently support perpetual cycles of product (re)use. Moreover, design choices necessitate zooming out to consider the ecosystem perspective and broader context in which a product and company operate (e.g. supporting standardisation to allow for interoperability between devices).

Many designers are used to navigating the economic trade-off between technical and cost performance, but today, environmental performance introduces a new dimension into this evaluation (Figure 5.7). Making design decisions within the context of these performance dimensions is particularly challenging in industries where technology is rapidly evolving, and products serve an increasing range of functions, all while facing limited transparency in the value chain. Take the consumer electronics industry as an example. Brands in this highly competitive market are continually developing more compact products, incorporating complex materials such as batteries, and integrating advanced

Figure 5.6. Circular design levels

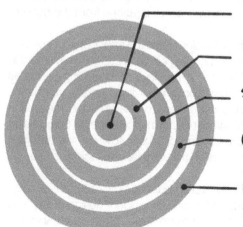

CIRCULAR BY DESIGN

MATERIAL LEVEL
Design for circulation of technical and biological resources in cycles

PRODUCT LEVEL
Design for resource productivity and extended product life, zero waste

SERVICE LEVEL
Design for addressing customer-centric problems and human needs

OPERATING MODEL LEVEL
Design for circular processes and operating systems for closed loops

ECOSYSTEM LEVEL
Design for tackling systemic inefficiencies, supporting standardisation and collaboration

Figure 5.7. Performance trade-offs in design

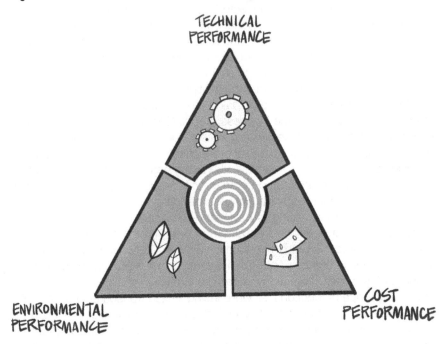

hardware and software features. Considering environmental performance early in the design process is crucial. Factors like energy consumption and compatibility with recycling systems are significantly influenced during the design stage. Design teams benefit from guidance on navigating challenging performance trade-offs, supported by tools and data, such as LCA and materials analysis. Providing designers with more freedom to optimise their designs as well as clear instructions of how to handle potential performance trade-offs – whether adjusting technical specifications or setting more flexible cost constraints – empowers them to integrate environmental considerations from the outset.

DS Smith is committed to playing a leading role in the transition to a low-carbon, circular economy. Next to incorporating circularity as a core element in their sustainability strategy the company has developed guiding principles for circular design. Their five principles combine environmental performance aspects (optimising materials and structures, maintaining and recovering materials) with economic technical/cost performance aspects (maximising supply efficiencies, protecting brands and products) towards the ambition to 'find a better way' for more innovative and circular packaging solutions.

IKEA's ambition to transform into a circular business by 2030 puts a spotlight on design. They have developed a 'circular product design guide' and eight 'circular design principles'. Those include designing for renewable and recycled materials, standardisation, care, repairability, adaptability to evolving needs, disassembly and reassembly, remanufacturing and materials chosen for recyclability. These principles aim to guide the design decisions and trade-offs, optimising for form, function, price, quality and sustainability.

Ecosystem partnerships

In the circular realm, ecosystems are not just essential, they are the lifeline. Without strong partnerships and collaborative networks, the realisation of effective circular business models remains an elusive endeavour. Delivering circular business models in time and at scale typically requires strong partnerships that shape new markets and systems.[7] Building trusted partnerships can significantly accelerate your implementation path, beginning with your internal ecosystem, which involves cross-functional collaboration and adopting an agile set-up. Beyond your intra-organisational ecosystem, consider collaboration in two essential dimensions: first, the solution ecosystem, which involves partnerships to deliver your offerings, and second, the enabling ecosystem, providing framework conditions and support networks (Figure 5.8). Winning circular ecosystem innovation particularly requires collaboration and experimentation.[8]

Internal ecosystem

To enable circular business models, some internal processes and collaboration need adjustment. Circular business transformations may encounter resistance, especially in organisations heavily organised in functional silos. It is

Figure 5.8. Ecosystem levels

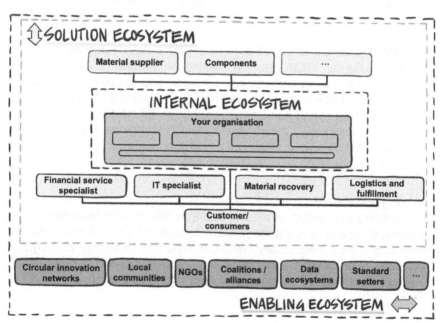

often necessary to fundamentally question product design, even if it has been done 'that way' for a long time. Circular innovation projects are often driven by sustainability teams or technical departments. However, for successful scaling, sales must also support new business models even if they may not initially be as lucrative. Internal partnerships are key and a prerequisite for the development and implementation of innovative circular business models. The People section (Section 5.3) will equip you with more information about the internal ecosystem, especially with respect to required skills and knowledge, as well as leadership mindset and support dynamics.

Solution ecosystem

Circular value chains require interconnection between internal and external stakeholders.[9] What are the specific partnerships that could help you to deliver circular solutions together with an ecosystem of suppliers, customers and specialists? First, think vertically based on your current value creation depth. This might involve forming supplier partnerships for a steady supply of recycled materials, and collaborating with material recovery partners for resource retrieval. Second, address logistics and fulfilment with strategic partnerships for managing reverse logistics flows. Third, consider forming alliances with financial institutions to secure competitive funding, navigating challenges like the balance sheet dilemma in Product-as-a-Service models, and employing risk assessments and insurance for effective risk management. Fourth, cultivate partnerships with data and IT specialists to establish robust data and digital information flows. This facilitates both the creation of data transparency (e.g. track and trace) as well as the efficient management of information throughout the full product life cycle or multiple cycles. Finally, establish deep partnerships with existing or new customers to collaboratively develop, test and optimise new business models.

> **TRUMPF** has introduced the pay-per-part business model for the TruLaser Center 7030 machine, aiming to provide a leading full-service solution in the manufacturing industry and to optimise resource productivity. At the outset, the success of this business model was underpinned by a strong partnership ecosystem. TRUMPF's solution ecosystem involved key partnerships with MunichRe, a global insurance and risk specialist, Relayr, an IT service provider, as well as Klöckner, a large steel distributor.

Enabling ecosystem

The enabling ecosystem serves to catalyse the circular business model activities, extending beyond the solution ecosystem. Consider your current position and think horizontally: Who can help you to strengthen regional relevance, push cutting edge innovation, drive a specific circular sector transition, contribute to the business-policy interface and standards setting processes, or co-shape the wider circular economy network? Diverse stakeholders constitute the enabling ecosystem, ranging from global circular innovation networks, such as the Ellen MacArthur Foundation or the World Circular Economy Forum hosted by Sitra, to regional and local networks like CIRCULAR REPUBLIC in southern Germany or circular city initiatives, and industry-focused network programmes (e.g. PACE Capital Equipment Coalition, Circular Consumer Electronics Program by Circularity e.V.). Collaborating with NGOs or coalitions can advance the thought leadership agenda, convening partners around a collective action plan. Beyond that, new data ecosystems are important to co-shape innovation and standards such as the Battery Pass, CATENA-X or Manufacturing-X. Finally, engaging at the business–policy interface (e.g. EU Circular Economy Stakeholder Platform) or contributing to standards setting (e.g. DIN Circular Economy Group) can help to co-shape external enabling conditions. Navigating these ecosystems often requires neutral facilitators or governing bodies to build trust among different parties. Such orchestrators can be key to shape the ecosystem's strategic direction and co-funding mechanism. They can set the drumbeat in collaborative projects and ensure progress towards impact.

Battery Pass is a consortium that produces the first content and technical guidance for digital battery passports as mandated by the EU. The group (founded by Systemiq, co-funded by the German Federal Ministry for Economic Affairs and Climate Action) includes a wide range of organisations key to the value chain, including BMW, Audi, Umicore and many more. The aim is to inform the innovators who are currently developing battery passports to implement the novel technology efficiently, maximise for environmental impact potential and support secure sharing of information along the battery value chain. It is a good example of how companies can build their enabling ecosystem to co-shape future data and information flows in their value chain, which can unlock circular business models.

Partnerships open the door to a broad spectrum of expertise and foster collaboration to translate the theoretical potential of the circular economy into practical, profitable business models. However, the substantial value of partnerships also comes with risks. Coalitions can be paralysing when searching for a common ground over extended periods. Partnerships can become inefficient and tie up many resources when the goal is not clearly defined, lack sufficient financial support or lack a coordinator. At the same time, it is clear that the transformation towards a circular economy can only be achieved collaboratively.

> **Food for thought**
>
> **How would you map your ecosystem?**
> You may use the ecosystem level framework to actively identify and map potential partnerships. Think vertically first, which partners could contribute some of the missing capabilities to your circular business model? Then horizontally, how could you link to relevant partners in your enabling ecosystem to accelerate your transition? This holistic approach ensures a comprehensive and strategic mapping of your collaborative landscape.

Data and technology

Digitalisation and technological innovation have undergone a radical acceleration over the past 2–3 decades, playing a pivotal role in unlocking circular business models (Figure 5.9). The synergy of digital innovation, such as data from supply chain track and trace systems or advanced data analytics, coupled with physical technology innovations, like sensor-based monitoring and novel recycling processing, holds the potential to significantly enhance commercial viability. This is a vibrant space for tech innovators and start-up entrepreneurs aiming to enable the circular transition. In this evolving landscape, the convergence of digital and physical innovations creates exciting opportunities for those who can navigate the intersection effectively.

Data and digital innovation

Managing advanced data and information flows can be a game-changer for the competitiveness of circular business models. However, in many industries, current data and information flows follow a linear logic, mirroring linear resource flows. A few solutions can help to turn this around.

- **Digital passports and supply chain transparency:** Digital product passports act as a digital identity card for products, summarising data on material origin, composition, sustainability indicators and performance data. Solutions like these are emerging across industries, such as mobility and batteries (e.g. EU battery regulation mandating digital passports for larger batteries starting 2026), textiles and fashion, construction, consumer electronics or plastics and packaging. Digital passports bridge the current information gap required for regulatory compliance and safe end-of-life recycling. Moreover, they unlock value for various value chain players, enabling more effective transport, informed purchasing decisions, digital administration and second use applications. Advanced tracking and tracing technologies can create the information base to monitor, manage and report circular value creation systems upstream and downstream. For example, this may include measurement, reporting and verification technology to track land use change and regenerative capacity.

Figure 5.9. Data and technology patterns enabling circularity

DATA AND DIGITAL INNOVATION ←——————————→ PHYSICAL TECHNOLOGY INNOVATION

DIGITAL PRODUCT PASSPORTS AND SUPPLY CHAIN TRANSPARENCY

Material or product passports as digital twins capturing product characteristics; tracking and tracing of supply chains; information technology for measurement and reporting

MATERIAL INNOVATION

New material solutions such as bio-based material, mono-material, lightweighting or performance materials that support more sustainable product design, resource productivity and energy efficiency

ADVANCED DATA ANALYTICS AND MANAGEMENT SOLUTIONS

Management and decision making supported by data analytics, simulation or machine learning; automation of transactions; consumer engagement; circular product and process design tools

PROCESSING TECHNOLOGY

Advanced processing solutions to close materials loops such as recycling technology, waste management, smart sorting; cost-efficient reman and refurbishment processes, additive manufacturing; robotics and automation to streamline processes

CONNECTED MONITORING AND MAINTENANCE OPTIMISATION

Connectivity for service optimisations; sensors and Internet of Things applications for performance monitoring; remote or predictive and preventive maintenance

CIRCULAR SUPPLY CHAIN SYSTEMS

Tech-enabled distribution and collection systems, smart and optimised reverse logistics flows; inventory planning, handling and management

Case examples: EON (cloud platform for product digitalisation and traceability), R-Cycle (digital product passport for packaging), Circulor (industrial supply chain traceability for metals or plastics), Circularise (digital product passport software), Makersite (product data and life cycle management tools for the manufacturing industry).

- **Advanced data analytics and management solutions:** Better data availability across the supply chain and the full life cycle, including usage data, can inform machine learning or simulation solutions, offering significant advantages for circular pioneers. Platform solutions reduce transaction cost by accelerating speed and enabling network effects, automating processes and improving efficiency. Process digitalisation can fundamentally enable automation and consumer engagement in circular business models (e.g. mobility solutions such as carpooling, peer-to-peer trading of goods for reuse).

Case examples: Faircado (data and information crawler to enable second-hand shopping), twig (digital bank of things reinventing payments with pre-owned items), twist (facilitating link between financial institutions and fleet operators), Resourcify (cloud-based recycling and waste management platform that connects corporations and local recyclers), Recyda (digital tool for packaging management), Pentatonic (legislation tracker for circularity), Circuly (enabling circular subscription solutions), Lizee (omni-channel platform to manage circular business offerings).

- **Connected monitoring and maintenance:** Connectivity for advanced monitoring and maintenance management may be enabled by built-in digital or technical features (e.g. sensors, IoT connectivity) and can optimise usage effectively. This, in turn, drives the impact of circular business models by ensuring a more efficient use phase and enabling predictive and preventive maintenance which extends product life and saves costs.

  Case examples: Relayr (industrial IoT platform), FixFirst (digital platform enabling repair services), iFixit (global repair community), Repair Rebels (platform for repair services).

Physical technology innovation
The enabling role of technology innovation can manifest in various forms, encompassing both novel cutting-edge advancements and also frugal innovations that make technology accessible at scale. Oftentimes the challenge lies not in developing new 'technologies that work', but to enable technologies to 'work at scale'. Key areas for innovation include:

- **Material innovation:** The spectrum of material innovation spans from new technical materials (e.g. material from sequestered carbon, performance materials), to bionics or biomimetic inspired materials (e.g. mycelium, seaweed, natural biopolymers, alternative proteins) and design innovation (e.g. monomaterial). Material innovation can emerge from new feedstock types with multiple potential applications. For instance, seaweed-based material innovation is relevant across various sectors including food, pharmaceuticals, cosmetics or bio-packaging.

  Case examples: Materiom (regenerative materials platform and community aiming to scale high-performance biomaterials), Carbonaide (technology to utilise and store CO_2 in precast concrete), Biotic (using macroalgae to create bio-based biodegradable polymer), Seaweed Solutions (scalable seaweed cultivation and supply).

- **Processing technologies:** Novel and more effective processing technologies are crucial to significantly improve unit economics in favour of circular systems. Technology at scale is required for advanced production (e.g. 3D/additive printing), cost effective remanufacturing and refurbishment technologies, as well as new waste management, sorting and recycling technologies (e.g. diverse new chemical, metallurgical or enzymatic recycling technologies).

Case examples: Greyparrot (AI solutions for material recovery facilities), Recycleeye (robotics and AI-based solutions for advanced waste segregation for material recycling facilities), Tozero (metallurgical battery recycling), Carbios (enzymatic recycling), Enzymity (enzymatic recycling), beworm (biocatalytic recycling), Cylib (metallurgical battery recycling), ROSI Solar (Silicon and metals recycling from photovoltaic cells), Ever Dye (novel dying process with bio-sourced pigments).

- **Circular supply chain systems:** Circular business and operating models often depend on tech-enabled supply chain management. Circular supply chains evolve into distributed and interconnected networks of partners. Innovative system solutions can support reverse logistics streams, automation and new information flows to manage such networks. This may also include tech-enabled inventory planning, handling and management.

  Case examples: Reverse Logistics Group (platform connecting reverse logistics value chain stakeholders), LiBcycle (full service B2B partner for battery dismantling, second life and recycling), Sensefinity (real-time connection and analytics for supply chains), ReBound (omnichannel logistics and returns management).

Food for thought

What are relevant technology innovations for you, and do you possess the digital backbone to realise your selected circular business models?
Can you build the solutions internally or – like many successful circular business models – do you need to forge partnerships with innovators in the field?

Organisational structures and processes

The best circular business strategies can fail if the organisational structure and processes are not set up for success, especially in larger organisations. The question of organisational embeddedness is a critical consideration when setting up or scaling new business model initiatives. Should they be seamlessly integrated into the existing structure or initiated externally? Success hinges not only on structural planning, but also on the allocation of sufficient human and financial resources to support the programme. Clearly defined roles and responsibilities are imperative. Finally, processes should be shaped to effectively guide the end-to-end deployment and scaling of new business models.

Roles and responsibilities

Establishing clear roles and responsibilities is important for the success of strategic initiatives within any organisation, and requires particular attention in the case of new circular business models. The interdisciplinary nature of developing and delivering these business models requires a specialised operational team entrusted with a distinct mandate – to bring together diverse functions. This team not only benefits from a connection to the overarching sustainability or circular economy programme, but also demands strong ties to the operational business units. Many organisations are composed of central functional units and decentral business units, with sustainability and circularity typically embedded within these organisational dynamics.

Special attention is also required if circular business models significantly challenge established legacy processes, such as procurement policies focused on radical product cost optimisation or sales processes solely optimised towards maximising unit sales. If you want to avoid radical innovation being hindered at the inception, you need to ensure a supportive governance structure. For example, this may involve the establishment of an executive steering committee and executive sponsors, as well as finding the right degree of organisational embeddedness for the initiative.[10]

The level of integration of circular business activities into an organisational structure has to carefully consider the broader organisational set-up for sustainability and also the specific needs of the projects. While circular business model initiatives should have (direct or indirect) links to the central sustainability and circularity programme, the structural integration depends on the needs of the prioritised business models. Practically, this results in a spectrum ranging from fully integrated set-ups led by a small central team, often linked to the sustainability team, to a more decentralised integration within business units or through cross-functional teams driving circular innovation projects (Figure 5.10). In cases where circular business models have a disruptive nature for the organisation, opting for a more independent set-up, such as a joint venture with partners or a corporate venture arrangement, may be advisable.

Siegwerk is a leading global innovator in inks and coatings. Many of their circular initiatives are steered by the global sustainability and circular economy team, but solutions are developed in close collaboration with the respective business units. The company enables circular packaging solutions that enhance recyclability or design based on renewable materials. Additionally, they operate Siegwerk Ventures, which builds independent ventures for digital and circular packaging solutions.

Figure 5.10. Organisational design questions

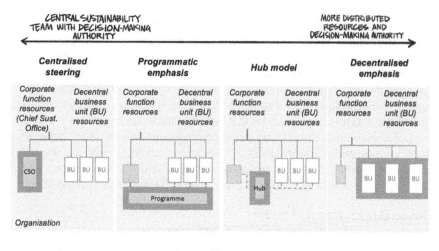

HOW ARE SUSTAINABILITY AND CIRCULARITY TYPICALLY ORGANISED?

CENTRAL SUSTAINABILITY
TEAM WITH DECISION-MAKING
AUTHORITY

MORE DISTRIBUTED
RESOURCES AND
DECISION-MAKING AUTHORITY

Centralised steering	Programmatic emphasis	Hub model	Decentralised emphasis

HOW CAN NEW BUSINESS MODEL INITIATIVES BE EMBEDDED?

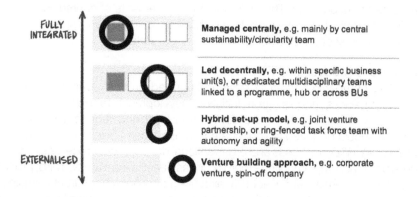

FULLY INTEGRATED

Managed centrally, e.g. mainly by central sustainability/circularity team

Led decentrally, e.g. within specific business unit(s), or dedicated multidisciplinary teams linked to a programme, hub or across BUs

Hybrid set-up model, e.g. joint venture partnership, or ring-fenced task force team with autonomy and agility

EXTERNALISED

Venture building approach, e.g. corporate venture, spin-off company

BlueMovement is a spin-off start-up initiated by Bosch Siemens Hausgeräte (BSH), Europe's largest manufacturer of home appliances. BlueMovement offers a rental model for Bosch and Siemens appliances for a fixed monthly fee. The initiative has been started in an entrepreneurial set-up to increase speed and allow for quick testing with a focus on the Dutch market, before expanding into the German market.

Decisions regarding organisational set-ups should be tailored to the respective business model initiatives and can also change depending on the maturity phase. For example, ring-fencing a new business model initiative through a more externalised set-up can enhance speed and agility. However, merging the initiative back into the right organisational set-up becomes crucial to ensure scalability and synergies. Regardless of the structural differences in set-ups, it is key to establish clear roles and responsibilities for that set-up with dedicated teams developing the business model. Conducting a *role crafting* exercise can assist the team in defining roles and responsibilities. A role comprises a purpose (i.e. intention), accountabilities (i.e. areas of action or decision) and domain (i.e. process or function link). It is important to note that one person may hold multiple roles.

Financial resources and budget
People on a mission with clearly defined roles, capacity and an entrepreneurial mindset are the driving force behind building circular business models. However, these individuals and teams usually require financial resources to fuel such initiatives. The team investing time and energy into early-stage projects requires a budget to develop the business model, covering aspects such as personnel cost, IT development or market research. Innovative approaches exist to ensure sufficient funding, including corporate co-funding models, incubation programmes with stage-gate funding processes, innovation competitions and allocated time budgets. The wider capital requirements of course vary among different circular business models, which will typically require a specific funding strategy (see section 'Business model strategy' earlier).

End-2-end processes
Leading companies carefully design integrated processes that enable new circular business models – from initiation, development, to execution. First, the processes triggering the identification of circular and regenerative business models should be linked to your strategic management practices, sustainability processes, R&D processes and organisational development processes. Second, developing and implementing emerging ideas benefits from agility. Third, process excellence is essential for actually executing and operating circular business models. For example, in a fully integrated set-up, process excellence involves establishing clear handover points and efficient interfaces between different organisational units. These units may already work well together based on other products and business models, or may be newly created functional units, such as those for reverse logistics or remote maintenance services. A proven tool for end-2-end process excellence is the RACI matrix, which structures the process along key tasks on one axis and key roles on the other. It designates which role is

responsible (R), accountable (A), and who should be consulted (C) or informed (I). This tool effectively combines the concept of clear roles with process excellence.

Tools, systems and KPIs

Effectively managing progress, performance and impact relies heavily on the use of metrics. Metrics serve as powerful tools for directing attention towards specific objectives and key results, forming a crucial aspect of performance evaluation. However, they can also be risky if they lead to narrow thinking, siloed optimisation or rebound effects. The principle 'what gets measured gets done' underscores the importance of clear targets aligned with overarching goals. Without this alignment, results may fall short, and the intended impact could be compromised. It's imperative to strike a balance between precise, tailored metrics and the need for a comprehensive, holistic approach to ensure that measurement practices contribute positively to the overall success of the endeavor.

Targets and measurement

Dedicated metrics should align with your crafted business model pathway and future circular vision. On the back of that, selected metrics should capture concrete impact figures. There is currently no universally agreed-upon standard set of circular economy metrics. On the macroeconomic level, popular metrics include Raw Material Consumption (RMC, per capita) or the Circular Material Use rate (CMU, the share of materials recovered and fed back into the economy) which are used by policy makers in national circular economy plans. At the company or product level, various metrics are available to measure circular and regenerative performance. Pioneering tools like Circulytics by the Ellen MacArthur Foundation, Circelligence by BCG and the CTI tool by WBCSD have shaped the relevant set of performance metrics for companies. In addition, the emerging reporting and disclosure system is also advocating for circular metrics.

On the one hand, there are voluntary standards and frameworks, such as the Taskforce on Climate-Related Financial Disclosures (TCFD) or Taskforce on Nature-Related Financial Disclosures (TNFD). On the other hand, there are more and more mandatory disclosure requirements, especially in Europe, such as the EU Taxonomy and Corporate Sustainability Reporting Directive (CSRD), which mandate companies to conduct a double materiality assessment and disclose resource-related metrics (see European Sustainability Reporting Standards, ESRS).

Figure 5.11 summarises a set of popular circularity metrics, building on insights from the leading tools and emerging standards. As a company, it is advisable to apply metrics that align with your ambitions and circular business model pathway while also considering your disclosure requirements. Your chosen metrics should enable you to monitor the progress and impact of your circular business activities.

Management steering systems and performance management

While there is generally no silver-bullet metric, it is important that decision makers integrate their targets and metrics into their management steering systems and tools. Select a suitable 'set of metrics' that not only captures your aspired impact *outcomes*, but also addresses specific considerations supporting the

Figure 5.11. Exemplary circular economy metrics and indicators

RESOURCE/ MATERIAL INFLOWS

- Reduce weight of **materials that are used to produce and package** the organisation's products and services
- Increase weight/share of input **materials used for the product/service that are recycled** (secondary sources)
- Increase weight/share of **input materials used that are produced through regenerative practices**
- Decrease weight/share of **inputs from high-risk ecosystems**
- Reduce amount of **water consumption** (generally and especially in areas at material water stress)
- Support **ecosystem restoration and protection**, such as size and location of habitat areas protected or restored

RESOURCE/ MATERIAL OUTFLOWS

- Reduce weight of **processing waste, packaging waste,** and also hazardous waste and other pollutants
- Increase **amount/share of waste diverted from disposal**
- Reduce **air pollutants** (such as SO_2 or NOx)
- Optimise weight/percentage of your outputs in terms of **product and services outflow of materials**
- Increase **recirculated processed waste/materials/products** and recovery potential

CIRCULAR PRODUCTS AND BUSINESS MODELS

- Increase weight/share of **products that are designed based on circular economy principles** (in portfolio)
- Prolong average **lifetime of products**, considering repairability and reusability
- Optimise amount/share of **revenue generated through circular business models** (transparent classification)
- Increase **material productivity** (revenue per tonne of material), or **product utilisation rate** (percentage)
- Increase **share of products with traceability**
- Increase **rate of reuse and recycling** considering the full product lifecycles

EMISSIONS (FOOTPRINT AND REDUCTION)

- Reduce **total GHG emissions** (metric tonnes of CO_2e), based on Science-Based Targets initiative and GHG protocol)
- Increase **share of renewable energy** in total energy consumption
- Increase **avoided emissions** through design and circular business model versus a comparable base case
- Reduce **GHG emission intensity** (such as metric tonnes of CO_2e per EUR)

implementation of your circular business models. For example, optimising towards the reduction of absolute resource use is always important, but tailoring metrics to your circular business needs, such as resource productivity in terms of utilisation, can be a powerful way to monitor performance in a dynamic way. To ensure sufficient management attention, prioritise the most important targets on a similar level as classic business performance targets. Ambitious targets should have visibility on the most relevant management steering dashboards within your organisation.

Evaluate your performance management to ensure alignment with circular business model targets. These formal mechanisms can contribute to behavioural change. Depending on your organisational culture, influential incentive schemes might be in place. For example, sales organisations are often incentivised through substantial variable compensation. Do these incentive schemes support or block the new business model? Similarly, procurement teams are often incentivised towards cost optimisation. Do these incentive schemes consider the design trade-offs behind your future circular product and operating model? Again, performance benefits should align with the intended circular business model pathway.

Philips, a leading healthcare technology company, is pursuing an ambitious strategic pathway centred around the circular imperative. Targets include generating 25 per cent of revenue from circular products, solutions or services by 2025, and offering a trade-in option for professional medical equipment. Philips publishes an extended range of sustainability metrics, covering circular materials management, waste reduction and water consumption. The circular revenue share metrics are reported as part of the key investor reporting.

Kering, the French luxury fashion group, has developed a circularity ambition named 'Coming Full Circle', addressing its entire value chain from raw materials and production processes to recycling and regeneration. New business models, particularly those extending product lifespan, are a key component of their programme. With respect to impact measurement, the management has introduced an environmental product & loss (EP&L) account, creating transparency and translating environmental outcomes into monetary value. Kering is also among the first companies to pilot the Science-Based-Targets for Nature (SBTN).

Food for thought

What is the right level of organisational integration for your circular business initiatives and how can you adjust your business steering and performance management to support and create tailwind?
Consider that adjustments to your organisational structures and processes should work in sync with the tools, systems and KPIs. There is typically not a single magic metric to steer a company towards circularity. What is the nuanced set of metrics that could be most effective in your organisation?

5.3 People

Building and empowering a high-performance team for your circular and regenerative business model involves focusing on the People dimension, which lays the basis for the essential skills and leadership mindset. So far, we have focused a lot on the circularity of *material resources*, but what about *human resources*? A team fuelled by passion and energy serves as the key driving force behind any circular business model initiative, working alongside financial and material resources. When assembling a dedicated team, it is essential to consider complementary skills and knowledge in the team composition, and also to foster an empowering and supportive leadership mindset. This is crucial from the early stages and continues throughout the journey of building new business models. Overcoming challenges and navigating complex paths require willpower and perseverance, often making it a collaborative effort. A famous African proverb wisely notes, 'If you want to go quickly, go alone. If you want to go far, go together.' For a high-performance team to thrive, a shared vision, trust, respect and mutual support are paramount. These elements create a foundation that fosters collaboration, innovation and the resilience needed to succeed in the dynamic landscape of circular and regenerative business models.

Skills and knowledge

High-performance teams are synergetic. They become unstoppable if they work in a *flow* and apply complementary skills towards the common goal of building a circular business model. But the team usually needs to be able to dedicate sufficient capacity to the implementation. A real strength lies in the ability of this core team to effectively integrate with the supporting ecosystem. In particular, when the team leverages a wider internal circularity community, and when this collaborative effort can also rely on a supporting knowledge management and learning environment, it becomes a superpower.

Team composition and talent capacity

The success of new circular business models is driven by talented individuals who channel their energy and passion into innovative projects. This encompasses a core team actively involved in the daily implementation of new business models, supported by tangential teams and an effective leadership team. A team is more than just a group of individuals; it is a collection of people with complementary skills united by a common purpose and shared goals.

The development of circular business models often demands a diverse skill set. *Technical skills* and functional subject matter expertise are essential. Beyond that, and especially when moving an idea from concept to action, unforeseen challenges are likely to arise, which is why critical thinking and *problem-solving skills* are needed to crack these nuts quickly. *Interpersonal skills*, including collaboration and effective communication within a team, play a pivotal role. These skills are especially vital when dealing with stakeholders holding opposing opinions and when steering the broader organisation towards adopting a circular mindset.

In composing a team, consider the individual skill factors aligned with the demands of the respective business model. This involves assessing the complementarity of skills, including synergies and adaptability, as well as diversity in terms of function, gender, culture and more. Staffing the right core team and supporting talent for implementing circular business models will typically require tapping into various functions within your organisation, such as strategy, development, sales and service operations. In cases where specific skills are lacking internally, external talent, such as LCA and decarbonisation experts, may need to be brought on board. Consider that a practical challenge is often capacity. Plan team composition while considering how much individuals can and should contribute to the team's success. If a circular business project remains a 'side topic' for key individuals or lacks critical support, the risk of failure increases significantly.

Capability building and knowledge management

Tailored learning programmes aligned with the vision of your circular business future are instrumental in helping all involved colleagues to develop relevant skills. The learning environment should support continuous improvement. Skills, in this context, refer to the practical capabilities required to apply knowledge (factual information) towards the aspired outcomes. In that sense, a dynamic learning ecosystem must consider both skill development and knowledge management, adapting to ad hoc needs and different project phases. For example, early stage business model innovation may prioritise systems thinking skills, such as system mapping and policy monitoring, while the implementation stage may demand entrepreneurial skills like sprint design and creating minimum viable products. Think beyond traditional learning formats and consider expert coaching as well.

Developing circular business models typically means tapping into new unknown territory. You can think of the knowledge gap in a T-shaped manner: covering broader general elements as well as deeper specific areas. On the one hand, there is a breadth of general knowledge required to help an organisation on its circularity journey, such as the basics around sectoral climate decarbonisation and circular economy principles, or the emerging regulatory landscape or new technologies and data solutions for circular supply chains. On the other hand, deep specific knowledge may involve technical expertise or context-specific knowledge within your organisation, such as understanding product carbon footprints or conducting life cycle assessments to inform product design choices. Making specific knowledge about supply chain constellations (upstream and downstream across multiple tiers) accessible can help to inform purchasing and circular operations. A traditional proprietary knowledge management system can be part of the solution to bridge the knowledge gap, but the complexity of knowledge areas often requires leveraging external sources and advanced technologies, such as artificial intelligence, machine learning systems, advanced enterprise search technologies and collaborative social tools.

The need for upskilling and effective knowledge management typically applies to all hierarchical levels of the workforce. C-suite and senior leaders require knowledge to navigate the wider sustainability transition within the industry, or understanding regulatory implications in terms of their risks and opportunities. Operational leaders and core teams need skills specific to the respective circular business model in focus. Some knowledge and skills may need to be built from scratch, while other areas may already exist within your organisation and be leveraged quickly. For example, industrial companies that optimised for lean production over the past decade may have lean champions who can swiftly contribute expertise in waste management and efficiency improvements.

MUD Jeans, a sustainable fashion innovator, offers jeans with circular design, incorporating organic cotton and recycled cotton, available through both traditional sales and a circular subscription model. The team actively invests in internal knowledge sharing and has established the MUD Jeans Knowledge Centre, which offers a learning environment for external audiences, especially students at schools, high schools and universities.

Talent acquisition

Quickly finding and onboarding relevant external talent can radically accelerate the development of circular business models. Especially if it is challenging to free up internal resources or if the required expertise is not readily available in-house, it may be essential to consider external resources. Consider ad hoc options such as expert networks and temporary solutions like freelancers if it is difficult or not required to onboard full-time capacity. In an increasingly global and competitive market for talent in sustainability and circularity, there is a set of best practices to consider: First, streamline the process for defining talent needs and creating attractive job descriptions. Second, establish partnerships with relevant networks, including dedicated sustainability platforms. Third, strategically incorporate circularity into your employer branding with a focus on your ambitious circular and regenerative future vision along with your emerging pathway and ecosystem. Finally, showcase your impact and initiatives to provide tangible, authentic success stories and inspire prospective talent about the work environment.

Internal community

Fostering an active internal community of change-makers can serve as a catalyst for your circular business model activities. This practically means creating space for an emerging internal community across all layers of the organisation, that can significantly boost employee engagement in new business model initiatives. Such a community can facilitate collaboration, breaking down organisational silos and leverage collective power to solve problems and share knowledge. Creating visibility for progress and achievements is also important.

There are several simple and effective tools and activities to build such a community. For example, an open internal communication channel can be established to share news and foster communication within (sub) groups. Hosting webinars is another approach, allowing for the collective advancement of knowledge, such as inviting external circularity experts or getting inspired by new insights that help to build a drumbeat and routine. Some organisations organise internal sustainability conferences or meet-ups to bring together like-minded colleagues. Sustainability and circularity have the power to convene people based on a strong shared social identity, creating a sense of identification and belonging with a group based on shared beliefs, values or goals.

Leadership mindset and culture

When Wilhelm Mauß assumed the role of managing director at Lorenz, a German manufacturer of water meters, the company was in a challenging position. Cost pressure increased and had already forced many larger competitors to shift their production to Asia. To stay competitive as a high-quality provider, a bold idea emerged: betting on modularity and developing a cost benefit by reusing parts through remanufacturing. However, this was a radically new practice, met with scepticism from employees about feasibility and potential sacrifices in quality. Wilhelm responded by initiating a co-shaping process that actively involved all relevant employees. Involving and empowering them to collectively address the challenge and run pilots to test the feasibility with customers became integral to his approach. Moving the mindset by co-shaping and proactively generating learnings to advance step by step turned out to be a key success factor for the transition to a circular business model. Over time, the team evolved the business model across multiple product generations, eventually transforming into a smart product with a full life cycle management approach. Fast-forwarding 20 years, Lorenz has experienced a quintuple increase in revenue and continues to advance its circular business models. The connected smart water meters are now offered through various models, including sale and take-back, rental and product-as-a-service. Under Wilhelm's leadership, the company transitioned from being analogue-linear to digital-circular.

Shifting leadership mindsets towards sustainability and circularity is a major enabler in the journey of building new business models. Formal leaders, including executives and senior managers, serve as crucial role models, and their support for a business model innovation agenda has a powerful signalling effect. They must foster understanding throughout the organisation regarding the necessary requirements for these new business models. Leaders play a pivotal role in transforming a 'team of stars', where individual contributions excel, into a 'star team', a high-performance team working together in a synergetic flow.[12] The impact of leadership mindset is not confined to the immediate circularity team but ripples across the wider organisation.

Shared vision

A shared vision and impact ambition for your circular business future will set the direction, but its effectiveness relies on company leaders actively explaining and inspiring that vision. In practice, this involves explicitly linking the shared vision to a collective ambition – a compass for human action. A compass that guides towards the aspired outcome and also emphasises the 'why'. The 'why' acts as a deep sense of purpose, which can unlock significant energy for the team driving the disruptive business model innovation, especially when navigating through difficult situations and uncertainty. It necessitates the establishment of a resilient management team that is ready and capable of confronting the challenges and setbacks that inevitably arise on the journey. Additionally, it might entail parting ways with individuals who are unwilling and/or unable to contribute to the transformation.

Be aware that internal elements around values and culture can also shape the shared vision and purpose behind your circular ambition. Corporate culture, while evolving, remains an important 'constant' for an organisation. Especially in times of uncertainty and change, a strong culture provides certainty. In that spirit, a strong culture may provide the reasoning of reinventing yourself and entering new business model exploration in the first place, or also may provide the backbone for mastering the required changes. The shared vision may challenge an organisation to move from an ego-centric to a more eco-centric perspective and mindset.[13]

Patagonia's founder, Yves Choinard, and his team have centred the company around the shared mission of "we're in business to save our home planet' and to '. . . use business to inspire and implement solutions to the environmental crisis'. This commitment empowers the company and its employees to champion the circular economy agenda, ranging from material-focused activities to testing innovative recommerce business models. This dedication to a shared vision was reaffirmed in 2022 when the family handed over the company to a new type of holding, consisting of a trust and non-profit organisation. As Choinard said: 'Instead of going public, you could say we're going purpose.'

Lombard Odier, the Swiss private bank, has developed a strategic focus on systemic sustainable change. Their approach, described as CLIC (Circular, Lean, Inclusive and Clean economy), underscores their commitment to supporting the transition to a more sustainable economy. The positioning and philosophy to Rethink Everything helps the firm to steer the team and its investment activities towards this vision. This means sustainable investing into systemic fields like net zero, electrification or eradicating plastic waste and also launching new sustainable investing ventures like holistiQ.

Mindset for transformational change

Leaders must embrace and endorse a mindset for long-term transformation and change. Leading for circularity demands individuals with cognitive flexibility capable of seamlessly transitioning between various time horizons, stakeholder groups and rationales for change. This multifaceted mindset is pivotal for navigating the complex landscape of circular business models.

Firstly, navigating different time horizons. Leaders must envision the circular and regenerative future they aspire to create, while concurrently managing the immediate present, characterised by intense short-term economic pressures for success. For example, challenging the conventional focus on quarterly returns may require courage and result in sleepless nights. In fact, transforming towards circular business models involves grappling with challenging considerations: How fast to exit certain markets or discontinue initiatives that face growing headwinds? How much to invest in new circular activities that are bound to be successful one day in the future, yet where the timing is uncertain? Leaders should aim to be ahead of the curve to be ready to catch the wave when the wave hits, yet being ahead of the curve for very long can be an uncomfortable situation in our current economic paradigm.

Secondly, cognitive flexibility involves a shift from a narrow focus on shareholder interests to a broader stakeholder perspective and systems lens. Embracing circularity necessitates leading within emerging ecosystems and partnering with sometimes fierce competitors. Striking the delicate balance between collaboration and competition becomes a nuanced challenge. Leaders must adeptly navigate the diverse interests and demands that come with this shift.

Thirdly, transformation and change programmes require navigating two components: a rationale aspect and an emotional aspect. On the one hand, a strong factual and logical case for change is imperative, encompassing elements like long-term business impact, desired outcomes through the circular business model pathway and a clear change agenda with a well-defined process plan. On the other hand, there is a need for a deeper psychological rationale that touches the emotions of the people, who are central to the change process.

Many transformation programmes fail because they fail to touch the people, their feelings and motivations. At the same time, particularly sustainability and circularity programmes require such an emotional component. Activating emotions for building successful circular business models involves triggering curiosity, connecting with risks and fears and fostering a culture that allows learning from failures. New business models often explore unchartered territory where it is critical to learn fast. Leadership can play a pivotal role by explicitly acknowledging the period of change and advocating for a 'fail fast mentality'. This approach encourages experimentation to quickly create evidence of what works, recognising learning and failure as natural elements of the transformation process. Achieving a transformational change around circular business models requires moving mindsets from linear to circular.

Ørsted successfully transitioned from a fossil-fuel utility to a leading renewable energy company within a decade. This remarkable green transformation is a testament to persistence and continuous change management that actively engages the stakeholders. As Ørsted aptly notes, 'What often seems to be a technological or financial challenge is in its essence a leadership challenge.'[14]

Empowerment by senior managers and shareholders

Strong support from senior leadership is paramount to empower new business model activities, particularly considering the significant organisational changes they may entail. The adoption of service-based business models, for instance, can challenge existing organisational set-ups and incentive structures within departments, such as sales or product management. Encouraging product management to adopt a full life cycle perspective means entering new territory upstream and downstream, which may be out of the comfort zone of the involved colleagues. Likewise, support for integrating new materials in R&D can disrupt traditional product development processes (e.g. radical cost optimisation) and practices that may have been optimised for years. Pushing circularity through revolutionary activities often carries an exploratory, high-impact-high-risk character, diverging from the exploitation focus found in many organisations (e.g. cash out on established business models through internationalisation).

Beyond internal management support, active shareholder backing might be a make-or-break point. Although shareholders sit outside of the classic organisational boundaries, they have a key lever and power, influencing core decision-making patterns. Radical change necessitates alignment with shareholders, especially when new business models introduce short-term financial pressure in pursuit of long-term impact potential and resilience.

Leaders and shareholders can empower the teams behind circular business models in several ways: First, internal support through active 'sponsorship' to increase the political weight behind specific projects and decisions. Second, creating a protected environment, such as ring-fenced initiatives, grants the core team members increased autonomy and psychological safety. Third, formally delegating specific responsibilities and decisions to trusted team members, coupled with active coaching, facilitates progress. Fourth, leaders can act as role models, which means to model behaviours that they expect from their team members. Fifth, celebrating successes and rewarding specific achievements like significant milestones during business model implementation (e.g. positive customer feedback or new partnerships) foster a culture of accomplishment and motivation.

Food for thought

How are your company leaders and some relevant shareholders involved in the circularity agenda?
What is their position towards the initiatives? If supportive, you can build coalitions or leverage them as multipliers. If the attitude is rather negative, how can they be convinced? Consider that the relevant stakeholders may have different personality types.

Chapter 5 – In a nutshell

- **Moving from idea to action requires an implementation plan and building a set of key enablers.** These key enablers strengthen your readiness and shed light on diverse challenges that could impede your successful circular business revolution, if they are not addressed early on.

- **The circular readiness framework and enabler landscape is structured along the three dimensions, strategy, execution and people, encompassing a set of 10 factors.** The strategy dimension provides directional guidance and visionary alignment on *where to play*. The execution layer builds the operational backbone for your journey, delineating *how to win*. The people foundation focuses on the essential skillset and leadership mindset crucial for driving change across the entire organisation, emphasising *how to empower*.

- **This comprehensive list of enabling factors should be interpreted within the context of your specific journey from evolution to revolution as well as the prioritised business model patterns.** Hereby the people layer, especially the leadership mindset, and the strategy layer, represent guardrailing conditions that ensure a successful pathway over the long run. The execution layer requires specific points of emphasis depending on your prioritised business model patterns, the respective implementation focus as well as your wider organisational set-up.

Epilogue

Congratulations on progressing on this exploratory journey, and thank you for allowing us to accompany you throughout this book. Have you reached your final destination on this expedition towards circularity? Likely not, circularity is a journey of continuous learning. It's an emerging future, and YOU play a pivotal role in shaping it. The decisions you make today carry profound implications for a world that aspires to be regenerative, circular and deeply collaborative. Just as the 2040 vision depicted earlier, your imaginative thinking, innovative strategies and creative problem-solving abilities can cultivate a business environment where hope and optimism drive progress.

Squaring the circle!

In the words of Hermann Hesse, 'You have to try the impossible to achieve the possible.' Driving real progress requires to radically challenge the boundaries of linear systems and business as usual. We hope that this book leaves you inspired, showing that a different way of organising is not only desirable but also economically possible. The wealth of practical tools and best practices aims to help you turn circular business models into a reality for your organisation and beyond. But driving the circular transformation is difficult. We are still locked into an economy marked by linearity, short termism and aggressive profit maximisation goals. Doing things differently within this rigid economic framework remains a significant challenge.

Don't let the fear of taking risks or dealing with uncertainty hold you back! Be bold and take on the ambitious projects that support a more regenerative and restorative future. 'If you think you are too small to have an impact, try going to bed with a mosquito', as Anita Roddick, the founder of Body Shop famously said. Change starts with one daring leader at a time, until we reach a 'tipping point'; the moment at which an idea, a trend, a product or, in our case, a new economic paradigm reaches critical mass and transitions from the invisible to seemingly ubiquitous, an unstoppable momentum. We hope that by conveying the following key messages, we can collectively drive the necessary cascade of tipping points toward circular and regenerative economic systems:

- **Seize transformation as opportunity:** The pressure for a shift towards a sustainable business future is immense, but within this pressure also lies a real business prospect. Embrace the transformation not just as a necessity but as a window of opportunity.

- **Circular economy as a powerful means:** The circular economy is not an isolated objective; it is a means to realise your sustainability and business goals. At scale, it's a delivery mechanism for more sustainable economic system design: decoupling prosperity from resource use to ensure a safe operating space within planetary boundaries.

- **Design circular models for aligned impact:** Circular business models are arguably the best – and perhaps the only – way to synchronise environmental and economic impact. Enabled *by design*, they offer you an opportunity to harmonise environmental benefits and responsibility – with profitability and resilience.

- **Imagine 'what if':** Set yourself an ambitious vision that serves as a guiding north star and inspiration for collective progress. A clear vision illuminates the pathway for your business model revolution. It creates clarity for your employees, customers, suppliers, investors and other stakeholders.

- **Inspire change and break with the past:** Be willing to break free from the constraints of the past and present. What got you here won't get you to a sustainable future. Embrace transformative change, adaptability and the courage to venture off the beaten track. Don't just passively wait for the economy to change; actively contribute to it.

Looking ahead

The circular business revolution has the power to make a more prosperous, resilient and sustainable economy reality. It's not impossible, rather, it's a conscious choice waiting to be embraced. The presented framework for designing your sustainable business models aims to facilitate that choice. Looking ahead through a systemic lens, it will be important that circular business endeavours address the key levers for change, emphasising the need for revolutionary systemic shifts. This approach is essential to scale up in response to global challenges and expedite the necessary pace of action. Achieving this requires leaders from diverse sectors, including business and government, to inspire collective action and foster societal shifts towards a circular and sustainable future.

Scaling systemic impact

Real impact demands a shift from niche to mainstream. Despite our enthusiasm and optimism that a circular economy is achievable, we need to acknowledge that it is still in its infancy, both within individual companies and on a global scale. Elevating these concepts to a scale where they can drive meaningful impact requires catalysts. At the company level, many circular initiatives lack a commitment to go all-in and remain at an experimental stage for years. Pioneers can catalyse change through lighthouse projects that signal change within and across sectors. Similarly, many countries have launched circular action plans and started to experiment with a fragmented landscape of initiatives. Yet, most of these experiments are not set up for success. Why? Circular endeavours demand systemic transformations, which small-scale initiatives struggle to effectuate. It's not enough if policy makers implement selected regulatory instruments (e.g. bans); they also need to put in place economic instruments and incentives that support circular business models. In essence, policy enablers have to shift the tax burden from labour to resources. Plus, to bring circularity to the forefront, investments and initiatives pushed by governments should focus on catalysing systemic change on a sectoral and regional level. New forms of collaboration between businesses, governments and communities become imperative, fostering an environment conducive to large-scale adoption of circular principles. Only through this concerted effort can we pave the way for a truly circular economy that transcends the boundaries of experimentation and becomes an integral part of our global ethos.

From 'me' to 'we'

Despite the undeniable importance of individual leaders serving as guiding lights into this new future, it's evident that circularity is not a solo endeavour for any single company. In envisioning a circular future, the paradigm shifts from celebrating individual successful companies to cultivating superior ecosystems. We've underscored the need for successful circular business models to adopt a whole-system perspective: one that dismantles internal silos, activates the solution ecosystem and leverages the enabling ecosystem. Business leaders should embrace the partnership mindset and culture conducive to building the coalitions that enable circularity to tackle real systemic challenges. This includes not only internal teams but also external collaborators such as suppliers, partners, entrepreneurs and even competitors. By doing so, you become a catalyst for an ecosystem characterised by cooperation, where collective efforts drive progress and innovation. Sometimes it is necessary to have pioneering initiators, moderators or orchestrators who step in and help to shape the alliances that confront systemic challenges head-on and place collaboration at the forefront of progress.

Navigating trade-offs

The human inclination for certainty often drives us to search for what we perceive as the 'right' answers. We tend to feel uneasy in the face of high ambiguity and uncertainty, where clear solutions elude us. The challenge with sustainability lies in its systemic nature. Everything seems to be interconnected – like the cycles in nature. This forces us into a continuous encounter with difficult decisions and intricate trade-offs. One of the most common dilemmas arises when attempting to strike a balance between long-term value and short-term pressures. Another prevalent trade-off emerges in the delicate equilibrium between environmental and social objectives, where progress in one area may come at the expense of the other. Also consider the performance trade-offs during design decisions that we discussed earlier. Trying to find a compromise between everything can result in stagnation. While there is no perfect answer to all these challenges, it's reassuring to realise that you are not alone in navigating this complex terrain. Engage with other leaders to exchange insights, discuss failures and share experiences and trust in your inner compass as you confront these challenges. As you navigate the intricate trade-offs on your circular transformation, remember that the journey is as crucial as the destination. Similar to entrepreneurial venture building, a key capability of innovators is to be agile and pivot based on learnings and failures. Your commitment to finding solutions, your willingness to learn from setbacks and your resilience in the face of uncertainty make for meaningful progress.

A global agenda for a circular future

While the agency of companies plays a central role in innovating for circular economy, it is important to underscore the significance of a comprehensive global agenda for its successful implementation. Despite notable advances, such as the inclusion of circularity in political initiatives like the European Green Deal or the US Inflation Reduction Act, a cohesive vision for a worldwide circular economy transition is still lacking. Just as no single company can single-handedly drive circularity in a sector, no individual country will be able to succeed in this mammoth task alone. Given the inherently global and fragmented nature of supply chains, reinventing our infrastructure necessitates a shared vision and collective effort. A critical next step is to forge stronger alignment between the circular economy and overarching global agendas and frameworks, such as the UN Agenda 2030 and the Paris Climate Agreement. Standardisation plays an important role, like the discussions around the need for a Global Circularity Protocol (similarly to the Greenhouse Gas Protocol). Importantly, the circular economy should not be treated as a stand-alone objective but rather be seen as a means to achieve broader goals, such as the 1.5°C climate target or the UN biodiversity objectives (30x30).

Harnessing natural capital

One thing is clear: humans have always depended on the services and fruits of nature for our survival. In fact, the global decline in natural capital and biodiversity is one of the greatest risks to our economies.[1] With climate change progressing, the global community and businesses are now realising that we need to cut emissions, but at the same time actively enable the power of natural solutions! Nature is part of the solution to mitigate climate change and design an economy that operates within planetary boundaries. We have outlined extensively how businesses depend on natural resources. The circular economy provides a holistic approach for optimising biocycles and technocyles to actively strengthen natural capital – and pioneers can use novel business models to unlock that regenerative power. Whether it is forests, soils, grasslands or oceans, the regeneration, restoration and preservation of natural systems can and must be considered to reinvent our business models. However, supporting this economic case will require further enabling conditions; for example, technology that is able to measure, monitor and verify the services of nature, and also, adjustments to global accounting standards as well as financial innovation to steer required investments into the land use transformation and nature-based solutions. This will create the tailwind for circularity to scale. The future success of businesses relies on the trajectory of nature's most productive cycles and superpowers.

Green growth or degrowth?

One of the central debates in sustainability revolves around the question of whether we can effectively address our social and environmental challenges through pragmatic green growth or if a more radical shift towards degrowth is needed. Interestingly, the circular economy emerges as a nuanced approach that could reconcile aspects of both perspectives. On one side of the spectrum proponents of green growth see the circular economy as a viable strategy to mitigate environmental impact. By reducing waste and optimising for resource productivity, it offers a pathway to decouple economic growth from resource extraction and inherent ecological harm. This perspective emphasises the possibility of expanding economic prosperity while minimising resource depletion and pollution. Conversely, advocates of degrowth argue for a substantial reduction in production and consumption to realign with the planet's ecological boundaries. From their viewpoint, the circular economy advocates for a simpler and more sustainable form of consumption[2] – one rooted in principles of sharing, repairing or reusing. The integral idea is to meet essential human and societal needs with sustainable resource use – which is also often described as sufficiency.[3] The shift from ownership to access becomes a central tenet, challenging the conventional narrative of perpetual growth to more conscious consumption patterns. The circular economy, therefore, serves as a unifying bridge between the seemingly disparate paradigms of green growth and degrowth. By integrating principles of 'closing the loop' and a more deliberate approach to consumption, it offers a holistic strategy to address both environmental concerns and the need for a more balanced, conscious society.

Towards an inclusive circular economy

Throughout this book, we have underscored the opportunity to converge environmental and economic impact – often considered an impossible marriage. Amid our focus on this powerful synergy, we must not overlook the crucial third element: social impact. The circular economy, given its revolutionary essence, carries the potential for profound changes and challenges in global supply chains. This may happen at the expense of low- and middle-income countries, or may reconfigure entire industries and labour dynamics. For instance, envisioning a reduction in our dependency on primary raw materials or building much more localised supply chains may inadvertently disadvantage countries heavily reliant on exports. A 'just transition' becomes an essential puzzle piece in managing the transformative changes on the horizon. This transition requires a careful and deliberate effort to ensure that the shift towards a circular economy does not create new or exacerbate existing disadvantages. It may be important to implement social protection mechanisms and strengthen international cooperation. However, the transformative journey also offers an opportunity to champion inclusive growth. It empowers us to envision a future where the benefits of a circular and regenerative economy are more equitably shared across countries. As we steer towards an inclusive circular economy, let us acknowledge the challenges but actively work to craft solutions that uplift the vulnerable and ensure a fair distribution of opportunities. By embracing a just transition and inclusivity, we can harness the potential to not only revolutionse industry practices but also to catalyse positive social change.

Your circular and regenerative future is built through your continued exploration, actions and decisions. May your journey ahead be filled with the spirit of a good disruption. A circular business revolution where hope and optimism drive meaningful change. A world that is better off because your company is in it.

Safe travels!

Notes

Chapter 1

1 Sharpe, B. (2013) *Three Horizons: The Patterning of Hope*. Dorset: Triarchy Press.

Chapter 2

1 European Parliament. (24 May 2023) 'Circular economy: Definition, importance, and benefits'. European Parliament Directorate General for Communication. Available at: https://www.europarl.europa.eu/news/en/headlines/economy/20151201STO05603/circular-economy-definition-importance-and-benefits

2 Nordic Innovation. (2022) *Nordic Circular Economy Playbook 2.0*. Nordic Innovation. Available at: https://www.nordicinnovation.org/2022/nordic-circular-economy-playbook-20#:~:text=The%20Nordic%20Circular%20Economy%20Playbook,in%20the%20Nordic%20manufacturing%20industries

3 Sitra. (2022) *Sustainable Growth with Circular Economy Business Models: Playbook for Businesses*. Sitra. Available at: https://www.sitra.fi/app/uploads/2022/12/sitra_sustainable_growth_with_circular_economy_business_models.pdf

4 Lacy, P. and Rutqvist, J. (2015) *Waste to Wealth: The Circular Economy Advantage*. London: Palgrave Macmillan.

5 Ellen MacArthur Foundation. (2017) 'A new textiles economy: Redesigning fashion's future'. Available at: https://archive.ellenmacarthurfoundation.org/assets/downloads/A-New-Textiles-Economy.pdf; Šajn, N. (2019) 'Environmental impact of the textile and clothing industry: What consumers need to know'. Briefing. London: European Parliamentary Research Service. Available at: https://www.europarl.europa.eu/RegData/etudes/BRIE/2019/633143/EPRS_BRI(2019)633143_EN.pdf

6 Ellen MacArthur Foundation. (2021) 'Circular business models: Redefining growth for a thriving fashion industry'. Available at: https://emf.thirdlight.com/file/24/Om5sTEKOmm-fEeVOm7xNOmq6S2k/Circular%20business%20models.pdf

7 Food and Agriculture Organization. (2019) *The State of Food and Agriculture 2019. Moving Forward on Food Loss and Waste Reduction*. Rome. Licence: CC BY-NC-SA 3.0 IGO. Available at: https://www.fao.org/3/ca6030en/ca6030en.pdf; UN Environment Programme. (2021) 'Food waste index report 2021'. Available at: https://www.unep.org/resources/report/unep-food-waste-index-report-2021

8 The Pew Charitable Trust and Systemiq. (2020) 'Breaking the plastic wave: A comprehensive assessment of pathways towards stopping ocean plastic pollution'. Available at: https://www.pewtrusts.org/-/media/assets/2020/10/breakingtheplasticwave_mainreport.pdf

9 World Economic Forum. (2019) 'Harnessing the fourth industrial revolution for the circular economy: Consumer electronics and plastics packaging'. White Paper. Available at: https://www3.weforum.org/docs/WEF_Harnessing_4IR_Circular_Economy_report_2018.pdf

10 Ellen MacArthur Foundation. (2017) A new textiles economy: Redesigning fashion's future. Available at: https://archive.ellenmacarthurfoundation.org/assets/downloads/A-New-Textiles-Economy.pdf

11 Systemiq. (2023) 'Circularity of PET/polyester packaging and textiles in Europe'. Available at: https://www.systemiq.earth/wp-content/uploads/2023/02/Systemiq-PET-Circularity-Europe-Synthesis-Report-High-Res.pdf

12 European Parliament. (2018) 'Microplastics: Sources, effects and solutions'. Available at: https://www.europarl.europa.eu/pdfs/news/expert/2018/11/story/20181116STO19217/20181116STO19217_en.pdf

13 McKinsey & Company and Global Fashion Agenda. (2020) 'Fashion on climate: How the fashion industry can urgently act to reduce its greenhouse gas emissions'. Available at: https://www.mckinsey.com/~/media/mckinsey/industries/retail/our%20insights/fashion%20on%20climate/fashion-on-climate-full-report.pdf

14 Remy, N., Speelman, E. and Swartz, S. (2016) 'Style that's sustainable: A new fast fashion formula'. McKinsey Sustainability. Available at: https://www.mckinsey.com/capabilities/sustainability/our-insights/style-thats-sustainable-a-new-fast-fashion-formula

15 UN Environment Programme. (2018) 'Putting the brakes on fast fashion'. Available at: https://www.unep.org/news-and-stories/story/putting-brakes-fast-fashion

16 Statista Consumer Insights. (2023) 'Most returned online purchases by category in Germany'. Available at: https://www.statista.com/forecasts/998730/most-returned-online-purchases-by-category-in-germany#:~:text=When%20asked%20about%20%22Most%20returned,than%20500%20industries%20and%20topics

17 European Environment Agency. (2023) 'EU exports of used textiles in Europe's circular economy'. Briefing. Available at: https://www.eea.europa.eu/publications/eu-exports-of-used-textiles#:~:text=Key%20messages,1.7%20million%20tonnes%20in%202019

18 Ellen MacArthur Foundation. (2017) 'A new textiles economy: Redesigning fashion's future'. Available at: https://archive.ellenmacarthurfoundation.org/assets/downloads/A-New-Textiles-Economy.pdf

19 Steffen, W., Richardson, K., Rockström, J., *et al.* (2015) 'Planetary boundaries: Guiding human development on a changing planet'. *Science*, *347*, 1259855.

20 Richardson, K., Steffen W., Lucht, W., *et al.* (2023) 'Earth beyond six of nine planetary boundaries'. *Science Advances*, *9*(37).

21 Huisman, L., Delivanis, C. and Schmidt-Traub, G. (2023) *Nature Risk is Business Risk*. Systemiq & Metabolic. Available at: https://www.systemiq.earth/wp-content/uploads/2023/11/Nature-Risk-paper-1123.pdf

22 United Nations Environment Programme and International Resource Panel. (2019) *Global Resources Outlook 2019: Natural Resources for the Future We Want*. Available at: https://www.resourcepanel.org/reports/global-resources-outlook

23 International Resource Panel. 'Glossary'. Available at: https://www.resourcepanel.org/glossary (accessed January 2024).

24 NielsenIQ. (2022) 'Sustainability: The new consumer spending outlook'. Available at: https://nielseniq.com/wp-content/uploads/sites/4/2022/10/2022-10_ESG_eBook_NIQ_FNL.pdf

25 GfK. (May 12 2022) 'Despite inflation: Consumers in Germany decide to buy sustainably'. Available at: https://www.gfk.com/press/sustainability-index-germany-may-2022

26 Economist Intelligence Unit. (2021) 'An eco-wakening: Measuring global awareness, engagement and action for nature'. https://files.worldwildlife.org/wwfcmsprod/files/Publication/file/93ts5bhvyq_An_EcoWakening_Measuring_awareness__engagement_and_action_for_nature_FINAL_MAY_2021.pdf?_ga=2.37861987.1577428094.1701211801-358578709.1701211800

27 McKinsey and NielsenIQ. (2023) 'Consumers care about sustainability – and back it up with their wallets'. Available at: https://www.mckinsey.com/industries/consumer-packaged-goods/our-insights/consumers-care-about-sustainability-and-back-it-up-with-their-wallets

28 FirstInsight. (2021) *New 2021 First Insight Consumer Spending Report*. Available at: https://www.firstinsight.com/press-releases/the-state-of-consumer-spending-gen-z-influencing-all-generations-to-make-sustainability-first-purchase-decisions

29 thredUP. (2023) 'Resale report 2023'. Available at: https://cf-assets-tup.thredup.com/resale_report/2023/thredUP_2023_Resale_Report_FINAL.pdf

30 Science Based Targets Initiative. (2023) 'SBTi monitoring report 2022'. Available at: https://sciencebasedtargets.org/resources/files/SBTiMonitoringReport2022.pdf

31 World Economic Forum. (2021) 'Net-zero challenge: The supply chain opportunity'. Available at: https://www3.weforum.org/docs/WEF_Net_Zero_Challenge_The_Supply_Chain_Opportunity_2021.pdf

32 EY. (2020) 'How will ESG performance shape your future'. Available at: https://assets.ey.com/content/dam/ey-sites/ey-com/en_gl/topics/assurance/assurance-pdfs/ey-global-institutional-investor-survey-2020.pdf

33 PwC. (2022) 'The ESG execution gap: What investors think of companies' sustainability efforts'. Available at: https://www.pwc.com/gx/en/issues/esg/global-investor-survey-2022.html

34 Serafeim, G. (2020) 'Public sentiment and the price of corporate sustainability'. *Financial Analysts Journal*, 76(2), 26–46.

35 Dealroom.co. Climate Tech. Available at: https://dealroom.co/guides/climate-tech (accessed December 2023).

36 Dhingra, N., Samo, A., Schaninger, B., *et al.* (2021) 'Help your employees find purpose—or watch them leave'. McKinsey & Company. Available at: https://www.mckinsey.com/capabilities/people-and-organizational-performance/our-insights/help-your-employees-find-purpose-or-watch-them-leave#/

37 PwC. (2017) 'Workforce of the future: The competing forces shaping 2030'. Available at: https://www.pwc.com/gx/es/publicaciones/assets/workforce-of-the-future-the-competing-forces-shaping-2030-pwc.pdf

38 BetterUp Labs. (7 November 2018) 'Workers value meaning at work'. Available at: https://www.betterup.com/press/workers-value-meaning-at-work-new-research-from-betterup-shows-just-how-much-theyre-willing-to-pay-for-it

39 Anthesis. (16 April 2021) 'Research reveals sustainability is vital for employee attraction and retention'. Available at: https://www.anthesisgroup.com/sustainability-vital-for-employee-attraction/

40 Doerr, J. (2021) *Speed & Scale: An Action Plan for Solving Our Climate Crisis Now*. Portfolio/Penguin.

41 Turner, J., Meldrum, M., Oppenheim, J., *et al.* (2020) 'The Paris effect: How the climate agreement is reshaping the global economy'. Systemiq. Available at: https://www.systemiq.earth/wp-content/uploads/2020/12/The-Paris-Effect_SYSTEMIQ_Full-Report_December-2020.pdf

42 Meldrum, M., Pinnell, L., Brennan, K., *et al.* (2023), 'The breakthrough effect: How to trigger a cascade of tipping points to accelerate the net zero transition'. Systemiq, University of Exeter, Bezos Earth Fund. Available at: https://www.systemiq.earth/wp-content/uploads/2023/01/The-Breakthrough-Effect.pdf

43 Krishnan, M., Samandari, H., Woetzel, J., *et al.* (2022) 'The net-zero transition: What it would cost, what it could bring'. McKinsey & Company. Available at: https://www.mckinsey.com/~/media/mckinsey/business%20functions/sustainability/our%20insights/the%20net%20zero%20transition%20what%20it%20would%20cost%20what%20it%20could%20bring/the-net-zero-transition-what-it-would-cost-and-what-it-could-bring-final.pdf

44 McFadyen, T. (2021) *Marketplace Best Practices: Transforming Commerce in the Platform Economy*. McFadyen Digital.

45 McGrath, R. (2013) 'Transient advantage'. *Harvard Business Review*. Available at: https://hbr.org/2013/06/transient-advantage

Chapter 3

1 Stahel, W. R. (2016) 'The circular economy'. *Nature, 531*(7595), 435–438.

2 Ellen MacArthur Foundation. (2015) 'Growth within: A circular economy vision for a competitive Europe'. Available at: https://www.ellenmacarthurfoundation.org/growth-within-a-circular-economy-vision-for-a-competitive-europe

3 McDonough, W. and Braungart, M. (2002) *Cradle to Cradle: Remaking the Way We Make Things*. North Point Press.

4 Stahel, W. R. (2010) *The Performance Economy*. Palgrave Macmillan.

5 Stuchtey, M. R., Enkvist, P.-A. and Zumwinkel, K. (2016) *A Good Disruption: Redefining Growth in the Twenty-First Century*. Bloomsbury.

6 Sitra. (2022) *Sustainable Growth with Circular Economy Business Models: Playbook for Businesses*. Sitra. Available at: https://www.sitra.fi/app/uploads/2022/12/sitra_sustainable_growth_with_circular_economy_business_models.pdf

7 Lacy, P., Long, J. and Spindler, W. (2020) *The Circular Economy Handbook: Realizing the Circular Advantage*. Palgrave Macmillan.

8 Ellen MacArthur Foundation. (2015) 'Growth within: A circular economy vision for a competitive Europe'. Available at: https://www.ellenmacarthurfoundation.org/growth-within-a-circular-economy-vision-for-a-competitive-europe

9 European Commission. (2018) 'Impacts of circular economy policies on the labour market'. Available at: https://circulareconomy.europa.eu/platform/sites/default/files/ec_2018_-_impacts_of_circular_economy_policies_on_the_labour_market.pdf

10 Ellen MacArthur Foundation. (2015) 'Growth within: A circular economy vision for a competitive Europe'. Available at: https://www.ellenmacarthurfoundation.org/growth-within-a-circular-economy-vision-for-a-competitive-europe

11 McDonough, W. and Braungart, M. (2002) *Cradle to Cradle: Remaking the Way We Make Things*. North Point Press.

12 Benyus, J. M. (1997) *Biomimicry: Innovation Inspired by Nature*. Morrow.

13 Stahel, W. (1981) *Jobs for Tomorrow: The Potential for Substituting Manpower for Energy*. Vantage Press.

14 International Resource Panel (ed.) (2011) 'Decoupling natural resource use and environmental impacts from economic growth', UN Environment Programme. Available at: https://www.unep.org/resources/report/decoupling-natural-resource-use-and-environmental-impacts-economic-growth

15 Stuchtey, M. R., Enkvist, P.-A. and Zumwinkel, K. (2016) *A Good Disruption: Redefining Growth in the Twenty-First Century*. Bloomsbury.

16 Circle Economy Foundation. (2023) 'The Circularity Gap Report'. Available at: https://www.circularity-gap.world/2023

17 Potting, J., Hekkert, M., Worrell, E., *et al.* (2017) 'Circular economy: Measuring innovation in the product chain'. PBL Netherlands Environmental Assessment Agency.

18 Henry, M., Bauwens, T., Hekkert, M., *et al.* (2020) 'A typology of circular start-ups: An analysis of 128 circular business models'. *Journal of Cleaner Production, 245*, 118528.

19 Walter R (2013), Policy for material efficiency—sustainable taxation as a departure from the throwaway society, Phil. Trans. R. Soc. A.37120110567. Retrieved from https://royalsocietypublishing.org/doi/10.1098/rsta.2011.0567#

20 Bocken, N. M. P., de Pauw, I., Bakker, C., *et al.* (2016) 'Product design and business model strategies for a circular economy'. *Journal of Industrial Ecology, 20*(5), 308–320.

21 Kirchherr, J., Reike, D. and Hekkert, M. (2017) 'Conceptualizing the circular economy: An analysis of 114 definitions'. *Resources, Conservation & Recycling, 127*, 221–232.

22 Osterwalder, A. and Pigneur, Y. (2010) *Business Model Generation: A Handbook for Visionaries, Game Changers, and Challengers*. John Wiley & Sons.

23 Science Based Targets Network (SBTN). (2023) 'Step 3: Measure, Set, Disclose: LAND'. Available at: https://sciencebasedtargetsnetwork.org/wp-content/uploads/2023/05/Technical-Guidance-2023-Step3-Land-v0.3.pdf

24 Polman, P. and Winston, A. (2021) 'The net positive manifesto'. *Harvard Business Review*. Available at: https://hbr.org/2021/09/the-net-positive-manifesto

Chapter 4

1 Osterwalder, A., Pigneur, Y., Bernarda, G., *et al*. (2014) *Value Proposition Design: How to Create Products and Services Customer Want*. Wiley.

2 Nußholz, J. L. K. (2017) 'Circular business models: Defining a concept and framing an emerging research field'. *Sustainability, 9*, 1810.

3 European Commission Joint Research Centre. (29 September 2023) 'Greenhouse gas emissions from manufacturing: What difference across countries?' News Announcement. Available at: https://joint-research-centre.ec.europa.eu/jrc-news-and-updates/greenhouse-gas-emissions-manufacturing-what-difference-across-countries-2023-09-29_en

4 Partnerships for Forests. (2020) 'Illipe nut: A new value chain with strong social and gender potential'. Case Study. Available at: https://partnershipsforforests.com/wp-content/uploads/2021/03/Illipe-Nut-A-New-Value-Chain-with-Strong-Social-and-Gender-Potential.pdf

5 Partnerships for Forests. (2020) 'A sweet taste for forests'. Case Study. Available at: https://partnershipsforforests.com/wp-content/uploads/2020/08/A-sweet-taste-for-forests.pdf

6 WWF. (2016) Living Planet Report 2016. Available at: https://www.worldwildlife.org/pages/living-planet-report-2016

7 UN Environment Programme. (2021) 'Food waste index report 2021'. Available at: https://www.unep.org/resources/report/unep-food-waste-index-report-2021

8 Braun, M., Herrmann, S., Kick, M., Kobus, J., Stuchtey, M. R. & Teuber, A. (2021). *Everything-as-a-Service (XaaS): How busiensses can Thrive in the Age of Climate Change and Digitalization*. SUN Institute Environment & Sustainability. Available at: *https://www.systemiq.earth/wp-content/uploads/2021/09/XaaS-Report-SYSTEMIQ.pdf*

9 Stahel, W. R. (2016) 'The circular economy'. *Nature, 531*(7595), 435–438.

Chapter 5

1 Lah, T. and Wood, J. B. (2016) *Technology-as-a-Service Playbook: How to Grow a Profitable Subscription Business*. Point B Inc.

2 Doerr, J. (2018) *Measure What Matters: How Google, Bono, and the Gates Foundation Rock the World with OKRs*. Portfolio/Pengiun.

3 Sinek, S. (2011) *Start with the Why: How Great Leaders Inspire Everyone to Take Action*. Penguin Publishing Group.

4 Osterwalder, A., Pigneur, Y., Bernarda, G., *et al*. (2014) *Value Proposition Design: How to Create Products and Services Customer Want*. Wiley.

5 European Parliament. (24 May 2023) 'Circular economy: Definition, importance, and benefits'. European Parliament Directorate General for Communication. Available at: https://www.europarl.europa.eu/news/en/headlines/economy/20151201STO05603/circular-economy-definition-importance-and-benefits

6   Ellen MacArthur Foundation. (2023) 'Circular design: Turning ambition into action'. Ellen MacArthur Foundation. Available at: https://www.ellenmacarthurfoundation.org/topics/circular-design/overview

7   Takacs, F., Stechow, R. and Frankenberger, K. (2020) 'Circular ecosystems: Business model innovation for the circular economy'. Available at: https://www.alexandria.unisg.ch/server/api/core/bitstreams/80845b25-a08c-4633-b118-3d2ae0682714/content

8   Konietzko, J., Bocken, N. and Hultink, E. J. (2020) 'Circular ecosystem innovation: An initial set of principles'. *Journal of Cleaner Production, 253*, 119942.

9   Eisenreich, A., Füller, J., Stuchtey, M., *et al*. (2022) 'Toward a circular value chain: Impact of the circular economy on a company's value chain processes'. *Journal of Cleaner Production, 378*, 134375.

10 Philip, F., Kühl, C., Braun, M., *et al*. (2022) *Organising for Circularity*. Systemiq. Available at: https://www.systemiq.earth/wp-content/uploads/2022/10/Organising-for-Circularity.pdf

11 BASF, Position on the circular economy, Retrieved from https://www.basf.com/global/documents/en/about-us/politics/BASF_Position_on_Circular_Economy.pdf.assetdownload.pdf

12 Jenewein, W. and Morhart, F. (2006) Sieben Manöver zum Teamerfolg. Harvard Business Manager. Available at: https://heft.manager-magazin.de/EpubDelivery/manager-lounge/pdf/47328793

13 Scharmer, C.O. (2007) *Theory U: Leading from the Future as It Emerges*. Cambridge: The Society for Organizational Learning.

14 Ørsted. (2021) 'Our green transformation: What we did and lessons learned'. Available at: https://orsted.com/en/insights/white-papers/green-transformation-lessons-learned

Epilogue

1   Johnson, J., Ruta, G., Baldos, U., *et al*. (2021) 'The economic case for nature: A global Earth-economy model to assess development policy pathways'. Available at: https://openknowledge.worldbank.org/server/api/core/bitstreams/9f0d9a3a-83ca-5c96-bd59-9b16f4e936d8/content

2   Potŏcnik, J., Spangenberg, J., Alcott, B., *et al*. (2018) 'Sufficiency: Moving beyond the gospel of eco-efficiency'. Friends of the Earth Europe. Available at: https://friendsoftheearth.eu/wp-content/uploads/2018/03/foee_sufficiency_booklet.pdf

3   Bocken, N. M. P., Niessen, L. and Short, S. W. (2022) 'Sufficiency-based circular economy: An analysis for 150 companies'. *Frontiers in Sustainability*, 3.

Index